D0477620

MEDUSA

MEDUSA

The Shipwreck,
The Scandal,
The Masterpiece

Jonathan Miles

JONATHAN CAPE
LONDON

Published by Jonathan Cape 2007

2 4 6 8 10 9 7 5 3 1

Copyright © Jonathan Miles 2007

Jonathan Miles has asserted his right under the Copyright, Designs
and Patents Act 1988 to be identified as the author of this work

This book is a work of non-fiction.
The author has stated to the publishers that the contents of this book are true.

First published in Great Britain in 2007 by
Jonathan Cape
Random House, 20 Vauxhall Bridge Road,
London SW1V 2SA

www.randomhouse.co.uk

Addresses for companies within The Random House Group Limited can be found at:
www.randomhouse.co.uk

The Random House Group Limited Reg. No. 954009

A CIP catalogue record for this book is available from the British Library

ISBN 9780224073035

The Random House Group Limited makes every effort to ensure that the papers
used in its books are made from trees that have been legally sourced from well-managed
and credibly certified forests. Our paper procurement policy can be found at:
www.randomhouse.co.uk/paper.htm

Typeset in Bembo by Palimpsest Book Production Limited,
Grangemouth, Stirlingshire
Printed and bound in Great Britain by
Mackays of Chatham plc, Chatham, Kent

Contents

For all those misled by their leaders

Illustrations

Théodore Géricault, possible likeness of *Alexandrine-Modeste Caruel*, in the Zürich sketchbook, Kunsthaus, Zurich, f° 47 r° © 2006 Kunsthause, Zürich. All rights reserved.

Alexandre Colin, *Portrait of Géricault in 1816*, lithograph, Musée de Beaux-Arts, Rouen © Musées de Rouen. Photograph: Catherine Lancien.

Théodore Géricault, *Le Chasseur de la Garde*, Musée du Louvre © Photo RMN – Hervé Lewandowski.

Anon., *The Frigate, The Medusa*, from *Le Petit Journal, Militaire Maritime* © Service Historique de la Défense – Département de la Marine.

Alexandre Corréard, *Plan of the Raft of The Medusa*, in Alexandre Corréard and Henri Savigny, *Naufrage de la frégate la Méduse faisant partie de l'expédition du Sénégal en 1816*, 5th edition (Paris: Chez Corréard, Libraire, 1821), between 52–3 © Photo Bibliothèque Nationale de France.

Anon., sketch on ms. report showing order of boats towing the raft, in *Service historique de la Défense*, Vincennes: Dossier BB⁴393.

Anon., *Shipwreck of the Frigate, The Medusa* © Musée nationale de la Marine.

Léon Antoine Morel-Fatio, *The Abandoning of the Raft of The Medusa*, in *France Maritimes*, Vol. IV, 281, mid-nineteenth century © Musée nationale de la Marine.

Anon., *The Finding of the Raft by the Argus*, in *Recueil d'événements maritimes*, 14 © Musée nationale de la Marine.

Anon., *Saint Louis in Senegal*, in René-Claude Geoffrey de Villeneuve, *L'Afrique ou Histoire, moeurs, usages et coutumes des Africains. Le Sénégal*, 4 vols (Paris: Nepveu, 1814), Vol. I, facing p. 63 © Photo Bibliothèque Nationale de France.

Théodore Géricault, *An Execution at Rome* © Photo École nationale supérieure des Beaux-Arts, Paris.

Théodore Géricault, *The Race of the Riderless Horses*, Musée du Louvre © Photo RMN – Gérard Blot.

Sébastien Cœuré, *Fualdès Being Dragged and Shoved into the Maison Bancal* © Photo Bibliothèque Nationale de France.

Théodore Géricault, *Fualdès Being Dragged and Shoved into the Maison Bancal*, Musée du Louvre © Photo RMN – Jean-Gilles Berizzi.

Théodore Géricault, *Studies of a Dancing Couple and a Centaur Abducting a Nymph*, London, Private Collection.

Théodore Géricault, *The Embrace*, Musée du Louvre © Photo RMN – Michèle Bellot.

Théodore Géricault, *The Kiss* © Museo Thyssen-Bornemisza, Madrid.

Théodore Géricault, *Lovers Reclining*, Private Collection.

Théodore Géricault, *Anatomical Fragments*, Musée Fabre, Montepellier Agglomération – Photo Frédéric Jaulmes.

Théodore Géricault, *The Severed Heads*, Nationalmuseum, Stockholm.

Théodore Géricault, *Study for Cannibalism*, Private Collection.

Théodore Géricault, *Drawing for the Mutiny on the Raft*, Amsterdams Historisch Museum.

Théodore Géricault, *The Raft of The Medusa*, Musée du Louvre, Paris/Bridgeman Art Library.

Théodore Géricault, *Study for the Figure of Corréard*, in the Zürich sketchbook, Kunsthaus, Zurich, f° 52 r° © Kunsthaus Zürich. All rights reserved.

C. Motte, *Valade the Police Commissioner Confronting Corréard in Prison*, in Alexandre Corréard and Henri Savigny, *Naufrage de la frégate la Méduse faisant partie de l'expédition du Sénégal en 1816*, 5th edition (Paris: Chez Corréard, Libraire, 1821), 442 © Photo Bibliothèque Nationale de France.

Anon., *The Shape and Dimension of the Places for the Slaves in the English Slave-Ship, Brookes*, in Thomas Clarkson, *The Cries of Africa to the inhabitants of Europe; or, a Survey of that Bloody Commerce called the Slave-Trade* (London, 1822) © The British Library.

Alexandre Corréard, *Posthumous Study of Géricault*, Musée de Rouen © Musées de Rouen. Photograph: Catherine Lancien/Carole Loisel.

Théodore Géricault, *Study for the Slave Trade* © Photo École nationale supérieure des Beaux-Arts, Paris.

Théodore Géricault, *Shipwreck*, Musée du Louvre © Photo RMN – Christian Jean.

Line drawings in the text

Every effort has been made to trace and contact copyright holders. The publishers will be pleased to correct any mistakes or omissions in future editions.

Note

Four ships left France in June 1816 to repossess Senegal from the British:

> *The Medusa*, a frigate and flagship of the expedition
> *The Echo*, a corvette
> *The Argus*, a brig
> *The Loire*, a supply vessel.

On board *The Medusa* were the following boats used during its evacuation:

> The Captain's Barge commanded by Midshipman Rang
> The Senegal Boat commanded by Ensign Maudet
> The Longboat commanded by Lieutenant Espiaux
> The Pinnace commanded by Ensign Lapeyrère
> The Governor's Barge commanded by Lieutenant Reynaud.

There was also a small skiff, and a raft was constructed out of debris from *The Medusa*.

Note

Although many facts are consistent in the various narratives and fragments left by the survivors of these harrowing events, there are, at times, discrepancies. Flawed memories – severely tested by the ordeal, weakened by the interval between the events and their chronicling, weighted by guilt or by passionate political agendas – account for these differences. In the few instances that it has not proved possible to corroborate, the most probable or trustworthy source has been used.

Acknowledgements

I would like to thank the staff of the *Bibliothèque nationale* in Paris, who are always most kind and helpful, providing an environment in which it is a joy to work. The staff of the Bodleian Library in Oxford, the British Library, the U.K. National Archives, the *Bibliothèque du Musée national de la Marine*, *Les Archives nationales*, *Les Archives départmentales* at Gap and *Le Service historique de la Défense* at Vincennes have likewise been helpful.

I am much indebted to the vision, guidance and dedication of John Saddler, my agent in London, and to the energy, counsel and enterprise of George Lucas, my agent at Inkwell Management in New York.

I feel a deep gratitude for the enormous enthusiasm, editorial acuity and care of Will Sulkin at Jonathan Cape and Joan Bingham at Grove/Atlantic, Inc., who have, in very different ways, contributed so much to the text – as have their alert and sensitive copy-editors. Drummond Moir at Cape has also been most helpful.

I would like to thank John and Claire Rickard, Amélie Louveau, Dr Eric Martini, Dr Michel Martini (enormously), Dr Patrick Chariot, Iradj Azimi, Jean-Yves Blot, Lucienne Ruellé, Anne-Marie Mahé, Régis Michel, Bruno Chenique,

Acknowledgements

Claire Lemouchoux and Mark Mullen. Also, immeasurable gratitude is due to my lovely Catherine, whose help has been invaluable, whose kindness is supreme; and to my daughter, Marjotte, whose bubbling enthusiasm for just about everything makes life a delight.

Paris, 2006

1

A Severed Head

AN agitated young man with a recently shaven skull and piercing eyes emerged through a monumental portico that fronted the hospital and turned into the chilly shadow of the street. Hitherto unfocused, in this bitter winter of 1819 he had a new-found sense of determination – a resolve formed not a moment too soon: although only twenty-seven, this striking figure would, within the space of five years, be dead.

The street into which he turned was not busy. He had chosen to install himself in a working-class, north-western suburb of Paris, close to the Hôpital Beaujon and away from society's babble. The quarter was tainted, as was every part of that damaged capital, by the bloodshed of a revolution turned vicious and, more recently, by the debris of an empire overthrown. A visiting English artist noted that there 'was scarcely a driver of a fiacre, a waiter at a café, or a man in middle life, who had not been in battle, served in a campaign, or been wounded by a shot'.[1] Mutilation was commonplace. Injured soldiers and amputees formed a macabre and length-ening procession that had dragged itself about the city since Napoleon's first conquests. Twenty years on, there were hoards of these invalids, retired on half-pay after 1814,

1

rejected victims of the restored monarchy's reduction of the once-feared *Grande Armée*. According to another English visitor, Paris was 'a vast mourning family', where 'three people out of five that one meets are habited in black'.[2] Its citizens had, after a quarter of a century, once again been made subjects, and discord grumbled round the capital.

Although the muslin parcel that he hugged in his arms was proving cumbersome, the young man attempted to quicken his pace. From his razored appearance and from the dark red staining the gauze, it would seem that his trade was perhaps butcher, or that his guilty secret was murder. The fabric was proving far from impermeable and he was obliged to reposition his load in order to prevent his coat from becoming bloodied.

If it seemed like madness to parade in broad daylight with a severed head clutched closely to one's breast – and indeed, neatly bound in the muslin sack was a human head, which had, until recently, been attached to a living, breathing body – it was nothing to the folly of the world into which Théodore Géricault had plunged. His new friend, Alexandre Corréard, had promised to call. He was an excitable person with strong convictions, a frankly litigious man with a recently acquired sense of self-importance. Corréard had been on board *The Medusa*. He had survived the infamous raft and had much privileged information to impart.

The severed head was already putrid, but the stench that greeted the young man as he climbed the stairs to his lodgings was emetic. It was fortunate that he was living an almost reclusive existence, for the stink was overpowering as he opened his front door and beheld the carnage. Surely the domain of a homicidal maniac, the space was ornamented with portions of death. Arranged lovingly, like delicacies on a small table, were the amputated arms and legs of some unfortunate person. If the young man was no murderer, then surely he was a psychopath, a cannibal who had decided to feast upon the dead.

The sound of quick, purposeful steps could be heard on the stairs and the expected visitor, Corréard, burst into the room. He showed no sign of shock at the butchery and neither did the reek of rotting flesh upset him. Corréard had, nigh on three years before, over a period of days while floating between life and death, eaten from the hacked-off limbs of dead companions. Since then, such sights had racked his dreams, but somehow, in the cold light of a winter's day, these scraps, arranged for purposes of research, seemed acceptable. Over the past few weeks, his host, Géricault, had been living with putrefaction as fragments of bodies had decomposed all about him, helping the artist to approach the horror precipitated by the wreck of *The Medusa*.

The flagship of a prestigious expedition to repossess the colony of Senegal, *The Medusa* had been driven onto a sand bank by its inept captain, a relic from the *ancien régime* who had been appointed leader of the expedition, not for any qualities of seamanship, but in recompense for past political services. Corréard, as a member of that ill-fated expedition, had been the victim of an avoidable shipwreck and a selfishly misconceived rescue plan. Adding insult to injury, when Corréard had sought compensation, he had been spurned by an indifferent government. Outraged by its callousness, he had embarked on that very modern tactic of turning himself into a kind of celebrity by publicizing his misfortune. To this end, Corréard had written *The Shipwreck of the Frigate, The Medusa* – a best-seller – and was visiting this stinking room to elaborate on certain visual details that were absent from his text. He was here to help create an image, to act as adviser to this disturbed young artist, who was deep in a painting with which he sought to make his name.

So gripping was the indictment of the French leadership in Corréard's book that it had been translated into English, German and Dutch, with an Italian translation forthcoming. The work, in its second French edition, had become more politicized in scope and Corréard visited Géricault, not only to reconstruct specific details of his terrifying days on the raft, but also to elucidate the sinister state of affairs. His argument, to which his own misfortune bore witness, offered a scathing appraisal of the Bourbon Restoration, which, he claimed, was intent on betraying the positive gains of nearly three decades of French political struggle.

Host and visitor began to talk, exploring the labyrinth of issues that led out from that supreme act of cowardice, the release and cutting of the ropes that were supposed to tow the raft of *The Medusa* to safety. One hundred and forty-seven people had been herded onto this makeshift platform because of a shortage of lifeboats. Abandoned by the leaders of the expedition, who fled to save themselves, all but fifteen had died on board.

Swept along by Corréard's intense and penetrating diatribe, Géricault listened attentively. He had begun to look about, in the streets and in the press, for something to excite his desire for relevance. He had come back early to Paris from his Italian painting trip, not with the usual copies of Michelangelo, but with scenes of carnival upheavals, executions, and a fistful of tortured erotic drawings. He had returned, searching for the kind of story that smacked of the moment, for an incident that thrilled the readers of the popular press of the day – one of those lurid news items that reported wide-ranging infamies, from criminal and sexual scandals to suicides, shipwrecks and cannibalism.[3]

Alexandre Corréard and Théodore Géricault, meeting in the midst of this butchery, had both suffered devastating setbacks, had scandals hounding them, had secrets to conceal and yet were determined to surmount misfortune: Corréard, tireless in his struggles for retribution and justice; Géricault, tackling his ambitious canvas with a fervour and single-mindedness that could be gauged from the hideous array of decomposing flesh with which he chose to populate his studio. It was a temporary space; he had rented it to paint the raft. Hence the strewn limbs, the sketches of the successive

4

outrages in the drama, the small model of the platform, which had been assembled for him by the ship's carpenter, a man who had questioned aspects of Corréard's account of their thirteen days adrift.

Catching sight of a bundle of studies for which he himself had posed, Corréard pondered them for a moment and then turned round to confront the large canvas on which Géricault had begun to work. He saw his own figure taking shape, centre stage, in pride of place, the star of the nightmare.

2

Voyages Out

For love and loathing

THREE fraught years earlier, in the summer of 1816, a summer that would change their destinies, Alexandre Corréard and Théodore Géricault appeared very different from the agitated, injured beings who would meet in that grisly studio during the winter of 1819. Both seemed, uncannily, so much younger. Géricault, in contrast to his later self, was very much the young man-about-town, handsome, well dressed, with an attractive head of reddish, light-brown hair. Corréard was lithe and sinewy, excitable and alert. These two men, who would become important figures in each other's lives, had urgent reasons to leave France. Love would drive Géricault away; loathing for what was happening to his country would send Corréard, as a pioneer, to Senegal.

Despite the costly failures during the final months of his reign, Napoleon had boosted the self-esteem of a great many Frenchmen. In 1814, the twenty-six-year-old Corréard was by no means alone in feeling dismay at his Emperor's defeat. Although a conciliatory constitutional monarchy was swiftly created, Louis XVIII was obliged to reward survivors from the *ancien régime*, counter-revolutionaries, and those who had been supportive to the Crown in exile. While the King was to preserve many of the improvements made in French

6

administration since his elder brother, Louis XVI, had been forced from the throne and guillotined, the year 1814 saw ennoblement on an unprecedented scale and witnessed the restoration of that emblem of an all-powerful monarchy, the palace of Versailles.[1] Such conflicting signals alarmed a country suffering from defeat and a formidable sense of collective loss.

During their childhood and youth, Alexandre Corréard and Théodore Géricault had known only the turmoils of revolution and the authoritarianism of the Empire. Alexandre had been born into a class that had prospered since the French Revolution and grew up in one of the grandest houses in the precariously hill-hugging town of Serres in the mountainous region of south-western France. On his father's side, the family had been merchants since the Middle Ages and his mother's family were middle-class professionals. Elizabeth, the mother of the ten children of whom Alexandre was the sixth, was fervently religious. She kept to her faith throughout the Revolution, which had, by turns, been unsympathetic or ambivalent towards the Church. Just as Alexandre's flair for enterprise suggests some measure of paternal influence, so Elizabeth's tenacity was reflected in the ardour of her son's subsequent struggles against the injustices of the state. He attended a military school in the imperial city of Compiègne, coming to maturity when Napoleon was at the height of his power. In 1812, as the tide turned against the Emperor, with food and anti-conscription riots at home, defeat in Spain and retreat from Russia, Corréard joined the *Garde Impériale*, in which he served until 1814.[2]

During those two years the military and domestic situation in France deteriorated rapidly. With so many men conscripted, wounded or dead, the women and children were to be found hard at work in the fields. Abroad, the unenthusiastic remnants of the French army in Spain were defeated at Vitoria-Gasteiz in June 1813, allowing the victorious Wellington to enter southern France. Napoleon was likewise defeated at Leipzig in October 1813, enabling the Prussians to push on towards the French frontier. By the early months of 1814, peasants were streaming into Paris with their carts and cattle, seeking refuge from the invading armies. The mentally disturbed were turned out of asylums in order to provide quarters for the retreating troops; hospital patients were driven from their beds to make way for the wounded. In March, famine and pillage threatened the capital, presaging complete social breakdown.[3] Dead bodies were heaped on the banks of the Seine and floated eerily in the river – a situation that the authorities duplicitously assured inhabitants would have no deleterious effect on drinking water. Mounds of the military dead were piled into mass graves and Paris took on the air of a sacrificial altar to a lost cause.

Then, at the end of March and the beginning of April 1814, it all changed. Throughout the city Allied troops paraded. In the Tuileries, along the Champs-Elysées and in the Palais Royal droves of curiously attired English tourists, along with a multitude of occupying troops, gave Paris the splendour of a fabulous extravaganza; a stroll through the capital would present the visitor with a:

> savage Cossack horseman, his belt stuck full of pistols, and watches and hatchets . . . the Russian Imperial guardsman, pinched in at the waist like a wasp, striding along like a giant, with an air of victory that made every Frenchman curse within his teeth as he passed him . . . the heavy Austrian, the natty Prussian, and now and then a Bashkir Tartar, in the ancient Phrygian cap, with bow and arrows and chain armour, gazing about from his horse.

The cosmopolitan mayhem of the occupation flashed visions of 'hopeless confusion . . . Russians, Poles, Germans, Italians, Jews, Turks and Christians, all hot, hurried and in a fidget'.[4]

To secure peace and stability in Europe, the Senate, at

the behest of the Provisional Government and acting on the wishes of the Allied victors, summoned the Bourbon Louis Stanislas Xavier, King of France, to return home after his interminable exile and accept his rightful place on the throne. The event was heralded in a fast-selling pamphlet in which the Royalist author, Vicomte de Chateaubriand, celebrated the Allies as liberators, denounced Napoleon as having had 'the sword of Attila and the maxims of Nero', and hailed the royal family as healers.[5]

Returning to France in 1814, the Bourbons may have been thoroughbred French with their line stretching back to the Middle Ages, but they were also an unprepossessing group who were coming to restore regal authority and order to a country that had run wild with bloodthirsty political experiment. Louis XVIII claimed that he had been *de facto* king since the death of his young nephew, Louis XVII, in 1795. By 1814, he was ageing, childless and deteriorating with gout, yet his uncompromisingly absolute attitude – a reaction to the execution of his brother, Louis XVI – had mellowed during his long exile. Not so, however, that of his younger brother, the dangerous and provocative Duc d'Artois, who would succeed Louis as Charles X. Artois surrounded himself with extremists, 'ultra-Royalists' who had no intention of letting renegade Republicans and Bonapartists have their say in Restoration France. These *ultras* were to prove the most problematic of all the political factions, launching intimidating affronts to Louis's rule.[6]

The Senate called Louis XVIII to the throne as a constitutional monarch on April 7th, 1814. The King arrived with a strong desire to heal his kingdom's wounds and to effect, as he put it, a 'fusion of two peoples'.[7] France was a nation in a state of shock and, as Louis's remark suggests, divided against itself. If a good number of people in many parts of the country welcomed the return of a king, the Army remained loyal to Napoleon. There was also a huge gulf between the spirit of the capital and that of the provinces.

Even Paris split along political lines. Dangerously, factions were testy and likely to clash.

Remembering Napoleon's rule as a period of opportunity, Alexandre Corréard noted that at the time of his fall, 'I wanted to distance myself as far as possible from France and so I engaged as an engineer in the military expedition that was going to retake possession of the French establishments on the African coast.'[8] As a geographical engineer, Corréard was appointed to identify a suitable location on Cap Vert, or its environs, for the establishment of a colony.[9] An expedition was set up in the late autumn of 1814 and participants began to assemble at Brest for a departure planned for the spring of 1815. The scheme for which Corréard enlisted, directed by the *Société philanthropique du Cap-Vert*, attracted a large number of Republican or Napoleonic sympathizers who were seeking to start afresh in a French colony.[10] In order to gain official support, the *Société* presented itself as an organization that had been created to prevent disaffected people from taking their capabilities and capital off to other countries. With a schedule for reimbursing the Crown for its initial support, it was a properly structured commercial venture with shareholders, annual general meetings, a committee of directors and projected profits.

As Corréard prepared to ship out, something unforeseen happened. On March 1st, 1815, Bonaparte, who had been smouldering away on the island of Elba, landed in Golfe Juan on the south coast of France with the 400 soldiers that he had illegally kept with him in exile. His reckless gamble seemed to be paying off when he entered Grenoble six days later, escorted by the very troops sent to check his advance. On March 10th in Lyon, Napoleon was greeted by crowds yelling, 'To the scaffold with the Bourbons! Death to the Royalists.'[11] Events followed swiftly. On March 14th, the Crown jewels were sent to England for safe-keeping. Louis addressed the Chamber of Deputies, claiming that he stood for peace and liberty, whereas Napoleon brought war. However, on March 19th, the King prepared to travel north into exile.

During the evening of the 20th, Napoleon arrived in the capital, at the head of yet more troops who had been sent to oppose him.[12] Unwisely, Louis had replaced the ever-popular *tricolore* – that rallying point for *liberté, égalité, fraternité* – with the white flag of the Bourbons. Upon Napoleon's return, the *tricolore* was unfurled with alacrity and shop-keepers exchanged their royal emblems for Napoleonic insignia, much as they had replaced Napoleonic eagles with *fleurs-de-lys* only nine months before. It was as if Louis had never happened; the reconceived monarchy had been still-born.

On June 12th, Napoleon marched his army north to engage the Allied troops massed under Wellington and the Prussian Field Marshal, Blücher. There were scores to settle and his new position to consolidate; although vast portions of the French population were loyal to the King, Louis now found himself in virtually unprotected exile. The future of the monarchy was, once again, in doubt until Napoleon's daring bid was, within the week, crushed by his defeat at Waterloo. By June 21st, Napoleon was back in Paris, where, the following day, he abdicated in favour of his son.[13] The period known as the *Cent-Jours* was at an end. To prevent himself from being captured by his enemies, Napoleon was persuaded to make haste for Rochefort, where two frigates would be waiting to enable his escape to America.

Forgetting earlier triumphs under Louis XIV against a united Holland and England, the French tended to under-value their navy. In a pitiful state when Napoleon first came to power, the Navy during the previous forty years had had a chequered history, although the loss of most of France's first colonial empire at the end of the Seven Years War in 1763 provoked a great period of naval reorgani-zation, ship-building and peaceful exploration – particularly in the Pacific. Louis XVI zealously sought a fleet that could wrest control of the high seas from the English and recover the French colonies lost under his grandfather, Louis XV. By 1780, France possessed seventy-nine warships, eighty-six frigates and about one hundred smaller ships. It was thus able to play a decisive but costly role in the American War of Independence. The French blockade of Chesapeake Bay in September 1781 prevented the Royal Navy from coming to the aid of Cornwallis, who was thus forced to surrender at Yorktown in mid-October. The Peace of Versailles in 1783 gave France minimal overseas territory, including Tobago and Senegal, yet the cost of helping the Americans to free themselves from the yoke of unjust English taxation had been punishing. The deficit in the Navy budget anticipated the ruin of the *ancien régime* itself.[14]

After the Revolution there had been a massive emigration and, by 1792, half of France's naval officers had disappeared. In 1793, when war broke out with England, the British sank the French fleet at Toulon. During the two following years France lost many vessels through bad seamanship as well as in combat, a sequence of disasters culminating, in 1798, in Nelson's crushing defeat of the French at Aboukir. Despite some reorganization under Napoleon, the Navy was again beaten on October 21st, 1805 at Trafalgar, where the smaller but remarkably well-trained English fleet beat their demoralized and badly equipped Franco-Spanish adversaries. The victors gained incontestable supremacy on the high seas and the subsequent blockade kept what was left of the French Navy starved of materials and largely port-bound.[15] After the Restoration, that blockade ceased to exist, but, towards the end of the *Cent-Jours*, the British Navy was again on hand to frustrate any attempt at escape.

The plan, in June 1815, was for Napoleon to set out for America on board the *Saale* while a frigate called the *Medusa* was to act as a decoy. This ship was the work of the acclaimed designer Jacques Noël Sané and construction had begun at Paimboeuf in April 1807. She was to carry forty-four cannon, each capable of discharging a two-kilo shot. The hull was reinforced to her waterline, with copper to protect it against molluscs and barnacles, and when ready for launch in July 1810, *The Medusa* was utterly up to date. Her maiden voyage in December of that year was the command of a small Franco-Dutch expeditionary force to Batavia.[16] She had an adventurous voyage out – she was battered by high seas, lost her convoy and was given chase by an English squadron. Shortly after her arrival in the Dutch East Indies, the islands were surrounded by British warships and Batavia surrendered. Julien Schmaltz, the quixotic adventurer who would later play such a shameful part in the *Medusa* scandals, was captured by the English in that action. Meanwhile, *The Medusa* and her sister ship, *The Nymphe*, gave the enemy the slip, sailed off and arrived safely back in Brest almost a year after they had left France.

The captain of *The Medusa* recorded that after various adventures during the voyage, he was in no doubt about the excellence of his ship. During 1812 and 1813 she put to sea a considerable number of times, given the blockade. Among her duties was the hunting of English ships returning from the Far East. Her career was distinguished; by February 1814, along with *The Nymphe*, she had engaged and destroyed a dozen enemy ships. Under the Restoration she served as a patrol vessel in the Caribbean, arriving back in Rochefort for a refit in February 1815. When the *Cent-Jours* ended ignominiously for Napoleon, *The Medusa* was nominated to draw the fire of the English squadron moored off Rochefort, while the Emperor would flee on board *The Saale*. The captain of the frigate, le Chevalier Ponée, believed that he would be able to distract and deceive the English for about three hours. After that, his frigate would be finished, but by then the Emperor would have put a little distance between himself and his pursuers. In the event, Napoleon gave himself up to the British Captain Maitland on board H.M.S. *Bellerophon* on July 14th, 1815. Ponée, understandably, lost his command with the coming of the Second Restoration and, only months after its refit, *The Medusa* returned to Rochefort to be disarmed.[17]

With the unforeseen episode of the *Cent-Jours*, Alexandre Corréard's departure for Senegal had been called off when the *Société philanthropique* 'momentarily suspended its activity'. Feeling that there were grounds, once again, for hope at home, he was in fact left in France merely to witness the swift and final failure of his Emperor and the subsequent eclipse of liberal prospects. After such an unexpected affront to European security, the subsequent occupation of France was more stringent than it had been in 1814, and the pressure on Louis to root out subversives even greater. With peace, however, the efforts of the *Société philanthropique* recommenced, helping 'peaceful men who were tired of exhausting their resources in conditions of social paralysis, and who, without ceasing to be French, wished to create a new country on land that is still untouched'.[18] For Corréard, the expedition – a chance to escape to a land uncomplicated by conflicting ideologies – seemed overdue.

In the summer of 1816, the date of Alexandre Corréard's eventual departure for Senegal, Théodore Géricault also wished to leave France. He signalled no immediate dissatisfaction with the Restoration; indeed, he played an active and positive part in the new regime. Born into a comfortable family in September 1791, Théodore spent his earliest years in Rouen, in a pro-Royalist household that was threatened during the revolutionary period. In those early years the boy quite probably absorbed something of the violence that characterized the Reign of Terror under the *Jacobins*, and it is likely that the Géricaults left for Paris in order to escape from local revolutionary unrest. In the capital,

Théodore's father, Georges-Nicolas Géricault, joined his brother-in-law, Jean-Baptiste Caruel, in his tobacco enterprise, while his son attended a nearby boarding school. Let out on Thursdays, the boy was much indulged by his grandmother, who lived with them in the faubourg Saint-Germain, and he threw tantrums when it was time to return to school. In 1806, Théodore entered the *Lycée Impériale*, where it soon became evident that he had more enthusiasm for horses than for school work; his eyes glazed over as he wrestled with Latin grammars, while his 'spirit was captivated by visions of imaginary cavalcades'. However, early on he did display artistic talent; a friend and fellow pupil, Théodore Lebrun, recorded Géricault's natural aptitude for drawing, commenting that he was already an artist without being conscious of the fact. Géricault used much of his recreation and study time to draw and, as a result, appeared somewhat of a dunce and was frequently thrown out of class.[19]

In May 1807 a family event occurred that would have immense repercussions on Géricault's life and art. In a union not unusual for the period, Théodore's fifty-year-old uncle, Jean-Baptiste Caruel, married a young lady of twenty-two. His chosen, Alexandrine-Modeste de Saint-Martin, possessed a lively interest in the arts, and, within the confines of her new family with its narrow focus on business, it was inevitable that the artistic leanings of her personable young nephew would attract her. An animated friendship grew up between them, which benefited from the blessing of Alexandrine's busy husband. When she met her nephew, she was keen to see his sketches and chat about art. He, at sixteen, was flattered, perhaps even a little embarrassed, by the attentions of an attractive young lady.

Within a year of Alexandrine's marriage, a death occurred that drew the young aunt and youthful nephew even closer together. In March 1808, Théodore's mother, a strong woman whom he had loved and by whom he had been much loved, died. While his father entertained practical and predictably safe ambitions for the boy, his mother had supported her son's budding artistic talent. After her death Théodore had even greater need of his aunt's understanding.

The boy and his father moved to the Right Bank, to a house only a stone's throw from the rich and luxurious establishment in the rue de la Grange-Batelière where the Caruels were installed. Alexandrine was particularly sensitive to the boy's grief, having lost her own immediate family during her childhood. She became a consoling presence who began to fill the emotional vacuum left by the death of Théodore's mother. He rejoiced in her sympathetic and vivacious spirit, and she delighted in the vitality of someone close to her own age who was still sufficiently young enough to become a kind of protégé. Easily distracted by his eagerness to become a man-about-town, Théodore responded warmly to the relaxed atmosphere generated by Alexandrine in the Caruel home. The extent to which and the swiftness with which he had become an important part of her world is indicated by the fact that in December 1809, Géricault was named godfather of the Caruels' second son, Paul.

As the bond grew between Alexandrine and her elegant, tall, well-formed nephew, she became the most important woman in his life. They became so close that they started to hatch secret plots, and deception became a part of their alliance. Théodore's father had continued misgivings about his son's desire to paint, so Alexandrine entreated her husband to provide a respectable cover for their nephew's artistic studies, persuading him to take the young man into his tobacco firm as a trainee accountant and turn a blind eye to the boy's absences. During these escapades, Géricault went either to a riding school or to class at the studio of the Anglophile and Royalist, Carle Vernet, an accomplished painter of history and horses. It was there that Théodore befriended Carle's son, Horace, whose own studio would, by contrast, and within the first few years of the Restoration, become a rendezvous for subversive Napoleonic and Republican liberals.[20]

On the brink of maturity and made financially independent by a substantial legacy from his mother, Géricault was much admired by women. Carle Vernet 'asserted that he had never seen such a good-looking man', going on to remark that 'his legs were, above all, superb'. Géricault was fashionable and becoming careful in his dress to the point of affectation.[21] Yet any vain posturing was 'tempered by a marked expression of gentleness'. His eyes twinkled, and such a dashing and accomplished young man, exhilarated by the thrill of horsemanship and beginning to take himself more seriously as an artist, proved a compelling companion for the youthful Alexandrine Caruel.[22]

One highly attractive place where he was welcome to stay and work was the magnificent property near Versailles that had been purchased by his uncle, Jean-Baptiste Caruel, in 1802. Adjoining the Parc de Trianon, the Château du Grand-Chesnay had once belonged to officers at the court of Versailles and was a typical purchase for a member of the bourgeoisie who had become rich after the Revolution. The château's park and its dependent agricultural holdings were sizeable and the house boasted a library of 1,400 classical texts and a collection of fifty pictures and engravings, mainly by minor Dutch and French artists.[23] While these indifferent images had little to offer the young visitor, the large house and extensive grounds gave Géricault the opportunity to enjoy privileged moments with his young aunt. She was becoming more than a strong ally against paternal caution, and the young man's attraction to her was developing into something more complicated than a mere replacement for maternal love and encouragement.

While at Grand-Chesnay, Géricault visited the nearby imperial stables to make paintings of three of the Emperor's studs. He also frequented the Trianon Gallery where he would study the works of art, and it was there that he would

meet and flirt with a certain Mlle Montgolfier, who mistook
the dalliance for a serious advance, a misunderstanding that
Géricault was, as the months went by, more than happy to
encourage. To be seen in the company of Mlle Montgolfier
and to be talked about would provide a useful camouflage
for the serious, dangerous and illicit adventure upon which
he was embarking.[24]

Not wishing to become a victim of the disintegrating
Napoleonic military machine, Géricault bought himself a
replacement for his military service. This was perfectly legal
and above board, and it meant that he could set out on a
course of study that would prepare him for the competition for that year's prestigious *Prix de Rome*, a four-year
scholarship to study at the French Academy in a city rich
in classical statuary and artistic heritage. Whether or not
Géricault entered the competition in 1812 has been argued
by historians and biographers; what remains important is
that, despite his youthful exuberance and dandyism, a new
strain of seriousness appeared in his approach to his work.
This, however, by no means suppressed his zest or volatility;
in May he was banned from the Louvre after abusing and
hitting a young student in the Grand Gallery. While the
incident reveals his passionate nature, it also vouches for the
fact that he was in the Louvre studying or copying. What
is more, it was not the first time he had fallen foul of the
museum authorities; Vivant Denon, director of a museum
richly swelling with Napoleonic booty, had occasion to ban
Géricault temporarily after he brutally resisted officials when
they attempted to repossess his membership card. Perhaps
the loss of his grandmother in April 1812, and the stress of
the developing triangle between himself, his kindly uncle
and his attractive aunt, help to explain such outbursts.

Left even wealthier by the death of his grandmother,
Géricault rented an empty shop in the boulevard
Montmartre, and there he began work on the first of his
few great projects, *The Officer of the Chasseurs*. Painted

between September and October of 1812, at a time when Napoleon had rashly driven his army deep into Russia with its infamous winter coming on, the tensions in the painting reflect the moment at which and for which it was painted. It questioned imperial military hubris by pitting the officer's splendid uniform, so out-of-place and yet worn with such bravura, against the inferno of the battle-field. Resonating with fear, the painting registered the degenerating military situation and its insight was prized. Géricault won a gold medal worth 500 francs in the Salon of 1812 with what was, in fact, his first submission. By the time the Salon shut its doors on February 13th, 1813, Napoleon had overreached his imperium and 300,000 of Géricault's compatriots lay dead in the Russian snow.

The Officer of the Chasseurs hinted at failure on a national scale, revealing that Géricault was already becoming sensitive to the political tensions that would transform him from the careless man-about-town into a shaven recluse, working with fanatical zeal on *The Raft of The Medusa*. Eschewing Napoleonic myth-making, and contrasting what attracted him to the military – the fine horses, opulent saddlecloths, shimmering uniforms – with the reality of battle, Géricault began to engage with the truth.

During 1813 his uncle, Jean-Baptiste Caruel, became the mayor of the village of Chesnay and, with his young wife, began to spend more time at their château. As he added mayoral duties to his already demanding business schedule, relations between aunt and nephew developed into a full-blown love affair. The Château du Grand-Chesnay provided an ideal setting for secret meetings and intimate encounters. Yet despite their rapture, the affair was understandably fraught. The underlying tension of deceits and stolen moments, along with the complication of Alexandrine's children and generous husband – the very man who had proved to be such an accommodating uncle to Géricault – placed enormous pressure on the lovers. For every moment of elation, for every afternoon of delight, they suffered acute pangs of conscience. Nonetheless, their affair seemed unstoppable, their love uncontainable.

Perhaps in an attempt to distract himself from this complicated relationship, Géricault decided to become a soldier. No sooner had Louis XVIII returned to France than the young artist joined the 1st Company of the Musketeers. By comparison with the dangers of Napoleonic conscription, the life of a soldier who was unlikely to be forced into battle pleased Géricault. The blade in him adored the red uniform and he was happy riding the fine grey chargers of the Musketeers.[25]

Embodying Louis XVIII's desire for unification and forgiveness, forty-one out of the 176 *Mousquetaires Gris* had served in Napoleon's army, including Géricault's captain, the Comte de Nansouty. Others, such as Géricault himself, and the poets Lamartine and Alfred de Vigny, were veterans of no cause, but simply rich, idling young men who were attracted by the prospect of playing soldiers. Their function was, however, taken very seriously by Louis XVIII, who believed that had his older brother surrounded himself with what was effectively a private army, he would not have fallen victim to the Revolution.[26]

When the *Cent-Jours* sent Louis into exile, Géricault – the toy-soldier musketeer, with his impulsive compassion for the underdog – followed the fleeing king through a dreary northern French landscape made even more depressing by an unrelenting downpour. Troops and wagons became bogged down in the mud of Picardy and many followers took the opportunity to desert. Even well-mounted horsemen could advance only with great difficulty as the paths had been reduced to muddy rivulets.[27] Ordered to disperse at Béthune, the Musketeers were free to return to their families or to follow the King into exile at Ghent.

There are several theories about where Géricault passed the remaining weeks of the short-lived insurrection. If he made for the Château du Grand-Chesnay, which would have been a likely destination, he would have been in contravention of the Imperial Decree of March 13th, 1815, banning all members of the *Maison du Roi* from residing in Paris, its outskirts or near the imperial palaces at Saint-Cloud and Malmaison. However, Géricault needed Alexandrine, and Napoleon's mind was on other things.

The *Cent-Jours* substantially altered the political direction of the Restoration. During his first year in power, Louis had proved a good strategist. In attempting to rule over a radically divided country, he was prudent. He willingly submitted to Allied demands for a charter that would provide the basis for the country's constitution. Devised by the King himself, the document aimed to guarantee political liberties. But the *charte* was, in effect, a vague document that offered with one hand and took away with the other. Article Eight was just such a piece of chicanery and one that would create great problems for Alexandre Corréard and his fellow liberals: 'Frenchmen have the right to publish and print their opinions, as long as they conform to the laws for repressing abuses of this liberty.' Declaring that the *charte* was granted 'by the free exercise of our Royal authority' in the 'nineteenth year of our reign' was a gauntlet thrown down to the left, as it effectively negated the political experiments that had changed the face of France over the previous twenty-five years.[28] But, above all, the liberal tenor of the document and its intentions were detested by the extreme right.

After the final fall of Napoleon, the elections of August 1815 yielded a surprising result.[29] Perhaps shaken by the swiftness and sureness of Napoleon's invasion, and manifesting their desire for stability, voters swung to the right, returning a Chamber that was predominantly ultra-Royalist. Louis retaliated by pointedly inviting the moderate Duc de Richelieu to lead his ministers as President of the Council.

Nevertheless, the government included a strongly *ultra* military axis: typified by the elderly Vicomte DuBouchage, who had served as a minister under Louis XVI and who now became Minister of the Navy. By contrast, Elie Decazes was a bright young politician who had so attracted Louis's admiration as the Parisian Chief of Police that the King appointed him Minister of Police. Decazes was an ambitious man of action, who proved to be a strong moderate presence in the government, rapidly declaring his opposition to the extreme right.[30] This did not, however, prevent him from introducing rigorous legislation that safeguarded the survival of the King. During the autumn of 1815, a series of laws was introduced that suspended habeas corpus for those plotting against the royal family and the state, suppressed inflammatory acts against the Crown and set up temporary criminal courts without juries, and which denied the right of appeal.[31]

Although such menaces can only have provided confirmation for Alexandre Corréard about the desirability, if not the absolute necessity, of leaving France, the true political situation was even uglier than the election result and subsequent legislation indicated. Having received slight comfort from the First Restoration, émigré nobility was full of bitterness and out for blood. Only two days after the abdication of Napoleon in favour of his son, the first major reprisal occurred in Marseille, where Napoleon's supporter, General Verdier, was removed from power. During the ensuing forty-eight hours, 250 sympathizers were killed in an orgy of retribution. There was violence in Avignon and about one hundred Protestants were slaughtered in Nîmes as the new White Terror began. There were mass purgings of the public sector; between 50,000 and 80,000 members of the civil service, about one-third of its total workforce, lost their jobs. Above all, untold numbers of people were murdered or tortured, particularly in the south where the ultra-Royalists entertained dreams of southern secession. As the contemporary observer, John Scott of Gala, put it, '*ultra-royalism . . .*

has raised its monstrous head, – professing to see in the last
disturbance the necessity for giving a stronger hand to
authority . . .' Politics descended into mob violence and
looting as the White Terror weakened the Bourbons and
their standing with the nation for ever. The 'demoralized
state of the public character', wrote John Scott, rendered 'it
impossible for the King, whose inclinations and principles
are decidedly moderate, to reckon on a substantial support'.[32]

The relaunching of the French monarchy promised a
turbulent passage fraught with conflict, and it was against
such an unpropitious background of stormy division and
strife that the newly repainted *Medusa*, with thirty cannon
removed to make way for extra troops and stores, was about
to set sail on her final voyage.

The expedition prepares

As a dangerous reminder of how things had turned against
the liberal and Republican cause at home, the crew, troops,
colonists and officers on board the flagship *Medusa* were to
be under the command of a political appointee, the haughty
Hugues Duroy de Chaumareys, a rusty relic from the *ancien
régime* who had not put to sea for about a quarter of a
century. Such ill-judged appointments were a hazardous fact
of the Restoration as the outmoded, old aristocrats, who
had remained loyal to the Crown, solicited just recompense.
The absurdity of their appeals is amusingly underscored by
a celebrated story of a petition brought to the government
by an officer of the Royal Navy who had not served since
1789. At that time the man had been a midshipman, but
now demanded the rank of Rear-Admiral, arguing that this
would have been his present position had his career evolved
normally. 'Tell him,' said the Secretary of State, 'that we
acknowledge the logic of his reasoning, but that he forgot
a key fact – he was killed at the battle of Trafalgar.'[33]

While the Restoration government was forced to suspend

more than 600 officers and numerous enlisted men on half-pay, or – worse still – make them redundant, the Crown was obliged to reward émigré naval officers. Some of these had gone so far in their fidelity to the Bourbons as to fight against their own country; manpower shortages in England's Royal Navy had led to the recruitment of French Royalists who had fought against Republican and imperial France. Obviously, the readmission of such men would rankle as the Restoration simultaneously checked the natural advancement of many of the officers who had distinguished themselves for the Republic and Empire. The situation was not only combustible, it was absurd. Veterans of great wars 'are vegetating on half-pay in ports, while brilliant commissions are given to those whose only merit has been to remain faithful to the Bourbons', sniped Gicquel des Touches, one of the other captains appointed to the Senegal convoy. Des Touches justly insists that fidelity 'can be rewarded by pensions, court appointments, and not by commands of ships on which depend both the lives of men and the honour of the flag'. Even the Minister of the Navy himself, the Vicomte DuBouchage, the man who was organizing the expedition to Senegal, had been retired from public life for a quarter of a century when he was appointed.[34]

As for Chaumareys, the man who was made commander of the convoy, his credentials were acceptable, but twenty-five years out of date. On his mother's side, Hugues Duroy de Chaumareys was related to one of Louis XVI's great maritime strategists, Admiral d'Orvilliers, whose example determined the young man's choice of career and greatly facilitated his advancement in the service. Hugues Duroy embarked as a midshipman under d'Orvilliers in 1779 and on April 17th of the following year saw action in the American War of Independence. Wounded in the head, but remaining at his post, he was subsequently promoted to ensign on the warship *Pegasus* and then rose swiftly to the rank of captain of a transport ship. If it had not been for the Revolution, it seems that Chaumareys, with that kick-start of a family connection and a demonstrable gift for advancement, would have made a tolerable career in the Navy. However, in December 1790 he became an émigré, and it was during this period as a refugee from the Revolution that he fabricated the tale that he would use to obtain his captaincy of *The Medusa*.[35]

What is established fact is that Chaumareys participated in the émigré landing on the peninsula of Quiberon on June 27th, 1795. The aim of the invasion was to rally support throughout Brittany and then march on Paris. It is likewise true that the insurgents were captured and transported to Vannes, where Chaumareys, unlike so many of his fellow Royalists, escaped being put to death. He avoided execution by lying. He swore that he was not an émigré, that he had not taken up arms against the Republic and that he had had no military function at Quiberon. He was subsequently imprisoned in a tower at Vannes from which he absconded, aided by sympathetic guards and by a local woman named Sophie de Kerdu. Chaumareys hid in the town for more than two weeks before escaping to the English fleet and thence to England, where he was treated as a hero and given the Royal and Military Order of Saint Louis on February 21st, 1796.[36]

Lavish praise and recompense were prompted by a self-aggrandizing narrative that Chaumareys published while in London. Selling in both French and English bookshops, the text made assertions that would be guaranteed to serve its author admirably in any future Restoration. Addressing those dead comrades who had, in fact, acquitted themselves more honourably than Chaumareys himself, he declares: 'There are still tyrants in my country . . . And you, touching victims of honour and fidelity, I saw your sublime devotion . . . You're no longer here; but you spilt your generous blood for your King . . .'[37] With sentiments worthy of a swash-buckling adventurer in the heat of escape, Chaumareys praises the courage of the young Sophie de Kerdu and, describing his leave-taking, swears that 'I will do nothing but devote my life to you'.[38] In the event, Chaumareys did not return to marry his brave Breton peasant and live happily ever after; within two years he married another Sophie, a Prussian baroness named Sophie de Azentrampf. Obviously such a match was socially and politically more serviceable.

Making his bid for celebrity with a self-serving rewriting of the failed uprising, Chaumareys's distorted version of events, which ran into three editions, propagated the myths on which he would rebuild the wreckage of his career. Returning to France in 1804, he sat out the Empire at his eighteenth-century family residence, the Château de Lachenaud in Limousin. During the first Restoration, using his relationship to Admiral d'Orvilliers, his service record, his inflated account of his participation in the Quiberon fiasco and slightly adjusting his age, Chaumareys solicited a commission. In a torrent of letters to the Minister of the Navy, the story of his escape from Vannes was further distorted to his advantage. The part played by Sophie de Kerdu was excised from his new account, which simply foregrounded Chaumareys's own incontestable presence of mind. In light of such bravery and composure, the Minister deemed him worthy of the command of a frigate, and Chaumareys was expeditiously awarded the *Légion d'honneur* in order to make amends for a ministerial gaffe in attempting to award him the Military Order of Saint Louis for a second time.[39]

When, with testimonials from his noble friends that were mistaken in matters of character and not always accurate in matters of fact, Chaumareys eventually secured his command of the Senegal expedition on April 22nd, 1816, he was to face understandable suspicion and opposition from the other officers appointed to the convoy, most of whom had served France during the previous decades. Gicquel des Touches found him, on first meeting, to be snobbish and ill-informed.[40]

In the aborted 1815 expedition to Senegal under Captain
Bouvet, Chaumareys was to have commanded a corvette.
Although this appointment would have given him ample
time to familiarize himself with the potential hazards of the
route, the Minister of the Navy urged Chaumareys to arrive
in Rochefort well in advance of the 1816 departure, in order
to profit from the experience of sailors who had navigated
the coasts of Senegal. It was a region badly charted and
notoriously treacherous, but there was an account that had
been published in 1789 documenting some of the dangers.
Sailing in the violent currents off the West African coast,
the author observed that the water around the ship became
steadily clearer. He urged the Captain of the *St Catherine*
to take a sounding, but was rebuffed: 'Why are you afraid,
we're 80 leagues from the coast?' That very night they were
beached and their tragedy was merely a prologue to attack
and capture; when survivors from the frequent shipwrecks
in the area managed to make it to the shore, they found
themselves on the edge of the interminable white sand plain
of the Sahara Desert and prey to hostile Moors.[41]

Apart from the strong currents, there was an ill-defined
and hazardous sand bank to contend with, but Chaumareys
appears to have been too high-handed to take the opportunity to learn from those with knowledge of the region.
Gicquel des Touches, in order to assert his superiority over
this man who, on first meeting, had treated him so contemp-
tuously, offered to give Chaumareys written instructions on
how to circumnavigate the notoriously dangerous Arguin
Bank. Upon receiving this offer of a helping hand,
Chaumareys immediately altered his attitude towards des
Touches, who observed that the commander of the expedition appeared much intimidated by the challenge of the
perilous shoal.[42]

A legitimate source of Chaumareys's anxiety was the inadequacy of the available maps. Hydrography was in its infancy
and charts were notoriously incomplete; many shoals, rocks

and reefs remained unrecorded because cartographers had an imperfect knowledge of the seas. This lack, coupled with a navigator's incapacity to correctly determine longitude, resulted in numerous shipwrecks.[43] In the case of the dreaded Arguin Bank, Bellin's map, which was supplied by the Ministry, was known to be defective in its tracing of the western perimeter of the extensive shoal, a fact indicated in the *Nautical Description of the African Coast*, which was sent to Chaumareys before the convoy set sail. This text, printed in 1814, was a ninety-eight-page document written by Admiral de Rosily, Director of the Navy Depot Hydrographic Service. It confessed that the French navy had minimal and imperfect knowledge of the West African coast, and a good deal of whatever information it did possess was the result of hearsay rather than serious study. It stated categorically that the 'maps of the western coast in *Bellin's French Hydrography* are flawed and it would be dangerous to trust them'. Above all, it claimed that 'For the greatest safety, you must take soundings as often as you can and proceed according to the depth and the type of sea bed that you discover.'[44] Such warnings would surely alert an insecure commander – if only his insecurity was not hedged by blinding arrogance.

A further source of concern for the leaders of the expedition was that Geoffrey de Villeneuve, in his authoritative history of West Africa published in 1814, urged that all Europeans 'who want to visit the African coast must aim to get there during November in order to acclimatize themselves before the onset of the rainy season which commences at the end of June and lasts until October'.[45] With an unpropitious date set for *The Medusa*'s departure, the avowed fallibility of his navigational aids, his lack of recent experience and the political hostility of his officers and men, Chaumareys was, from the first, a captain under stress.

When Charlotte-Adelaide Picard, one of the eldest daughters in a family of nine colonists bound for Senegal, approached Rochefort at the end of May 1816, she found it bustling with activity. There was the clatter of the workmen in the shipyards and the clanking of the enormous chains that yoked convict dock-labourers together as they dragged the heaviest loads along the wharves.[46] There were soldiers, stevedores, port officials, sailors, and officers like Chaumareys, strutting self-importantly about, attracting sneers and snide remarks from those condemned to drink away their enforced retirement in cafés, dreaming of glorious, old, imperial days. There were blacks from Africa, mulattos from the West Indies, and the buzz and hubbub of a recently revivified naval port.

Charlotte Picard had left Paris on the morning of May 23rd, and even the earliest stages of her journey had proved to be not without misadventure. On the first evening, the innkeeper almost burned down his establishment while preparing an omelette for the travellers. The following night their driver got completely drunk, and between Niort and Rochefort the road was so bad that they got stuck in the mud. These incidents must have given her pause; if such misfortunes could happen on home ground, then what lay in store for her in a wild and distant land? The spirited young lady, wondering if she would ever see her own country again, gazed with deep affection at the lush, fertile green of France's beloved Loire Valley, as her coach sped on towards her port of embarkation.[47]

Arriving in Poitiers on June 1st near the end of his journey to Rochefort, Charles-Marie Brédif, a mining engineer who kept the only surviving notes of *The Medusa*'s voyage written during the trip, checked to see if the Fortin Barometer that he had entrusted to his friend, Dechatelus, was intact after the bumpy ride. To his great chagrin he found it broken and, registering a rare note of pessimism, he remarked that 'our voyage has really begun badly'. To his further dismay, he found his chronometer was not working and hoped to be able to have both instruments repaired at Rochefort, where he arrived on June 4th, the same day as Colonel Julien Schmaltz, the future Governor of Senegal. Brédif lodged, like Schmaltz, his wife and his daughter, at the *Coquille d'Or* and found Rochefort, which stood near the mouth of the Charente River, attractive and astir. Brédif and Dechatelus set about having their instruments repaired and had the pleasure of meeting with several old friends from their student days at the respected *École Polytechnique*.[48]

Alexandre Corréard, in his second determined attempt to escape from France, along with the other colonists supported by the *Société philanthropique*, were arriving in Rochefort, eager to depart, all seeking the fresh air of a new start. The climate in Senegal may be oppressive, but the chance to get away from the stifling constraints of Restoration France filled them with optimism.

On a showery and windy June 9th, Brédif boarded a boat to carry him downriver to *The Medusa*, which was in the roads, a sheltered area offshore where ships could safely anchor. After a while, the rain became steady and the passengers were forced to take refuge in the sailors' quarters or in the hold. Despite a high tide, the incompetent pilot managed to beach them near some chalky rocks ominously known as The House of the Devil. It took an hour to free the boat, by which time the tide had gone out and they touched bottom again. This second time, the crew were unable to dislodge the boat from the mud and so the passengers spent the night stranded on board.

Enduring a dirty bunk and devoured by fleas, it was with some relish that Brédif, a stranger to the sea who was having second thoughts about voyaging into a dangerous unknown, lovingly recorded the details of the meals he took when they disembarked the following day at Verjou, only half a league from Rochefort. Lunch consisted of a milk soup, an omelette and soft cheese, his supper of 'peas and excellent little fresh fried sardines'.

At Verjou, they took on more passengers bound for Senegal, including the Picard family, and then went sailing out of the Charente in a good wind that speeded them along towards the ships at safe anchorage off the Île d'Aix. Among these, they discerned the newly repainted black and white hull of the flagship *Medusa*. By 9 a.m., Brédif and the Picards had boarded the frigate, where they found everything in complete disorder. Bad weather had prevented the ship from being notified as to their arrival, and matters were further complicated by the recent embarkation of 161 unruly soldiers from the Africa Battalion.[49]

Three days later, on June 13th, everything was shipshape, and the officers, in full dress uniform, welcomed Governor Schmaltz, his wife Reine, his daughter Eliza and their maids on board. Reine was of a nervous disposition and a patient of the celebrated and revolutionary mental specialist Dr Esquirol. She was immediately alarmed to find out that one of her great doctor's disciples, Falret, who was to have sailed on *The Medusa*, had cancelled his passage at the last minute.[50]

It was a motley collection of vessels assembled for the voyage out. There was the corvette, *The Echo*, detailed for a hydrographic and reconnaissance mission along the Senegalese coast. There was the supply vessel, *The Loire*, a flute built in India and, according to the Director of Construction in Rochefort, too slow and unwieldy to participate in such an expedition. There was the brig, *The Argus*, the former H.M.S. *Plumper*, which had been captured from the English. *The Argus* was a type of ship normally employed for short coastal trading voyages, a function she was intended to fulfil upon arrival in Senegal. *The Echo* was weatherly and fast, but both *The Loire* and *The Argus* would soon find it impossible to keep up with the convoy's flagship. Originally another ship, *The Elephant*, had been designated to lead the expedition, but in the event she was appointed to other duties, a fate that did not allow her to escape from the incompetent appointments of the Vicomte DuBouchage.

After delays caused by strong headwinds on the 15th and 16th, as the convoy finally got under way, Brédif noted that *The Medusa* did not hoist all of her sails in order not to leave *The Argus* and *The Loire* behind. By three o'clock on that first afternoon, *The Loire* sent signals that she was drifting badly, and Chaumareys gave the order to drop anchor. It was hardly a promising start for a convoy urged by the Minister to make all possible haste for Saint Louis in Senegal. The colony was to be repossessed as rapidly as possible as there was this year's valuable gum harvest at stake.[51]

Towards the end of the eighteenth century, West Africa had been considered simply a loading stage for the slaves captured, largely by Moors, from the interior; the continent was seen as little other than 'a mine of men to exploit'. Restoration France, trailing behind England in its abolitionist thinking, and suspicious that the moral stance of its recent enemy masked commercial intentions, vacillated over the legality and acceptability of the trade. Nonetheless, the avowed intention of Louis's government was to re-establish a legitimate colony in Senegal, and the Crown thus offered grants of African land to the colonists who were going – or escaping – to start a new life. There were projects for the growing of cotton, cocoa and sugar cane and plans to profit from the lucrative gum trade. With its laxative and anti-haemorrhaging properties, gum was valuable in medical applications. It was also an ingredient in the manufacture of inks and dyes, and a substance much used by confectioners.[52]

The commanders and crew of the various vessels were as heterogeneous as the ships themselves. A man of identical rank and sharing Chaumareys's loyalty to the Crown was the captain of *The Echo*, François-Marie Cornette de Vénancourt, who, descended from American plantation colonists, had been born in Martinique in 1778. A Monarchist like Chaumareys, during the *Cent-Jours* his crew on board *The Actéon* mutinied in favour of Napoleon while anchored in the roads of Fort Royale, Martinique.

Vénancourt was wounded trying to restore order and became a prisoner on board his own ship. Nevertheless, he dissuaded the sailors from hoisting the Napoleonic *tricolore*, which would have put them at risk from the English ships patrolling those waters. When they eventually sighted an English brig, the mutineers pressed their prisoner to take command of an attack. Pretending to acquiesce, Vénancourt merely signalled his difficulty to the English, who promptly escorted *The Actéon* to Martinique. Safely arrived, Vénancourt began a campaign to rid the island of Napoleonic supporters and further the Royalist cause in the West Indies. If sympathetic to Commander Chaumareys's politics, Vénancourt clearly resented the superior appointment held by an inferior mariner.[53] Not only was Vénancourt a more experienced sailor, but he had been recently and demonstrably brave in his loyalty to the Crown.

Gicquel des Touches, captain of the unwieldy *Loire*, was of the opposite political persuasion. He had also revealed an exemplary courage unknown to Chaumareys. Aged ten, he had been on board a ship sailing for Guadeloupe when she was given chase by the English. The captain beached the ship in order to give the enemy the slip, but the young boy was denied a place in the lifeboats. Left on board the wreck with a handful of unruly sailors who started to drink themselves to death, the young Gicquel discharged a cannon in the direction of the enemy, which achieved the desired effect. The English approached and boarded the French wreck and took the plucky young Gicquel and his mates prisoner. He was, at length, transported back to England in the stifling 'tween decks of an old frigate, in conditions resembling those of the slave ships, where air was in short supply, the odour rank and the insects legion. After a year in prison in England, he returned to France to fight for the Republican cause. Gicquel des Touches served at Trafalgar, after which, once again, he was taken to an English prison. Having persistently revealed his audacity and his presence of mind, and with two of his brothers dead in the service of the Republic, it is hardly surprising that des Touches took exception to the airs put on by an undeserving émigré such as Chaumareys.[54]

The Captain of *The Argus*, Léon Henry de Parnajon, was, like Vénancourt, of colonial origin and, like des Touches, had fought at Trafalgar. Later captured by the enemy, he had languished in an English prison from April 1809 until August 1811. Apart from that brief interruption, he had been sailing since 1799, so he too was more seasoned than the expedition's commander.[55]

On board *The Medusa* herself, the official second-in-command was the Republican, Lieutenant Joseph Reynaud. His career against the English had been lively. In 1804 he had been shipwrecked on the French coast after an engagement with two enemy frigates. During a mission to Santa Cruz in 1805–6, he had captured H.M.S. *Calcutta* after a two-hour battle. Latterly, however, his duties had involved protecting coastal shipping, and so in his present rank of lieutenant he had little experience of long voyages. What is more, his politics made relations with his captain awkward.

The second lieutenant on board *The Medusa*, the 'very knowledgeable and zealous' Jean-Baptiste Espiaux, had been wounded twice in the wars with England and had been captured by the English in the Bay of Cádiz in June 1808. He escaped while being transported to England, courageously diving off an English ship and returning to the siege of Cádiz. Later, aboard *The Medusa*, participating in Napoleon's escape bid to America, Espiaux witnessed the humiliation of his Emperor's ultimate surrender to the English. Such an officer can have had but a slight regard for his obsolete, out-of-touch captain, a man sustained by the discredited idea that he was capable simply because he was of noble birth.[56]

Ensigns Chaudière, Lapeyrère and Maudet had all fought against Britain and all spent long periods in English prisons.

They made no secret of their contempt for their captain, a disdain generously reciprocated as these officers had all sprung from the bourgeoisie.

Only the most forceful and knowledgeable commander would have been able to harness officers and men so dangerously at odds with him. The clamour of contradictory voices on board *The Medusa* echoed the discord that resounded throughout France, where divisiveness, selfishness and suspicion were the upshot of thirty years of ideological struggle. If passions ran high at home, emotions intensified in the creaking confines of an overloaded frigate, just forty-seven metres from prow to stern, twelve in its beam, and sailing into the tropical heat at the height of summer.[57]

A captain no longer in command

At 7 p.m. on June 17th, the convoy weighed anchor once again, cleared the Straits of Antioch and finally set sail. But only hours after this second start, the wind dropped, *The Medusa* became ungovernable and lay stranded in the lull before the storm. Slowly, the sky darkened, the sea swelled and strong gusts of wind squalled about the ship. Suddenly and quite violently, the frigate tacked in order to avoid drifting onto a reef, an accident that would have ensured her destruction. For those on board who were aware of what had happened, such a brush with calamity can hardly have added to what little faith they had in their dubious captain.

The departure roll call on board *The Medusa* listed 166 officers and crew, sixty-one passengers, ten members of the frigate's artillery, 161 soldiers in two cosmopolitan and volatile companies of the Africa Battalion, and the wives of a couple of these soldiers – a neat total of 400 souls. The passengers on board *The Medusa* included explorers and geographical engineers, such as Corréard and Dechatelus, the naturalists Lachenault and Kummer, the mining engineer Brédif, and clerks, administrators and settlers such as Picard with his prodigious family. There were the professionals and tradesmen needed to build and maintain a colony: pilots, gardeners, scouts, schoolteachers, bakers, hospital directors and surgeons. There were twenty-three colonists sailing under the auspices of the *Société philanthropique*: carpenters, cabinet-makers, locksmiths and two women with three young children.[58] Among the passengers, there was also Gaspar Mollien, a man who later made a name for himself as an outstanding geographer and who, usefully, prefaced an account of his travels into the interior of Africa with a narrative of his eventful voyage to Senegal. Besides Mollien, there were several people on board, who, for a variety of motives, would provide records of their adventures. Brédif kept his diary regularly. Charlotte Picard published, under her married name of Dard, a narrative of the voyage and its aftermath. By far the most exhaustive version of events was the result of a collaboration between the ship's second surgeon, Henri Savigny, and Alexandre Corréard, whose observations were subsequently challenged in print by Lieutenant Anglas de Praviel of the Africa Battalion. As for the cargo on board the frigate, it included munitions, supplies, state papers, statute books, travel writings about Africa, a bust of Louis XVIII intended to preside over the Governor's residence and, in the hold, three casks containing 90,000 francs in coin.

During the following days, passengers who had never been to sea, such as Corréard, Brédif and Charlotte Picard, variously adapted to the pitching and rolling and heaving and groaning. They marvelled at the optimism and thunderous splendour of sails unfurling. They found the sharp, salt sea breezes bracing, the speed and the spin drift exhilarating. They were awed by the lateral tilting of their tall ship in a squall. They learned the hard way that they had to stoop, supporting themselves against unexpected jolts as they moved around the dimly lit and encumbered spaces between decks. They adjusted to the smells of those confined spaces as the frigate moved south. They became attuned to the creaking of her joints, to the noise and flurry of the changes of the watch when sailors scurried up and down vertiginous ratlines as if they were doing it in their sleep. When the winds changed, they observed a great buzz of activity. Charlotte Picard noted that 'the crew was busy everywhere, climbing the rigging, perching on the extremities of the yards, climbing the highest masts, bellowing as they rhythmically and forcefully pulled on certain ropes, swearing and whistling' as 'the yards were turned on their pivots, the sails were stretched and the ropes fastened'. The sailors seemed to be in control of what appeared to be giant bundles of laundry fastened by myriad stays, strung about every which way from deck to mast and from mast to mast in seeming confusion. The passengers experienced in the abrupt reports – 'Sail ahoy' and 'Two points off the starboard bow' – and in the sudden order – 'Lower away on the main' – strange and novel incantations which promised, in their mystery, that this vessel would indeed deliver them safely to their exotic destination.

When the wind dropped on June 18th, Brédif, struck by the fact that he could see nothing but water encircling him as far as the great disc of the horizon, recorded that the sea was 'extremely calm and of an indigo blue'. But by one o'clock the weather was changing and that evening, when he dined with the commander at a table meticulously laid and amply provided, he wasn't sure that he would be able to hold his meal down: 'the movement of the boat is more pronounced in his quarters and it made me feel unstable. After dinner, the walk which we took with the ladies on the quarter-deck made me feel better and I went to bed feeling fine.'[59]

Many passengers were, indeed, seasick and Charlotte Picard was, at times, terrified by the new sensations surrounding her. During the night, she went up onto the

37

quarter-deck and 'watched with horror as the frigate flew across the water'. There were 'sounds of cracking from every corner as this large mass of wood seemed ready to smash under each wave that thwacked us in the side'.

The commander's indecisiveness was made dramatically apparent in his slowness to react when, at sunset on June 23rd, a fifteen-year-old sailor slipped off the breech block of a cannon and through a forward port-hole. When the cry 'Man overboard' was heard, many of the crew and passengers were on the poop and at the bulwarks, being entertained by the antics of a school of porpoises. A bo'sun's mate managed to grab the boy by the neck of his jacket, but had to let him go lest he too was pulled into the sea. Buffeted in the waves, the boy grabbed at a dangling rope, but the rapid motion of the frigate ripped it from his hands. Sailors attached themselves to ropes and plunged into the sea – but in vain. When an attempt was made to signal *The Echo*, it proved to be too far off and so it was decided to fire a cannon as a substitute, but none of the fourteen on board was loaded.

At length a lifebuoy was thrown, the frigate hove-to, her sails were shortened and trimmed, and a skiff was let into the water, from which three sailors began to search the heavy sea. They pulled towards the lifebuoy, disappearing under the billows, reappearing on the crests of each wave until they were forced to give up. Brédif remarked on the considerable 'disorder in the manoeuvre', with excited passengers impeding the efforts of the sailors. In the narrative of the voyage to Senegal that Corréard and Savigny felt compelled to bring before an astonished public, they commented that the 'manoeuvre was long' and that 'we should have come to the wind as soon as they cried "man overboard"'. The failing light, which slowly obliterated all hope of rescue, darkened the spirits of the helpless onlookers as the youth, who should – and perhaps could – have been rescued, was left to drown.[60]

Already the expedition was beginning to fall apart. The recently modified *Echo* was a match for *The Medusa*, but *The Argus* and *The Loire* were starting to lag behind. Chaumareys was torn between his duty to keep a convoy together and the wishes of DuBouchage and Governor Schmaltz to reach Senegal as swiftly as possible. By the time the Captain of *The Loire* lost sight of the command ship, des Touches had received no indication regarding the route. Maintaining his course for several hours in the hope of sighting *The Medusa*, des Touches then decided to set his own. Vénancourt, the captain of *The Echo*, who kept close enough to Chaumareys to receive communications, noted a discrepancy between the prescribed course and the actual navigation of *The Medusa*. He thought it wise, at that stage, to follow what Chaumareys did rather than what he signalled. When, on June 24th, Vénancourt and Chaumareys compared their respective estimates of their position, they were out by eight minutes of longitude, or nearly six nautical miles, and forty-six minutes of latitude, a measurement equivalent to the identical number of nautical miles.[61]

The disorderly manner in which the Captain had reacted to the fatal accident set passengers and officers whispering. The rougher soldiers and humbler sailors began to mutter their superstitions, and Chaumareys would find small groups falling silent as he approached. Increasingly, he found himself isolated and excluded. The pull between innate and excessive arrogance, and his desire to hide his inadequacy from those whom he had been appointed to lead, meant that the commander was acting erratically from the start. Among the passengers at his table, however, was a member of the *Société philanthropique*, a man by the name of Antoine Richefort. An ex-mariner and a braggart with a clouded history, Richefort claimed great knowledge of the west coast of Africa. Finding himself an outsider on his own ship, Chaumareys turned increasingly to this man, ignoring the advice of his unsympathetic officers. With seeming relief, Chaumareys placed his unqualified trust in this blusterer.

Once the gloom over the lost sailor boy had begun to lift, the usually optimistic Brédif recorded many agreeable moments of life on board: how he delighted in climbing onto the bowsprit while *The Medusa* was ploughing through the foaming sea at ten knots, white spray showering up about him; how the crew and passengers took great pleasure in catching tuna with fishing lines that the sailors dangled from various parts of the ship; how there was great excitement as a stowaway was found on board – Marie-Antoine Rabaroust, an infantry surgeon's junior assistant who had resigned after the *Cent-Jours* and who wished to escape France to start afresh in Senegal – and how, once discovered, he was swiftly assimilated into the Governor's retinue as a domestic.[62] People marvelled as they sailed south, at the stars that hung above them, stars of a different world, another hemisphere. It was a splendid adventure, the chance of a lifetime.

Chaumareys had predicted that they would sight Madeira by the morning of June 26th. As it was not until sunset that land was eventually spotted, his margin of navigational error had increased; his calculations – or perhaps those of his side-kick, Richefort – were now off by a whole degree, or sixty nautical miles.[63] That night *The Medusa* tacked so as not to draw in too close to the islands, and on the following morning she sailed along the southern coast, past Ponta do Sol towards Funchal. Disparaging the advice of his officers with whom he was politically at loggerheads, and placing his complete trust in the boastful Richefort, Chaumareys allowed *The Medusa* to be directed too close to the coast. In lee of the land, there was a sudden calm and the frigate was at risk of being swept ashore by the strong current.[64] After a lively exchange of views, Lieutenants Espiaux and Reynaud prevailed and *The Medusa* made for open sea and a fresh wind. As a result of such a perilous, inept and time-wasting manoeuvre in the bay of Funchal, Chaumareys decided against sending a boat ashore for provisions. The crew and passengers were left with a passing impression of an island whose fertile slopes were covered with vineyards, orange and lemon groves and fields bordered with banyan trees. The fiery colour of the volcanic earth and the fragrance of citrus fruits blowing out to sea made a powerful appeal to those inex-perienced voyagers who hankered for land and who had never before glimpsed such extravagant vegetation.[65]

By the evening of June 28th, the highest point on Tenerife came into view, the peak aflame with sunset. As they approached the island the following morning, the fiery crown had given way to a misty veil through which *The Medusa* sailed into the bay of Santa Cruz. At 7 a.m. a boat was lowered, and a party, including Lieutenant Reynaud, Ensign Lapeyrère and Midshipman Sander Rang, was chosen to go ashore. They suffered as they sat in their boat awaiting the completion of landing formalities; loud, incessant bells tolled for the Feast of St Peter and, as the morning mists cleared, a fierce sun beat down upon them. At length the French sailors were allowed to disembark and were introduced to the Governor, Don Pedro de Rodriguez, a Francophile and Royalist who was curious about the political situation in Europe. After this meeting, the shore party set about making purchases and were aided by some French inhabitants. The Spanish wife of one of these urged the sailors to stay and make some amorous conquests on the promenade that evening. They were tempted, but they declined. Their captain and Governor Schmaltz were eager to make haste for Senegal and so they were back on board *The Medusa* by late afternoon.[66]

Towards midday, while the party was ashore, *The Echo* rejoined *The Medusa* and Vénancourt came aboard. His log somewhat reproachfully makes it clear that he considered it injudicious to have put a boat ashore in such a strong breeze.[67] While on board the flagship, he was an appalled witness to the dangerous trust that Chaumareys placed in the loud-mouthed Richefort. In what seemed to be a repeat of his vainglorious performance along the coast of Madeira, Richefort decided that it was unsafe to stay at anchorage off Santa Cruz, and again Chaumareys took his advice. Charlotte Picard accused Richefort of changing route:

> for no other reason than to show that he knew how to make the necessary manoeuvres to tack. Every moment . . . we came, we went, we came back again, we drew near to reefs in order to defy them . . . All this went on so long that after a while the sailors refused to obey the scheming pilot, saying loudly that he was nothing but a vile impostor.

Indeed, several officers 'complained to the Captain that it was shameful to place his confidence in someone unknown', adding 'that they would not obey a man who didn't have the temperament to command'. Chaumareys scorned this intimation of mutiny, and, according to

Charlotte Picard, 'was, without doubt, relieved to have someone else doing his job'. To that end, he ordered the crew and pilots to obey his self-appointed surrogate. Adrift, among officers more competent than himself, Chaumareys was now dangerously out of his depth.

Even before reaching Tenerife, Brédif had started complaining about the 'insupportable sun'; now the weather had become heavy, giving him a headache and making him feel sick. Nonetheless, he claimed to be in good health generally, possessed of a hearty appetite and, despite the continual creaking and straining and heaving of the boat, he slept well. The heaviness and the headaches were signs that *The Medusa* was sailing into the tropics at the very hottest time of the year. Charlotte Picard recalled how, as they neared the Tropic of Cancer, the sun seemed suspended directly above their heads and 'the burning wind blowing off the Sahara' offered its parched welcome to a strange land.[68]

From the maintop a ringing was heard, and a raucous hunting horn broke in, followed by a shower of pulses and dried peas, which hailed down onto the deck. These announced the 'Lord of the Tropic', who would preside over the ritual festivities that accompanied the crossing of the Tropic of Cancer. When the hard rain halted, a booted courier, whip in hand, arrived on the quarter-deck and delivered a dispatch to Captain Chaumareys, who seemed mildly flattered to be the centre of such attention. At last, a sailor disguised as the despotic Lord, covered in skins like a Lapp, yet shivering in the sweltering heat, arrived, interrogated the Captain and said that he would visit him at ten the following morning. At this point Chaumareys, happy to have any release from the disquieting concerns of navigation, granted a day of festivities on the morrow.[69]

Waking at 2 a.m. on July 1st, Brédif was astonished by the thousands of points of reflected light that surrounded him. Slowly, he understood that his little cabin was covered in five centimetres of water, which, he later discovered, had flooded from the gutters of the ship. Going up on deck, he marvelled at the lucent wake and the brilliance of the sails, appearing as if they had been lit by torches from beneath. Moonlight on the foam and billows had ignited the sea into a thousand flames and, with myriad stars milking the sky, it seemed the most sublime privilege to be aboard that ship that night.[70]

By morning, the baptismal vat was ready. Into it would be plunged any passenger refusing to pay tribute to the Lord while crossing his Tropic for the first time. Sailors dressed as priests heralded the ancient Lord in his twelve sheepskins and hempen wig, accompanied by a sailor disguised as his wife with scandalous protuberances and scaly hands. The couple was dragged on an old gun carriage by two sailors disguised as bears. At each side, to the front and back of their chariot, processed sailors representing the Four Corners of the World: Europe with plumed hat and epaulettes, Asia, Africa and America variously blacked or bronzed by a mixture of soot and tar. Sailors who were crossing the line for the first time were embraced by both their majesties, after which the passengers were rushed through a friendly baptism. But just as they thought they had escaped the worst, a signal sounded and thirty bucket loads of water held in reserve on high rained down on the quarter-deck. Everybody was soaked – passengers, sailors, officers. The Four Corners of the Earth were blanched as water splashed and gushed in every direction. In this uproar, the defrocking of the Lord of the Tropic began. His beard, his diadem, his sceptre were all torn from him; even the excessive breasts of his travesty of a wife were ripped from her body and tossed about from sailor to sailor.

While Chaumareys played his part as the Captain of a ship participating in a time-honoured ritual, Richefort was strutting on the forward deck, casting his untutored eye on a treacherous coast not half a cannon shot off the port side. This charlatan was pumping himself up with his own rhet-oric – bragging that he had already saved *The Medusa* from certain shipwreck, boasting of his experience of this coast and vaunting his knowledge of the perilous Arguin Bank.

Within the previous twenty-five years, at least thirty ships of differing nations had been wrecked on the stretch of the African coast between Cap Bojador and Cap Blanc, along which *The Medusa* was now sailing. Not eleven months earlier, the American brig *Commerce* had been wrecked near Cap Blanc and the crew taken into captivity by hostile Moors.[71] While Chaumareys was so enjoying his carnival-esque diversion, that humble echo of the court burlesques of the *ancien régime*, a maritime disaster that would shake the fledgling Restoration was in the making. Given the conflicts on board, the mutterings of discontent, it seems most appropriate that the shadow-play subversion of the masque should act as a prologue to tragedy.

The officer of the watch, Lapeyrère, knowing that *The Medusa* was sailing too close to the coast and was much at risk from the strong onshore drift, put an end to the celebrations and changed course without consulting the Captain. This unauthorized initiative resulted in a brisk exchange with Chaumareys, but saved the frigate from running onto a reef that stretched half a league out to sea. The commander of the expedition, having mistakenly identified Cap Barbas earlier that morning when *The Medusa* was still to the north of that cape, had already set in motion the miscalculations that would result in the loss of his ship. Even a land-lubber like Brédif correctly recognized the cape as they doubled it at midday.[72]

Throughout that afternoon *The Medusa* sailed at a safe distance from the coast as *The Echo* followed off the stern on the port side. Towards evening the weather became hazy, and anxious passengers watched as the shore melted into the mist and darkness.

The Echo spent the early part of the night of July 1st–2nd signalling to *The Medusa*. Until 11 p.m. she remained off the port stern, but then she overtook the frigate. Vénancourt, wanting to maintain contact in these dangerous waters, lit extra lights and sent up a flare. He also took soundings, finding a depth of forty fathoms at 11 p.m. and forty-five fathoms at midnight. Losing sight of *The Medusa* shortly afterwards, he sent up a second flare, but, getting no response, he wisely continued to steer west-south-west.

It was Ensign Chaudière's watch from eight to midnight. At ten, he took a sounding of thirty-five fathoms and at twelve he registered a depth of forty-five. Chaudière did not inform Captain Chaumareys when *The Echo* disappeared from sight. This was irregular, but perhaps, by that time, Chaudière questioned the utility of communicating anything of importance to his captain. Henri Savigny was on deck when Reynaud took over the watch at midnight and was surprised that the lieutenant failed to reply when a signal from *The Echo* was, at last, sighted. *The Medusa* once again lost touch with *The Echo* at 3 a.m. and this fact, along with the information that *The Echo* had overtaken *The Medusa* and was now off the starboard, or offshore bow, was communicated neither to Espiaux, who relieved Reynaud, nor to Captain Chaumareys.[73]

By now mistrust was running so high that a group of officers attempted to dupe Chaumareys in order to secure a wider margin of safety. The accepted wisdom was that to reach Senegal – avoiding the dreaded Arguin Bank which extends out into the ocean from the bay to the south of Cap Blanc – a ship simply sights that cape and continues sixty-six nautical miles south-south-west before changing to a course south-south-east. Officers, anxious about the competence of their commander, could thus indemnify themselves against any errors that he might make, simply by 'moving' Cap Blanc farther south. Several of these conspirators went to rouse the Captain at 5 a.m. on the morning of July 2nd and persuaded him that a huge white cloud in the distance was, in fact, Cap Blanc itself. Although Chaumareys had already claimed to have identified it the previous afternoon, a perfectly logical consequence of having 'identified' Cap Barbas well in advance, they succeeded in their deception without the least difficulty.

But they had not counted on the arrogance of Richefort, who thought it necessary to sail only thirty nautical miles after sighting Cap Blanc before setting a southerly or south-easterly course. The cunning group had taken the trouble to dupe a captain who was no longer in command.

People's nerves were frayed; an officer who dared challenge the competence of Richefort was arrested. Ensigns Lapeyrère and Maudet calculated that they were heading straight for the dangerous shoal and, when they challenged Richefort, they received the blithe rebuff: 'Never mind, we're in eighty fathoms.' The colonist Picard, who had made two previous trips to Senegal, sought out the Captain to alert him that the ship was making straight for the ill-defined sand bank. As with the protestations of the officers, Picard's opinion was ignored. Richefort patronizingly asserted, 'We know our job, get on with yours and rest calm.' Seeing that he would not prevail, and hopeful that Providence would keep them from danger, Picard went down to his cabin and tried to bury his fears in sleep.[74] When, at half-past seven, a sounding gave a depth of 120 fathoms, a course was set south–south–east.

During the morning, even those passengers with no previous experience of the sea noticed a steady change in the colour of the water. Corréard observed that deep blue had given way to green. Shoals of fish flashed just beneath the surface. Then they detected sand scrolling in the little waves, agitated by the gentle breeze blowing from the north. The sailors set about catching large numbers of fish, delighting in a sport that distracted them from the other telltale signs of shallow waters: the kelp, appearing in great quantities, floating on the surface; a sea becoming clear.

At midday, Ensign Maudet and Midshipman Rang took over the watch, in little doubt that they were on the fringes of the Arguin Bank. Brédif had measured the temperature of the sea at eight o'clock that morning; taking a reading after lunch, he found that the temperature of the water had, alarmingly, risen by more than four degrees centigrade in as many hours. A sounding was taken that gave only eighteen fathoms. Chaumareys was informed. He hastened up on deck and gave the order to steer a quarter to starboard. Everyone became silent. Another sounding was taken. Ten fathoms. Brédif watched as Rang turned pale. Two quarters to starboard. Six fathoms. The frigate's sails swelled with a sudden gust of wind. There was a shudder. A scrape. A jolt. A roar from the keel rasping against some undesired obstruction. *The Medusa* lurched to a halt. An absolute silence was broken only when a sudden panicked clamour resounded throughout the stranded vessel. On the quarter-deck, officers were shouting orders. The Captain alone was unable to speak.[75]

Politics and passion

Whether Louis XVIII was a liberal at heart or merely appeared to be one, because that is what the situation dictated, is unclear; certainly, in 1815–16, he seemed happy to uphold sentences that condemned his subjects to the guillotine for political crimes. In July 1816, the month in which *The Medusa* came to grief, three men accused of participation in a Bonapartist conspiracy had their right hands severed, prior to being guillotined before a huge crowd in front of the Hôtel de Ville in Paris. And still the *ultra*-dominated Chamber criticized the government for not rooting out sedition.

Throughout the early stages of the second Restoration, the person whom Louis XVIII increasingly came to treasure was Elie Decazes, the Minister of Police. To gain such favour, Decazes had played the part of devoted young man, eager to learn the ways of government from a master. The ruse worked and Louis began to consider Decazes a disciple, a spiritual son – even perhaps the offspring he never had. Decazes, a political animal who won favour by telling Louis what he wanted to hear, was also a clear-headed tactician who believed that he knew what was good for the Crown and hence for the country.

Anxiety had been mounting among the liberal ministers that the reactionary policies of the *ultras* would lead to the downfall of the monarchy. During the cold and rainy summer of 1816, which gave rise to a serious famine in many parts of France, Decazes set out to turn the King against the hostile and reckless policies of the extreme right. A threat to the *charte*, to national security and to sovereignty itself, the *ultras*, Decazes suggested, would push as far as civil war in order to realize their reactionary aims. Carefully selecting what he brought before the King and Richelieu, the leader of the government, Decazes presented the picture of a country suffering at the hands of a right-wing Chamber. During the summer recess, with support from Pozzo di Borgo, the Ambassador to Russia, and even from Tsar Alexander I himself, Decazes persuaded Louis XVIII that the Chamber must be dissolved to make way for autumn elections that could reduce the parliamentary influence of the *ultras*.[76]

Théodore Géricault's shift from dandy and man-about-town to serious and dedicated artist took place against this ministerial struggle for the safety of the realm. Géricault's political attitudes were beginning to mature and his decision to leave the Musketeers at the end of 1815 had been influenced by his realization that there was a good deal of arrogance and vanity in his devotion to the royal family.[77] He had settled in the rue des Martyrs, in a part of Paris that was too bourgeois to be called bohemian, but was nonetheless a quarter occupied by the painters, writers, politicians and wits who were agitating against the status quo. The young painter's change was also part and parcel of a pervasive shift in the attitude of middle-class youth that was beginning to occur in France. In the Chamber of Deputies, citing young men born between the early 1790s and the early 1800s, Benjamin Constant spoke of a generation 'Less frivolous than that of the *ancien régime*, less passionate than that of the Revolution' and 'distinguished by its thirst for knowledge . . . and its devotion to truth'.[78]

The young painter's decision to leave the King's service was prompted by his desire to do more serious work in preparation for the 1816 *Prix de Rome* while, at the same time, juggling the logistically difficult affair with his aunt.[79]

On March 18th, 1816, along with twenty-nine painters and fourteen sculptors, Géricault sat for the first round of the competition. With seventeen others, he made it through to the next round, but on March 30th Géricault was informed that he had failed to make the list of ten finalists, and the contest was eventually won by an artist who, as is so often the case with these prizes, fell into obscurity.[80] Apart from the kudos of an award, the independently wealthy painter had no need of financial assistance in order to go to Italy and, as this was considered to be an important part of an artist's education, it is what Géricault decided to do.

An incident that took place not long before his departure testifies to Géricault's growing embarrassment with his image as a bright young thing. Théodore Lebrun, who was to have accompanied Géricault on the two-year Italian trip, called to see him and found Géricault making elaborate preparations for a ball, with his hair in paper curlers, intended to give it added bounce. When Lebrun was forced, for reasons beyond his control, to cancel his journey, Géricault assumed that he had done so merely to avoid travelling with so vain and frivolous a companion.[81]

The role of winsome man-about-town had, to a degree, become a mere façade for the intense affair that embroiled Théodore and his pretty aunt. Yet Géricault had become a divisive presence in Alexandrine's comfortable life and he was rattled, distracted, unable to fix and maintain a course of work. A substantial motivation for his Italian trip was the belief that he must distance himself, physically and emotionally, from the turmoil of his relationship.

On August 15th, 1816, the *Préfet de Police* issued Géricault with a passport for Switzerland and Italy. The young painter obtained a highly laudatory letter of recommendation from his teacher, Pierre-Narcisse Guérin, who claimed that Géricault 'is one of the pupils on whom must rest our greatest hopes'. And so Géricault was off to Italy in search of inspiration. He was fleeing the wreckage of his emotional life and he was leaving France at a time when the *Medusa* scandal was breaking. Obviously he had his mind on other things, but for Elie Decazes, eager to change the government and set a new course for France, the news of the shipwreck fell like manna from Heaven.[82]

3

The Wreck

AFTER the silence of the shock, after the shrieks of panic and the inaudible commands, came the volley of recriminations. Increasingly, during the voyage, murmurings of discontent had escaped from the quarter-deck, down through the moaning confines of *The Medusa*, to where veteran sailors vouched that they, 'by guess or God', would have a better chance of steering the frigate to its destination than this toffee-nosed Hugues Duroy de Chaumareys. This shipful of grousing erupted into accusation and affront when the frigate ran onto the Arguin Bank. Ensign Lapeyrère darted up onto the bridge and confronted the Captain's man, Richefort: 'You see, sir, where your pig-headedness has led us!'

Groups formed, intent on convincing themselves that they were not in danger. Others speculated on the exact nature of their dilemma, while nearly everybody proposed extravagant theories about what should be done. Only Chaumareys, stunned into silence, seemed incapable of coming up with a plan. Loath, in any case, to pay much heed to their captain, the officers, all with differing ideas, issued a barrage of conflicting orders, and a chaos of activity squandered the afternoon and evening of July 2nd. Certain necessary steps were, nonetheless, taken: Midshipman Rang, who never doubted that they would refloat *The Medusa*, set about executing the orders that he had been given. Studding sails, set on the outer parts of the topgallant and topmast booms, were pulled in, the topgallants dismantled, and preparations made to lower the boats, an operation interrupted while the Longboat, ignored in the rush to dispatch the expedition from Rochefort, was of necessity recaulked.

Lieutenant Espiaux went out in the skiff to take soundings. *The Medusa* drew five metres and, although it was high tide when she beached on the sandy bottom, skilful seamanship would be able to disengage and save her; it would take merely a modicum of informed humility to set matters right. A kedge anchor was dropped. This device, designed specifically to haul a ship into deeper water when she has run aground, did not produce, with this first attempt, the desired result. During the night, Sander Rang put out a boat to move the kedge farther from the ship, but at 4 a.m., when the tide was once again high, another attempt to pull off the bank resulted in the anchor – rather than the frigate – tearing free. The plan to drop the much heavier bower anchor was delayed, as the only boat capable of transporting such a weight was the Governor's Barge which was also discovered to be in a bad state of repair. Time was wasted while she was patched and sealed and, even then, empty barrels had to be fastened to the barge to give her the extra buoyancy needed to bear the bower's great weight. When it was at last dropped into the sand, mud and shells of the bank, the sea was so shallow that one fluke remained above the water, while the purchase of the other fluke on the shifting bed proved so tenuous that this attempt also failed.[1]

Despite Brédif's impression that everything was being done in complete disorder, several worthwhile measures were in fact taken by the lieutenants and the ensigns in their attempt to refloat the frigate. The hull was proving mercifully resistant to the shocks of the billows, although it was necessary to repair damage to the hold, where water was entering. The dismantled topmasts were put overboard, but the lower yards were left in place to act as crutches, should the ship list dramatically. To prevent this happening, barrels of powder were thrown into the sea and the cannon were moved to the port side to compensate for the tilt of the frigate. Lightened by the jettisoning of the powder, *The Medusa* nearly floated on the high tide and, had they ditched the artillery, there would have been a strong chance of success. Stubbornly, Chaumareys refused to sacrifice the cannon of the King, unable, it seems, to comprehend that the frigate herself was His Majesty's possession!

As the chances for successful rescue now seemed slight, a council was convened.[2] With Richefort shamed and Chaumareys in disgrace, it was at this moment that Governor Schmaltz began to take control. If the Captain proved unequal to his task, Schmaltz, by contrast, seemed able to adapt himself to almost any situation. He was a survivor, his every action motivated by his overwhelming desire to succeed. While Chaumareys's incapacity starkly revealed itself, Schmaltz's manoeuvres were more shadowy and his responsibility for the events that followed less easy to determine. In a fictionalized account of the wreck of *The Medusa* published in 1929, the author, Auguste Bailly, has Chaumareys sitting on the poop deck with Schmaltz when he hears a sailor singing the Marseillaise, the fervent Republican anthem that Napoleon so perceptively appreciated 'would save many a cannon'; a Royalist, Chaumareys is furious and orders the man to be clapped in irons, at which point the 'debonair' Schmaltz has a discreet word in the Captain's ear and the incident is forgotten.[3] Illustrative of the way Schmaltz could smooth things over, it also suggests that the Governor, who was happy to blow with the prevailing wind, was a less zealous supporter of the Bourbon monarchy than he pretended. He was dubbed 'an amphibious reptile' by a contemporary satirist, and his sudden ardour for the monarchy in 1814 had simply smacked of opportunism.[4]

His father German and his mother half-Gascon and half-Irish, Julien Désiré Schmaltz grew up in the cosmopolitan world of Lorient, a thriving port in Brittany. In 1797, when he met and married Reine, 'merchant' appeared as his profession on their marriage certificate.[5] A daughter, Eliza, was born the following year, but six days after giving birth, Reine suffered a severe post-natal depression that developed into manic rage, during which she took an aversion to her husband and daughter.[6]

With this apparent liability in tow, Schmaltz departed for the Dutch East Indies, where his advance was rapid and his life colourful. Despite Schmaltz's lack of military training, Governor-General Daendels promoted him to the rank of Lieutenant-Colonel in May 1808. But, after presumptuously sending the Governor-General an essay on the defence of Java, Schmaltz was suddenly retired in January 1809. Showing his ability for cunning readjustment, he recalled that 'I set myself up in manufacture and I trained several slaves that I owned, making of them good labourers. Both my wife and I worked with our hands and we succeeded.' After several months of manufacturing haberdashery, Schmaltz was happy to be recalled to strengthen the defences of the port of Surabaya. When the English attacked the town in September 1811, Schmaltz was taken to Bengal as a prisoner of war. Madame Schmaltz, who had suffered a second breakdown in 1805, succumbed to a third as the result of a terrible sea voyage and the imprisonment of her husband. At the end of 1812, Schmaltz was taken to England, whence, a year later, he was repatriated; Royou's *Biographie pittoresque* insinuated, rightly or wrongly, that Schmaltz had traded privileged knowledge about the island of Java for his freedom.[7]

With the return of the Bourbons, Schmaltz enjoyed an incredibly swift rise. On July 8th, 1814, he was confirmed in the grade of *Chef de Bataillon* and in August appointed

Lieutenant-Colonel. He was awarded the *Légion d'honneur* and assigned to Guadeloupe as commandant of Basse-Terre.

The destabilizing episode of the *Cent-Jours* served Schmaltz well. While in Gaudeloupe he let it be known that he harboured *Jacobin* sympathies, yet a daring bet on the failure of Napoleon's adventure gave him the appearance of a diehard Royalist. During a period of vacillation among the administrators of the island, a schooner, *The Agile*, arrived from France, persuading all except Schmaltz to back Napoleon. Schmaltz's refusal meant that he was arrested and sent for trial. But *The Agile* had arrived in Guadaloupe only three days before the Battle of Waterloo; by the time Schmaltz arrived in France, Louis was back on the French throne and the commandant of Basse-Terre was in a position to cash in on his fidelity. He was thus confirmed in his appointment as Commander for the King and Administrator of Senegal on April 25th, 1816, promoted to a Colonel of the Infantry, and on May 22nd further decorated as a *Chevalier de l'ordre royal et militaire de Saint Louis*.[8]

In November 1815, Reine Schmaltz suffered another attack of mania and it was then that she came under the care of Dr Esquirol, whose treatment appears, in the short term, to have been reasonably effective. She was not only able to accompany her husband on the expedition to Senegal, but what is more she appeared calm and even insensible to the danger in which *The Medusa* found herself in the first hours after running aground.[9]

In the council on board *The Medusa*, plans were discussed for the evacuation of the frigate. Given the enormous number of shipwrecks during this period, it was incredible that the small craft carried on ships were often unsuitable as lifeboats. Frequently in bad shape, they were intended for light duties in and around the ship, such as the laying out of a kedge anchor; there was no dedicated navigational equipment, no food or water ready to be loaded in case of disaster. Given

such insufficiencies, one of the most intelligent ideas put
forward at the council was to ferry the passengers and crew
to the inhospitable shore in a series of round trips.
Reassembled into a troop, armed against the hostile Moors,
and provisioned from the boats that would follow the castaways along the coast, they would thus march together on
foot to Saint Louis in Senegal. Another creditable idea was
to lighten the frigate as much as possible and dispatch the
most seaworthy of the boats post-haste to Senegal for help.
Another idea, the construction of a raft capable of carrying
a large number of men and all the supplies, was proposed
by Governor Schmaltz. At mealtimes, the six boats, which
would be carrying the rest of the passengers and crew, would
approach the raft and collect their rations. This suggestion,
seconded by Captain Chaumareys, was thus adopted and
construction began at once: the sea was becoming rougher
and the winds wilder, reminding all the frightened souls on
board that the stormy season would soon be upon them.

During the evening of July 3rd, another attempt was made
to position the anchor. The crew struggled with the capstan
to pull the frigate free; efforts met with a sudden, universal
shout of joy as those on board felt the first strains and stirrings of success. But the clamour of exultation suddenly
collapsed into deadly silence as the sailors were ordered to
stop. Night was falling, the sea had become heavy and the
attempt to free *The Medusa* would have to be postponed until
the morning tide.[10] The frigate groaned, the sea pummelled
the ship, pounding and punishing the hull as sailors vigor-
ously pumped out the seepage and the carpenters made all
possible haste to advance the construction of the raft.

The crying of the wind in the cordage, the yelping of
badly disciplined men, the contradictory commands shouted
and swallowed by the night, terrified the already frightened
passengers. Song – rarely heard under Chaumareys's
command – echoed through the vessel as soldiers and sailors,
oiled by drink, went on the rampage. They ransacked trunks

and strong boxes in search of fine clothes and precious objects. They boasted of how they had broken into the Captain's cabin, preferring his wines and liqueurs to his safe. Nobody mustered for meals; everyone grabbed what they could, as life on the ship rapidly descended into anarchy.

There was another burst of optimism when, on the morning of July 4th, a further attempt to float the frigate appeared as if it might succeed. A kedge anchor was dropped on the port side to pull against the bower anchor off the starboard and swing *The Medusa* round so that she could float back into deeper water. The operation began encouragingly. The ship began to turn and, with breath held, the hopeful passengers watched as she swung about completely, leaving only her stern on the bottom. Ensigns Lapeyrère and Maudet wanted to jettison every possible object to lighten the vessel, but they were stopped. Schmaltz even forbade the dumping of barrels of flour, claiming that hunger was a huge concern in the European trading posts. The ultimate failure of the refloating operation underlined the fatal inadequacy of the leadership. As Savigny and Corréard commented, 'only half measures were adopted, and in all the manoeuvres, great want of decision prevailed'.[11]

The construction of the raft, which had been designed by Schmaltz, was put under the charge of that accomplished mariner, Lieutenant Espiaux. The boom, masts and yards from *The Medusa* were lashed together. A prow to aid navigation was fashioned from two topgallant yards, and in the main body of the raft spars were placed at intervals onto which planks were fixed. Long pieces of wood were placed laterally and projected three metres on either side to give the craft stability. A little raised deck was constructed with some spare planks and fixed with large nails and rope. The two-metre-long prow was not solid enough to support people, and neither was a portion of similar length in the stern, so – although the craft was a sizeable twenty metres long by nearly seven metres wide and therefore nearly a quarter of the size of the main deck of *The Medusa* – an eighth of its surface was all but useless. Barrels were placed in the corners and an ineffectual railing, just forty centimetres high, ran around the raft. The inadequacy of these defences made it immediately clear that those who designed the craft were unlikely to assign themselves to its care.[12]

As soon as the makeshift platform was finished, Schmaltz and Chaumareys, standing before the white Bourbon flag, promised the assembled company that the five largest boats would tow the raft to the coast, and there, equipped with provisions and firearms, everybody would make for Senegal on foot. But these were a politician's promises. Anglas de Praviel, the infantry lieutenant, recalled that a secret order of disembarkation had been drawn up by those in command, who assigned themselves to the safest places in the boats. When the allocations were, at last, made public, the Picard family – already much distressed by the violent scenes of drunken plunder – found, to their horror, that they had been assigned to the raft, along with a grab-bag of rough, drunken soldiers and sailors, assorted Cap Vert colonists, and several officers who were out of favour with Chaumareys or Schmaltz. Picard was indignant and swore that if they were not given a place in one of the boats, his family would stay on board the frigate, which remained well provisioned and showed little sign of breaking up. Although, as Charlotte Picard reflected, he was probably considering only how posterity would judge him, Schmaltz at last relented and promised them a place in one of the boats.[13]

The evening of July 4th began so agreeably that Brédif decided to put his mattress up on the quarter-deck and lie there under the unfamiliar stars. This brief respite was soon interrupted by a freshening wind, which, towards midnight, became very strong. Waves struck the hull with a new vigour, until the frigate began to crumple amidships as the keel split in two. The sudden violence of these shocks and jolts, and the hunch that they were about to be abandoned, unnerved the fiery soldiers of the Africa Battalion. They ranked in battle formation and threatened to shoot anybody they caught trying to escape secretly. Schmaltz came up on the quarter-deck to calm them. When they seemed disinclined to heed his words, he mustered all the troops, crew, officers and passengers and, once again, repeated his vow to abandon no one. Everybody, he insisted, would be transported to the shore. Assembled as a caravan, 400-strong, they would all make their way on foot to Senegal.

Rather than these doubtful reassurances, it was the raft breaking loose from its moorings and drifting out to sea that re-established calm. Watching as their chance of rescue started to float away, the troops and crew – some constricted in their movements by the five or six stolen jackets they wore and were loath to surrender – united in an operation to recover the raft.[14]

All available pumps were working flat out when, at 3 a.m. on July 5th, the master-caulker informed the Captain that the frigate had taken in a dangerous quantity of water. The increasing anxiety that the remaining masts would fall and crush people, when the hull finally collapsed, prompted the officers to finalize their evacuation plans amid the ruckus of a ship's company crazed with drink or fright. Sailors and soldiers continued to carouse as if all time were theirs, ignoring the Captain who had, in any case, informally been relieved of his command by a confused and drunken consensus. Pillagers were stumbling about carrying plate and candlesticks and other objects unlikely to aid their escape or survival, decked in finery that made it seem as if the whole misadventure were merely an extra episode in the tropical burlesque that had been in full swing such a short time before.

Between 5 and 6 a.m. the water reached a sufficient height for Governor Schmaltz to order the evacuation. The list that had been drawn up on the previous day was little heeded, as those with rank or power sought the best means of saving themselves. Provisions had been carefully prepared and placed in iron-hooped barrels, but such was the lack of leadership and panic in the face of disaster that many of these were left on deck or flung indiscriminately into the sea.[15]

The soldiers were the first to leave; Anglas de Praviel, supervising their descent onto the raft, took pains to ensure that any swag and, most importantly, their weapons were left on board the frigate. Another officer, observed by Charlotte Picard, 'whose brain seemed severely affected, mounted on the bulwarks as if on a horse and, armed with two pistols, threatened to shoot anybody who hesitated to descend'. Standing on the quarter-deck, Rabaroust, the stowaway, was assigned a place on the raft. Convinced that to accept would prove fatal, he refused to budge. When Chaumareys chivvied him, he retaliated, 'I prefer to die on the frigate. I'm at least allowed to choose my own manner of death.'

By the time forty men had clambered aboard, the raft had sunk by more than half a metre in certain places. Provisions that had been put on board the night before, barrels full of necessary supplies, were rolled off into the sea. Only six tubs of wine and two containers of water were left after this rash attempt to lighten a craft that would only sink further under the weight of the next hundred bodies. To supplement the few provisions left on board, an eleven-kilo sack of biscuit was thrown from the frigate – only to land in the sea. By the time it was retrieved, the contents had become a soggy, salty paste that would, nonetheless, prove invaluable in the days ahead.

De Praviel followed his men down onto the raft, but was unable, through the glut of 150 bodies, to reach the little deck that had been constructed in the centre, where other officers, along with the surgeon, Savigny, and Corréard had formed an impregnable nucleus of command. Blocked in the sunken stern with water up to his waist and waves sweeping over his head, de Praviel decided to jump into the sea and clamber back on board the frigate.

Unable to move and thus incapable of checking what now

remained on board the raft by way of provisions and instruments for navigation, Corréard hailed Lieutenant Reynaud:

– Have we got the necessary instruments and charts?

– I've provided you with everything you need.

The exchange was difficult against the ocean's roar, but Corréard persisted:

– Is there an officer coming to take charge?

– It'll be me. I'll be with you in a moment.

And then, having urged an unconscionable number of souls aboard the makeshift structure, Lieutenant Reynaud went off to take his place in one of the boats.[16]

Throughout the confused evacuation, the frigate's ladder was insufficient, so men slithered down ropes or made a jump for it. Despite the sea swell, they all made it to the raft or the boats and, in all the undisciplined chaos, it is remarkable that no one seems to have been seriously hurt. Apparently unruffled by the crisis – and wrapped in a large fitted coat, protecting her from the wind and the spray – Reine Schmaltz, together with her daughter, was lowered into the Governor's Barge, a nine-metre-long, fourteen-oared boat whose command was entrusted to Lieutenant Reynaud, the very officer who had promised to captain the raft.[17] As for Governor Schmaltz, whom Charlotte Picard credits with 'taking care of nothing but the wish to save himself', he was lowered in an armchair suspended from a hoist, and was deposited in the well-provisioned barge, where he joined his wife, daughter and dearest friends. When five or six sailors who had jumped into the sea approached this barge and pleaded, in the name of humanity, to be picked up, they were repelled by the thick, curved sabre of Schmaltz's aide-de-camp. Settled comfortably among the other thirty-six passengers, who were well distributed in a barge capable of taking fifty, the Governor's family viewed this incident with complete indifference. Fearing for their lives, the repulsed sailors scrambled to get back on board the frigate.[18]

The Picard family was still stranded on the deck of *The*

Medusa. Charlotte yelled to the captains of the boats, who appeared to be abandoning them, and when the Governor's Barge circled the frigate, as if to take on more passengers, Charlotte hoped against hope that the Schmaltz ladies, who had taken an interest in her family during the voyage, would make room for them in their boat. But as the barge pulled away again, Chaumareys opined disdainfully that they would not wish to overburden themselves.

M. Picard then hailed Lapeyrère, who had been ordered to take the family on board the Pinnace, but his boat continued to distance itself from the ship. When the skiff came alongside, M. Picard beseeched the sailors to take them to Lapeyrère's boat, which was as sizeable as the Governor's Barge and far from full. When they refused, he snatched a rifle and threatened to shoot whoever rebuffed him, adding that the skiff was the property of the King and that he and his family must profit from it as much as anybody else. The sailors wisely capitulated and accepted the large complement of four small children, four women and Picard himself. Precious papers, clothing and two bottles of ratafia were seized from them and thrown into the sea by the sailors; the Picards had been forced to leave all their other possessions on *The Medusa*. As they drew close to the Pinnace, they were greeted by a volley of excuses from an embarrassed Lapeyrère, who claimed that he had been ordered to go off without them. Not necessarily believing such protestations, for the family constituted a large and obvious liability, the Picards were nonetheless relieved to be rescued.[19]

With the boats now beginning to move off for fear of becoming overloaded, Chaumareys decided, against all the laws and usages of the sea, that it was time for him to leave the frigate. Petit, a non-commissioned officer, confronted the Captain with the utmost composure: 'Since you are leaving us, at least give us the pleasure, if you reach France, of giving our families the news.'

Chaumareys descended by a forward rope, escaping onto

the Captain's Barge, where Midshipman Rang was already installed and in charge. Rang claims that the Captain's intention was to put himself in a position from which he could rally and regroup the less-laden boats. But, from the deck of *The Medusa*, it appeared otherwise. Anglas de Praviel, furious at the selfishness and cowardice of the leaders of the expedition, grabbed a rifle and threatened to open fire. Midshipman Rang hollered from the Captain's Barge that the boats would return for them. Cheered by such comforting news, those on board *The Medusa* hoisted a white flag and started shouting 'Long live the King' and 'Long live the Governor' – cries which passed along the convoy that was forming in order to tow the overloaded, half-submerged raft. The Captain's Barge, with its mizzen hoisted, was at the head of the line, followed by the Senegal Boat. This was commanded by Ensign Maudet and had its full compliment of twenty-five people. Next came the Pinnace, under Ensign Lapeyrère, leaving the Governor's Barge, under Lieutenant Reynaud, closest to the raft.

Realizing that he and the other sixty-three men remaining on *The Medusa* had been abandoned, de Praviel became delirious and threatened to take his own life. An infantryman raised his rifle to take aim at the cowardly Chaumareys at the head of the convoy. Rabaroust, thinking the man crazed, tussled with him and spoiled his shot, to the dismay of the incensed and stranded victims. Believing that there was space for everybody in the boats, Engineer Brédif had not hastened to leave the frigate and was left among this increasingly irate and drunken rabble.

Although the wind had dropped and the sun was breaking through the clouds, the tide and current were dragging the heavy raft – which, in turn, pulled the convoy of four boats, in a north-westerly direction, away from the shore to the east and from Saint Louis in Senegal to the south.

The Wreck

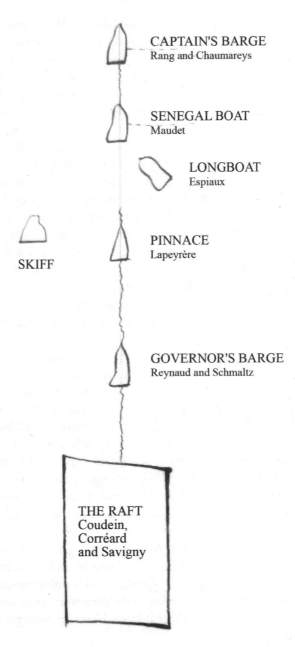

CAPTAIN'S BARGE
Rang and Chaumareys

SENEGAL BOAT
Maudet

LONGBOAT
Espiaux

SKIFF

PINNACE
Lapeyrère

GOVERNOR'S BARGE
Reynaud and Schmaltz

THE RAFT
Coudein,
Corréard
and Savigny

65

The ship's skiff was too small to form any useful part of
the convoy and Lieutenant Espiaux's Longboat, though sizeable, had not joined the towing operation. Alone among the
officers, Espiaux decided to return to the ship. Conscientious
and brave, he believed that his comrades in the Longboat
would rather die than abandon the helpless. Drawing close
to the frigate with considerable difficulty, Espiaux was
surprised to find that there were upwards of sixty soldiers
and sailors remaing on *The Medusa*. His plan was to ferry
everybody to the other, less-laden boats, and he managed
to embark, at his peril, all but seventeen.

De Praviel and Brédif found themselves in the fragile and
overladen Longboat among nearly ninety people, the sea on
the point of pouring over the sides and submerging them.
Approaching the Governor's Barge, hoping to place nine of
their number on board, Espiaux met with a blunt refusal.
Schmaltz claimed that he had accepted too many already
and that his barge was taking water. Espiaux then approached
Lapeyrère in the Pinnace, but was also refused, one hard-
hearted officer interjecting that as Espiaux had gone to
rescue the others, he would have to look after them.

The derisive cry resounded from boat to boat that the
Longboat was going to sink them all. Indeed, Espiaux's
encumbered and unwieldy craft appeared to be on the point
of colliding with the Senegal Boat, when its commander,
Ensign Maudet, in order to avoid this accident, was obliged
to release the towrope attaching him to the Pinnace. This
divided the line of towing boats into two. Maudet hailed
Chaumareys:

– Captain, take the towrope again.

The blithe reply came back:

– Yes, my friend.

Now, only the Governor's Barge and the Pinnace were
towing the raft, and before the Captain's Barge and the
Senegal Boat were able to rejoin them, the whole line was
surprised by the cry:

– The Governor is abandoning the raft.

From the sinking platform, it was clear what was happening. The sudden confusion caused by the manoeuvres to avert the collision gave Reynaud his chance. Standing up in the stern of the Governor's Barge, he raised his arm like an executioner. The hatchet in his hand came down in hard, repeated blows on the thick rope, hacking until he had severed their last threads of hope.

The Captain's Barge came within earshot of the Governor's Barge and Chaumareys called out:

– What are you doing?

The reply came back:

– The towrope has broken.

– Get hold of it again.

– We're abandoning them.

– We didn't hear you.

– We're abandoning them.

Clanet, the pay-master of the frigate who was on board the Governor's Barge, repeatedly protested against the chopping of the towrope, but to no avail. Lieutenant Reynaud had cut it on the order of Governor Schmaltz. Several men in Espiaux's Longboat, understanding what was happening, took aim at the culprits in readiness to open fire, but Espiaux prevented them.

As several of his friends were aboard the Longboat and facing an uncertain fate, Picard renewed his appeal to Ensign Lapeyrère to take them on board their boat, which could easily accommodate a few more souls. Indeed, Picard was already enthusiastically holding out his arms, in order to help them, when suddenly Lapeyrère released the rope that tied them to the Governor's Barge and rowed away towards the east. At that instant, all the boats imitated this manoeuvre in order to distance themselves from the foundering Longboat. As Gaspar Mollien put it, surveying the scene from Maudet's boat, 'egotism and cowardice triumphed' and, in their scramble to distance themselves, the raft was forgotten.

Cries erupted from those stranded on the makeshift structure:

–The towrope's broken! The towrope's broken.

Hollow, desperate screams of 'Long live the King' and 'Long live France' reached the ears of Charlotte Picard, as the Pinnace rapidly pulled away from all immediate responsibility. The leaders and commanders in the other boats took up this cry, which, ironically, seemed to vitalize them. Chaumareys, obviously exhilarated to be rid of his unhappy command, was gaily waving his braid-trimmed hat.[20]

After a few moments, the cries from the raft died down as the silence of apprehension settled on its ill-fated occupants. The half-submerged structure, void of sails, oars, ropes, anchors, instruments and charts, was abandoned, ungovernable, in the middle of the sea.[21] It was 11 a.m. by the time the boats pulled away from the raft; the chaotic and cowardly evacuation had taken upwards of five hours, and those stranded on the platform were stunned by the realization that the twice-sworn solemn promises of their leaders, made so recently on the deck of *The Medusa*, had been broken.

Brédif, crammed aboard Espiaux's Longboat, had managed to save his diary from the general jettisoning that ineffectively attempted to lighten the craft. He recorded the cutting of the ropes and the distancing, under full sail, of the less-hampered boats, adding with sarcastic stoicism, 'Whew! My friends, since that's the way it is, leave us to our fate' as he looked out at the increasingly empty and desolate ocean.[22]

4

On a Scorching Shore

Storms and breakers

As the overloaded Longboat was unable to aid the raft, let alone rescue those on board, she too pulled away to the east. Within four hours land was sighted. At 3 p.m. on July 5th, as he made his diary entry, Brédif recorded that 'all is well, the weather is good and there's hope of saving our lives'. With nearly ninety people straining the frail craft well beyond its capacity, this observation exhibited a laudable optimism, which was soon put to the test. In the early evening, the Longboat struck bottom. The night came down, closing in with thick mist, and it was not until 9 p.m. that the sailors disengaged their craft. Once off the shoal, all on board received a small quantity of water and a biscuit, their third distribution of rations since leaving *The Medusa* that morning.

Steadily the wind had been strengthening, blowing off the mist and whipping up a storm. Crouched down in the cramped Longboat, his earlier confidence undermined, Brédif described it as a 'night of distress and fear' as wave after wave threatened to engulf and drown them. But they survived the turbulent night. As day broke under a fresh wind on a heavy sea, they struggled eastwards, using their drenched bodies as a shield against the overwhelming waves.

With the coastline once again visible, the majority of those aboard decided to take their chances on the dry, inhospitable land, rather than risk uncertain navigation in a sinking Longboat. Lieutenant Espiaux thus put ashore fifty-seven people at Cap Mirick on the southern point of the Arguin Bank. Lieutenant de Praviel was among those who went ashore to contend with the blistering heat on a desert march of more than 320 kilometres south to Saint Louis in Senegal.

Lieutenant Espiaux, along with Brédif and the twenty-five others left on board, put out to sea.[1] About an hour later, they sighted some of the other boats from *The Medusa*. Espiaux, always thinking of how best to manage things, hailed them, offering to take people on board in return for water. Incredibly, he was refused. Nobody on the other boats believed his story about the landing. How would men be so crazy as to elect to march through the desert to a likely death from dehydration, or into captivity and enslavement by the Moors? Suspicious, the occupants of the other boats believed Espiaux's band to be concealed under the seats, ready to surprise them and steal their rations. While such distrust was undermining all sensible attempts to coordinate the rescue, the small skiff was beginning to break up and fifteen passengers, including Rabaroust, were taken on board by Espiaux.

Towards evening, the weather deteriorated once again and Brédif, facing another stormy night, impassively awaited his fate. Hanging his head over the side of the Longboat, he succumbed to much-needed sleep. The roar and splatter of the waves smacking against the hull provoked a dream about a pure alpine torrent, to which the parched victim was running in order to plunge his head under its fresh-water spray and quench his thirst. In the manner of such dreams, he never achieved his goal, but woke to find his lips stuck together by a crust of salt, his tongue glued to the roof of his mouth and his mind possessed by the most terrible desire to end his nightmare by throwing himself into the sea.

By midday on July 7th, the temperature was unbearable. Brédif wanted to dangle his feet in the sea to cool them, but as sharks had been sighted, he did not dare. Portions of the coast they followed were, from time to time, obscured by thick red sandstorms, which blew out over the sea, dusting them and leaving a boatload of terracotta bodies immobile in the oven-hot afternoon. Drinkable liquid was already scarce, as some unruly sailors had downed the several bottles of Madeira that were on board, and so everybody sucked on little balls of lead to keep their saliva circulating.

That afternoon, they sighted the Senegal Boat. After the break-up of the convoy, this craft under the command of Ensign Maudet soon lost sight of the others. During the first stormy night she was tossed about wildly, up onto the crests of immense waves and then, stomach-scoopingly, plunged into chasms over which giant arcs of water reached to engulf her.

When, on the afternoon of July 7th, those in Maudet's Senegal Boat were scared by the sight of what they took to be Moorish pirates, they were relieved to discover that it was, in fact, *The Medusa*'s Longboat. Their only rations, a small cask of wine, had been lost overboard by a sailor, scared out of his wits by the high waves. They were thus deeply grateful to Lieutenant Espiaux when he handed them two bottles of eau-de-vie.

About six o'clock they discerned a group of Moors on the beach, mending their fishing nets. Frightened by the sight of two strange boats, the fishermen went off on their camels. At this, two brave – or desperate – men decided to take their chances with the breakers and swim ashore to see what food they could scavenge. Successful, they feasted on the dried fish and fresh water left behind by the Moors and then struggled back to the boats.

The following morning, Maudet's Senegal Boat was carried towards the coast where she was swept into the breakers, which threw her up on the beach. People scrambled onto the sand and scattered to search for fresh water. Observing this, the sailors aboard the Longboat angrily pressed Espiaux to go ashore. A sail was hoisted, and the Longboat likewise sped into the breakers and crested up onto the sand where she beached, plunging people overboard into the waves. Brédif found his diary notes miraculously intact and returned to the Longboat several times to stuff his pockets with sodden, salt-watery biscuits. Back on the hot sand, he found a group of sailors broaching the only remaining barrel of water. Fighting through the desperate group, he wrestled to get his mouth on the bung-hole, managing only a couple of gulps before it was torn away – two swigs must have seemed like two litres to a body that, for three days, had taken in dangerously little liquid.[2]

Staggering from a phantom pitch and roll, the legacy of three weeks at sea, the castaways from Espiaux's Longboat joined the crew and passengers of Maudet's Senegal Boat. Some drenched, others already covered with sand and without shoes, they could hardly recognize one another, standing in the odd scraps of clothing they had managed to snatch from the frigate before or during the evacuation. This sorry, ragtag band began to move south along the coast and had walked for only about half an hour when they saw the Pinnace speeding towards the shore.

Under Ensign Lapeyrère, the Pinnace had kept in convoy with the Captain's and Governor's Barges as they descended the coast. Both Schmaltz and Chaumareys had insisted that they sail straight for Senegal, and there had followed a lively exchange in which the dearth of supplies on board the Pinnace, the need to make for land and their obligation to return to save those on the raft and still on board *The Medusa* proved useless arguments against the egotism of the Governor and the commander. If the plan to proceed to Senegal by sea was to be respected, the Pinnace needed to take on some of the excess of supplies provisioning the barges. Chaumareys, between great gulps of wine, which he swigged from a huge demijohn, nonchalantly informed Lapeyrère that they didn't have sufficient supplies for themselves. At length, the leaders of the expedition forbade the Pinnace from making a landing, reiterating their wish to make for Senegal by sea and, to that end, they dropped anchor for the night.

By 6 a.m. on July 6th, when the convoy once again got under way, several sailors demanded to be put ashore. Entreaties flared into threats, and it was only the firmness of Ensign Lapeyrère that quelled a mutiny on board the Pinnace. By midday they were blinded by the hot grains of sand blown out to sea by infernal desert winds, colouring the sun a hellish red and coating the insides of their mouths with grit. In the late afternoon, a north-westerly breeze cleared this storm and, with a second meal – a little glass of water and a soggy biscuit – spirits rose. But the breeze freshened to a wind and, throughout the night, waves threatened to submerge them, washing overboard one of their sails and those few effects that several people had managed to sneak on board. A large hole opened in the stern, through which water was pouring. Trousers, sleeves of shirts, strips of dresses, shawls, hats – everything available was used to plug it. As the sea rose, with its white foam tracing deep black chasms, Picard broke down and started to cry with fear for the safety of his family. Wanting to suckle her baby, his wife found that her milk had dried for want of nourishment.

The compass broke during the night and the boat meandered first to port and then to starboard, until the first streaks of morning light gave them their bearings. Land was sighted and the sailors, once again, agitated to be put ashore. This time, with the craft rapidly deteriorating, Lapeyrère agreed to navigate the Pinnace towards the beach, at which point whoever wanted to could plunge into the waves and swim ashore. In the attempt, faced by the size of the breakers, the eleven men who had insisted thought the better of it. Pulling away from the shore, they received their third distribution of food since leaving *The Medusa*. With only two litres of water and a dozen sodden biscuits left on board, the question of putting ashore in search of sustenance was being seriously debated when the sight of a caravan of Moors dissuaded them. Lapeyrère now thought it best to continue by sea, reckoning that they would reach Senegal the following day.

The sun set the air ablaze and people, in desperation, capitulated to the dangerous urge to drink sea water. To alleviate desiccation, some started to consume their urine, cooling it first in the sea. The youngest Picards cried incessantly and little Laure, aged six, lay on the verge of death at her mother's feet. Devastated by this sight, Picard pulled out his knife. Staring at his daughter, he brought the blade down purposefully onto his arm. He was on the point of slitting a vein – so that his blood might assuage the thirst of his child – when he was stopped.[3]

The freshness of the evening offered some respite and the Pinnace anchored a little distance offshore while people slept. Ravenous as dawn broke on July 8th, stranded without even a whisper of wind on a dead sea, they tried to row in the direction of Senegal, but were too weak to make any headway. A fourth and final distribution of food was a mockery: six waterlogged biscuits and two litres of water were eked out among the forty-two people on board. Again, Moors appeared on the shore and the boat distanced itself a little, until someone noticed a small troop of men standing on a hillock, gesticulating wildly. Recognizing them as castaways from *The Medusa*, they hoisted a white handkerchief by way of acknowledgement and decided to make every effort to reach the shore.

Rolled and tossed by the surf, the Pinnace sped towards the coast. When the helmsman misjudged the crest of a wave, the boat was all but capsized. So an older, more experienced pilot took over and ordered the mast and sails to be thrown into the sea. Having successfully navigated the boat through the storm, he took charge in order to get the frightened passengers safely ashore. A towering wave remained between them and the beach. As the boat angled to ride the crest, she lurched and plunged into the wave, which swallowed them and rolled her over, splintering oars and ramming the vortex of debris up onto the sand, where it was battered by successive breakers. Sailors tried to hook the grapple anchor in order to secure their landfall, as others threw themselves into the surf to rescue the children. Engineer Brédif pelted down the beach and into the waves to help save the Picard ladies and, after a few moments of hectic effort and confusion, Charlotte Picard found herself standing on the firm sand beside her mother and her half-dead brothers and sisters.[4]

The tattered band

The castaways found themselves on a scorching shore under a lacerating July sun without water, without food and with many of the exhausted and famished party nearly naked. The immense expanse of undulating sand that stretched before them appeared every bit as daunting as the heaving sea.[5] All the warnings given in published accounts about the dangers of sailing the African coast had not saved them from shipwreck, and all the stories of the menacing desert could only have raised their apprehensions about a region where the Moors viewed all ships and boats thrown up on their coasts as gifts to them from the heavens.[6] Whatever practical difficulties the castaways faced, their perceptions – moulded by ignorance, prejudice and limited experience – prepared them for the worst; over and above their desperate physical situation, they anticipated the perils of enslavement and, worse still, cannibalism.

History provided examples of expedient cannibalism, and cautionary tales made use of it as a symbolic punishment, but only since the days of the great European explorers had cannibalism appeared as a real threat.[7] The subject had thus come to fascinate and terrorize the so-called civilized world. Published in London by Henry Colburn, who was to produce the English edition of Savigny's and Corréard's best-selling account of the *Medusa* saga, a book by the German doctor and explorer George Heinrich von Langsdorff provided a kind of traveller's *Good Food Guide* to the human species:

> Incredible as it may appear, there have been, and are still, particularly in South-America, and in the interior of Africa, as well as upon its western coasts, people who feed upon human flesh merely on account of its delicacy, and as the height of gourmandise. These nations not only eat the prisoners they take in war, but their own wives and children; they even buy and sell human flesh publicly. To them we are indebted for the information that white men are finer flavoured than Negroes, and that Englishmen are preferable to Frenchmen. Farther, the flesh of young girls and women, particularly of new-born children, far exceeds in delicacy that of the finest youths or grown men. Finally they tell us that the inside of the hand and the sole of the foot are the nicest parts of the human body.[8]

Charles Cochelet, shipwrecked on the West African coast in 1819, described some indigenous figures as barely human,

writing that 'I should have looked upon them as apes of
the most frightful species, had not their bodies, which no
clothing concealed, possessed the human form.'[9] So widespread were such reactions and their attendant fantasies of
cannibalism that Louis-Marie-Joseph de Grandpré had, in
1801, set out to dispel 'the disgusting absurdity' that 'the
Congo is governed by a King who feeds on human flesh'.
Grandpré claimed that Africans were not cannibals and that
it was, ironically, on board European slave ships   chained
and clapped in irons, and watching the sailors drinking
blood-red wine and dark, dried meat that the fear of cannibalism gripped the minds of the captured Africans being so
inhumanely transported. They agonized that they would
soon be served to their rapacious captors.[10]

Whatever hardships the castaways from *The Medusa*
confronted, they would encounter no cannibals among the
indigenous people that they met during their arduous march
to Saint Louis. However, the far more real fear of captivity
was ever present to the almost defenceless and severely weakened troop of eighty-six people who came ashore near the
deserted trading post at Portendick, about halfway between
where *The Medusa* ran aground and their destination in
Senegal. There were many stories about the savage treatment of shipwreck survivors at the hands of Moorish slavers.
In 1814, Geoffrey de Villeneuve had documented a particularly ferocious tribe, the Azounas, who wandered between
Cap Bojador and the River Senegal, plundering whatever
they could find either from shipwrecked boats or, further
south, from black villages along the river. They were armed,
hated, and enslaved their captives.[11]

As the clothes of the castaways were in tatters, and fearing
that the women might be at greater risk, several gallant officers proposed their uniforms to the Picard ladies. Charlotte
inexplicably declined, but soon discovered that her torn dress
afforded her legs little protection against the prickly shrubs
that punctured the desert sands.

77

They were, at once, forced to abandon a man whose legs had been smashed coming ashore; they laid him out on the sand to an almost certain, lengthy and painful death and set off into the desert to look for fresh water. Their saliva sticky and tongues furred, they eventually found clumps of foul-smelling and thorny vegetation and started to dig, crazily pawing and scraping at the sand like dogs. Down they dug into the clay-like earth to a depth of almost a metre until they discovered a whitish, stinking liquid, which Brédif dared to sample. Finding it to be saltless, he called out that they were saved. Several other holes were dug at once and the parched survivors gorged themselves on more of the stomach-turning water.

After slaking their thirst, some people set about gathering bunches of purslane, a herb that had been known in the Middle Ages as an anti-aphrodisiac. Although reputed to 'mitigate great heat in all the inward parts of man', it was unlikely to afford protection against the blistering swelter of the desert sun. It did, however, help to keep the famished troops alive. The drenched ship's biscuit had by now dried as hard as stone; they tried to eat it, but it stayed solidified in their mouths until they spat it out.[12]

The group rested for another hour before setting off in a southerly direction, with the women and children in the front of the party and Brédif carrying one of the youngest on his shoulders, in the hope of inspiring the sailors to do the same. For those still shod, the fine, burning sand poured into their shoes and boots as their feet sank deep into it, making each step impossibly hot and heavy.

With the arid, sand-filled air caking their eyelids and firing their throats, they were happy once again to cross the dunes that gave way to the sea's edge. The wet sand soothed them as they stopped to rest. They drank a little of the sulphurous water that they had carried with them from their first stop and, as the sun fell, the temperature cooled. It was obviously less arduous to travel after sundown, in the early morning or at night, but it was then that they felt most vulnerable, easy prey for the fierce tribes and wild animals that haunted the coast.

On that first night ashore, after their rest with sentries posted to guard against marauders, the bedraggled band began their journey again at three in the morning. Those without shoes were stabbed and cut by the shells strewn along the beach. They halted every half-hour at Picard's behest; his intense anxiety for the weaker members of his family made his attitude somewhat imperious and, in his wearied state, he lacked sufficient reserves to manifest his gratitude for these rests. Two officers, believing that only the greatest drive and determination would get them to their goal, grumbled that the family was dangerously slowing their progress. Picard immediately sprang to the defence of his kin, who were, unfortunately, at that moment straggling at the rear. With nerves frayed by fatigue, bodies tested by the extremes of climate and with the question of their survival at stake, the argument grew fierce and swords were drawn. The older members of the family, shocked once more by the selfishness that had spread through the ill-fated expedition like an epidemic, pleaded with their father to stay with them in the desert rather than travel on with people they judged more barbarous than the dreaded Moors. Captain Baignères, a leader of one of the companies of the Africa Battalion, intervened, shaming those who wished to abandon the family with notions of honour and duty and discourses on what it meant to be French, a quality that had been aired and tested and rolled uncertainly around in the minds of many of the *Medusa* victims.

As the day declared itself, burning off the dawn chill, the party searched behind the nearest dunes for more edible plants. A green creeper, strung across the sand, was found to be bitter. Other plants were identified as poisonous. So further quantities of purslane were gathered and devoured voraciously. One plant, milkweed, with its silky white plumes, played havoc with human perception. Waving in the distance, it looked to several people like clumps of Moorish tents. Determined to find fresh water even at the cost of enslavement, they started to stagger off in that direction, only to realize that it was a mirage. Others saw distant pools or wide, rapid-flowing rivers and hastened to reach what their stricken minds were swiftly forced to accept as a trick of the dazzling sun rebounding off the white, burning sand.

The naturalist M. Kummer, one of the delegates of the *Société philanthropique*, recklessly decided to leave the group and strike off into the burning interior of the Sahara in search of Moors who might feed him. Two days later his friend, M. Rogery, also a delegate of the company and an ex-infantry officer, would suddenly and secretly leave the band in order to trace a parallel path deep into the desert.

Again wells were dug, yielding the now-familiar fetid liquid with which the castaways refreshed their sand-choked mouths and moistened their cracking lips. At first, this strange arid environment had seemed a sea of silence after the ocean's incessant roar, but slowly the group adjusted to the desert's sounds: the grating of the fine crystals against their bodies and their clothes, the whispering as the wind chivvied the sand into little rills, the moaning and growling of a storm.

After their rest, they set off back over the blazing dunes to the succour of a fresher, harder surface that had been cooled and compacted by the action of the waves. Such zigzagging was adding distance to their journey, but it was necessary and they gratefully lay down in the water and caught some large crabs, which gave them sustenance as well as moisture as they sucked on the claws.

On the night of July 9th, when the weary group halted between dunes, they heard the sounds of what they thought were leopards and decided to spend a good part of the threatening night bunched in the safety of a tight group. When someone thought he spotted a lion, people roused themselves to take a look. After staring intently into the desert for some time, they realized that the lion swayed, but didn't move, and that it was nothing but the moonlight playing tricks with the ruffled milkweed.

Despite the risk of wild animals, they moved off long before dawn. At about 6 a.m. they had their first encounter with human predators, a small bunch of Moors who seemed content to rob some of the stragglers and then disappear. Several men had been hatching a plot to kill the officers in order to seize the gold they vainly imagined them to be carrying. Others fantasized about robbing everybody and running off to become marauders. Slowly, the sun's disabling heat burned off these thoughts as, parched and swollen-footed, they stumbled along with the rest of the tattered band. At length, they sighted and approached a humble camp of shabby tents. Gaspar Mollien observed that the Moorish women inhabiting the camp, with their stick legs, sunken torsos and withered breasts, were hardly less alarming in appearance than the wizened castaways themselves. This second meeting with the feared Moors proved a little expensive, but not dangerous. The black servant of one of the officers acted as an interpreter and the women sold them goat's milk, fresh water and millet. Picard purchased two kids from them to feed the group, but unable to wait for the animals to be cooked, the sailors tore off half-raw morsels, which they devoured, leaving hardly any meat for the officers.

While Picard was busily seeking contributions towards the cost of the animals (being denied only by Richefort), suddenly, out of nowhere, a small band of blacks and Moors charged at the group. Grabbing their rifles, several soldiers ranked in formation as if to defend the castaways from the assault. When the assailants abruptly halted without attack, two officers and the interpreter, covered by several soldiers, went to speak to them. What had appeared as menace proved to be nothing more than commercial enthusiasm, as the would-be attackers offered their services as guides to Senegal, suggesting that they set off at once.[13]

As they traversed the spiky shrub-covered dunes, Charlotte

Picard's feet and legs were scratched till they bled and her
dress was snagged and torn. She struggled to keep up as the
guides led them to their camp. When at last they arrived
exhausted, they were not welcomed, but viciously taunted
by a horde of women and children who swarmed around
them, showering the sorry visitors with sand. Dogs snapped
at their raw and blistered shins. The women pinched them,
tugging at their hair to inspect it, ripping all the shiny buttons
and braid from the uniforms and spitting with delight into
the faces of the frightened Europeans. After what seemed
like an interminable barrage of abuse, the guides shooed off
the vicious gang so that water could be distributed and dried
or rotten fish and bitter milk sold to the castaways.

– Hey, Picard, don't you recognize me, it's Ahmet?

The sound of French tumbling from the mouth of a large
young figure swathed in Arab costume startled the hungry
band, and Picard turned to find himself greeted by a goldsmith whom he had employed on one of his previous trips
to Senegal. Appalled by their wretched state, Ahmet arranged
for more milk and water to be distributed without charge.
As the weather was turning, he also set about constructing
a tent of skins to shield the Picards; forbidden by his religion to lodge Christians in his own house, he was anxious
that the family of his old employer should be protected
against the ravages of a desert storm. Lighting large fires to
comfort the frightened Europeans, Ahmet and his fellow
tribesmen bid them goodnight, assuring them that the
Christian God is also that of the Muslims.

By midnight, the weather had improved, so they decided
to set off with the Picard women and children balanced precariously on donkeys. They now rested every quarter of an hour,
fuelling resentment against the Picards, as such frequent stops
were thought to risk the safety of the group at large.

Brédif began to experience extreme fatigue in the early
hours and was so comatose that he nearly slept as he walked.
Happy to hear the command 'Halt', he collapsed onto the

sand, dreading the moment that came after all too short a break when they were urged up and on their way. During one such interlude, Brédif fell into a particularly profound sleep and failed to hear the command to move on. Consigned to captivity or certain death, he lay asleep, unobserved as his compatriots moved off. Only by chance was he spotted by a man at the back of the caravan, who returned to revive him.

On their strange, snaking journey, the frayed group reached the coast once again at dawn. The donkeys, after their labours in the shifting sands, became so excited to set their hooves on the firm wet shore that they galloped, out of control, into the surf; the one Charlotte Picard was riding almost crushed her as he rolled over in the foam. In this spree, one of her young brothers was nearly carried off on the backwash, but she scrambled up in time to save him.

Soon after this reviving frolic, another uplifting event, the sighting of a sail, raised the spirits of every member of the shattered band. As she pulled closer, those on shore identified her as a French brig. The vessel had set about lowering her sails and had put a boat in the water. The brig was, at length, recognized as *The Argus*, last seen by these people an eternity of just three weeks earlier, in the Bay of Biscay, before the convoy had broken up shortly after setting sail from France. A white handkerchief was hastily fastened to the bayonet end of a musket that a soldier stretched to wave on high. The ship acknowledged the signal, and Lieutenant Espiaux scribbled a message, which was stuffed in a bottle and hung around the neck of one of the five Moorish guides who courageously rushed into the dangerous waves. About half an hour later, the Moors, who had reached the longboat that was fighting unsuccessfully with the current, reappeared floating three little barrels in front of them and carrying a reply stoppered in a bottle, from Captain Parnajon to Lieutenant Espiaux. *The Argus*, having arrived safely and without incident in Senegal, had been dispatched to search the coast and to find the lost *Medusa*.[14]

The barrels appeared to the castaways like a gift from Heaven: wine, Dutch cheese, brandy and biscuits. They set upon the cheese, which was beading with sweat in the vibrant late morning, and cupped the wine in little shells they found along the beach. Despite the tropical heat, the women, with the exception of Charlotte Picard, eagerly downed the brandy. Preferring liquid in quantity to a liquor capable of softening pain, Charlotte swapped her ration for more wine. There was a great relief, a feeling that their luck had turned. Although the breakers prohibited the weary band from attempting to reach *The Argus*, at least they had been sighted. Their whereabouts were known, they had fed on familiar food and help would surely soon be on its way. They signalled all the elation that their wasted bodies could muster, and a new sense of hope rekindled a spark of purpose and possibility. People who, on the punishing sand and in the intolerable heat, had somehow found the energy to quarrel with one another, became at a stroke more tolerant. Smiles painfully broke the cracked lips of the children for the first time in days.

The appearance of the ship had also drawn the attention of a large group of Moors, who now approached the castaways, curious about these half-naked, burned and blistered remains of human beings who seemed, despite their state, so deliriously happy. Among the Moors were women keen to sell milk and butter, offering at high prices further sustenance to these deprived bodies, who had fortunately escaped from *The Medusa* with a little cash. The cost of camel's milk was variously recorded by Charlotte Picard and Charles-Marie Brédif at three and ten francs a glass. Perhaps the women took pity on a young girl in tatters, judged Brédif to be better off, or simply took advantage of his assumption that he was certain to be fleeced.[15]

Having provisioned the tattered band, *The Argus* sailed off on its mission to find *The Medusa*. As the march recommenced, the morning's unexpected bounty and delight gave way to the realities that stood between the castaways and

their destination. Whenever the wind blew from the east,
the horizon became like a white-hot furnace, and, as they
marched, the relentless sun burned their blistered skin. Brédif
was filthy: his trousers, without braces, kept slipping and he
was covered from head to toe by a thick coating of sand.
His ragged clothes, a knife and fork – hardly useful here
where the diet was purslane and rank water – a watch and
his small diary were all that he possessed in the world.[16]
Commenting on the behaviour of the sailors, whom he
found so unruly as to be of danger to the rest of the group,
Brédif wrote that if he were a naval officer, he 'would like
to shoot more than ten of the scoundrels' for they were 'real
animals, beasts that should be driven with a cane or led with
a rope. They are a thousand times unworthy of the kindness or the care of their officers whom they do not respect.'[17]

The dawns evaporated into mornings, mornings burned
into afternoons, which melted into dusk and darkness. The
castaways were beginning to lose all track of time. Picard was
showing signs of complete exhaustion, and Charlotte and her
mother stayed with him while the other members of the
family went on with the donkeys. Resting beside him,
watching their kin disappear, they gave in to fatigue and fell
asleep. Waking up to find the sun gone down, Picard realized
that, despite all their efforts since leaving *The Medusa*, despite
the promising start to the day, his ultimate weakness in submit-
ting to a fatigue that he had fought with such determination
had finally brought them to their end. There could be no
rescue for those who had been reckless enough to break rank
and fall behind. Disturbed by his agitation, the two ladies
awoke, only to fall back in a faint, overcome by the sight of
several large, bearded Moors towering above them on camels.
Their shock, however, was momentary as one of these fear-
some men began to speak to them in tolerable French:

– Madame, reassure yourself, beneath this Arab costume
is an Irishman come here to help you.

He told the astonished Picards that the rest of the tattered band was waiting for them some eight kilometres down the coast. His name was Kearney and, as he lived among the peoples of the region and knew the lie of the land, he had been dispatched to search for the castaways by Colonel Brereton, the English commander in Senegal. They were told that a camel, loaded with supplies, had already been sent north in the direction of Portendick to look for other groups that might be struggling down the coast.

Finding themselves in a landscape in which the dunes were lower, their surroundings greener and where there was fresh water, the main body of the group planned to rest until the small hours. Under Kearney's guidance, the straggling Picards soon joined them.

The castaways began to sense that the end of their troubles was in sight. Not wishing to risk any threat from the wild animals they had heard on the previous evenings, they asked the soldiers to gather bracken and start a fire to keep danger at bay. Bloody-minded and wasted, the soldiers refused. Kearney gently calmed everybody's nerves by assuring them that experienced Arab guides would be on guard while they rested.[18]

Journeying through the second half of the night, by early morning on July 12th they had passed from Moorish territory into that of the peaceful black tribes who inhabited the region of the Senegal River. The donkeys suddenly started to act up again. Standing rooted to the ground, they hee-hawed, bucked their riders into the spiky bushes and ran off. The heat now grew so intense that the frazzled group were, once again, obliged to cross the dunes in search of shelter. Without a donkey and barefoot, Charlotte Picard likened the temperature of the sand to that of an oven at the moment when a baker opens it to withdraw his bread.

Their speech had become slurred and, although they were exhausted, there were scraps, scuffles and all kinds of combustible moments between half-crazed people seared by the heat. Perhaps they imagined that if Chaumareys and

Schmaltz could do it, others too might try to deceive them. The blistering trek was drawing on their last reserves of strength, but they pushed on – not, Charlotte Picard adds, 'without cursing the person who was the first cause of our sufferings'.

The worn-out band was forced to stop and shelter from the savage heat under some acacia trees and wait while the tide, which blocked their progress down the coast, receded. The furnace-hot air refused to refresh them. Charlotte feared that after overcoming so much hardship, she was, at last, going to surrender to death. A blacksmith called Borner handed her a little of the muddy water that he had conserved in a small barrel and she readily accepted it, taking great gulps of the nauseating solution. The ever-attentive Captain Baignères, guessing at the repulsive aftertaste, offered Charlotte some crumbs of biscuit that he had preciously conserved in his pocket. She chewed at the mix of bread, dust and tobacco, but, unable to swallow it, gave it all mushed up to one of her famished younger brothers.

While Kearney went in search of supplies, black women arrived with water and some excellent cow's milk for sale. Everybody drank their fill, but few had the energy to eat when Kearney rejoined them, not with the promised ox, but with rice and dried fish. Despite the intense heat of the afternoon, when the tide had receded, they went down to the shore where they found their obdurate donkeys and where they cooled themselves in the waves that streaked up onto the beach. When Charlotte and her sister, after bathing in the sea for a good half-hour, went to rest in the shade, one of the Moorish guides who accompanied Kearney, thinking them asleep and fascinated by the braid and buttons on the uniform worn by the sister, crept up close in the hope of detaching one or two of these trappings. Realizing that the ladies were just resting, and that he had been detected and recognized, he seemed content merely to inspect at close quarters.

As they took up the march again, they sighted several

groups of Moorish raiders, notorious slavers who operated along the frontier of the River Senegal. Poorly armed and completely exhausted, some of the soldiers brandished their swords in the air to make the marauders think that they were fighting fit and well equipped – gestures that success-fully sent the tribesmen on their way.

The breeze picked up and clouds filled the sky. Thunder roared and a storm threatened. Again the marchers decided to stumble over the dunes in search of shelter. The sighting of an English schooner detained them on the shore as three blacks were sent out in a canoe to meet the ship, which had indeed been dispatched by the English governor in Saint Louis to search for castaways. Returning from the schooner, the canoe was overturned, and though the blacks made it back to dry land, the supplies did not. Happily, however, Kearney had by then returned with the promised ox, and the troop trudged behind the hills to set up camp in a little clump of gum trees beside several fresh-water wells. The ox was slaughtered, skinned, divided and grilled over a fire, and these raw remnants of people, sand-blasted by endless swirls of grit, sat like ghouls in the flickering flames of the camp fire, chomping on dripping morsels of meat.

Some stretched out and tried to sleep, only to be plagued by a new menace – mosquitoes. Charlotte Picard had fallen into a kind of delirium. She imagined her companions depicted on canvas as cannibals. She trembled at the distant roars of wild beasts and, only after much tossing and turning, fell asleep.

The group set off in the early hours in order to reach Saint Louis as soon as possible. About 7 a.m. Charlotte found herself towards the back of the caravan, when she saw several aggressive Moors approaching, armed with lances. A ship's apprentice – a boy of ten or twelve years – who walked a few paces away from her turned, and in a frightened voice murmured, 'My God, they've come to capture us.'

As the Moors encircled them, one of them reigned in Charlotte's donkey and yelled into her face with violent gestures. The ship's apprentice had scampered off, and Charlotte started to cry as the Moor showed no signs of relinquishing his grip. By his gesticulations she guessed that he was asking where she was headed and so she shouted, at the top of her weakened lungs, 'Ndar!' — Saint Louis — the only word of his language that she knew. At this, the angry marauder dropped the bridle and rejoined his friends, who all burst out laughing. Charlotte, mercifully, was free to rejoin the castaways.

The River Senegal was now only about eight kilometres away. They were moving through a greener, lusher terrain in which parrots and promerops perched in the sheltering trees. Humming birds buzzed in the morning air. Where they had seen only white-hot sand, sky and sea, now a roof of green relieved their sore and dazzled eyes. The softness of the vegetation and signs of sympathetic life provoked the most intense relief and stinging tears tumbled down over their red-raw cheeks.

In the final descent to the river's edge, Charlotte's donkey stumbled, throwing her into a spiky bush, tearing at her already tortured skin. While Kearney, accompanied by two officers, went ahead to alert the authorities in Saint Louis that a group of about eighty survivors had made it to their destination, the castaways rested in the shade and, despite the crocodiles, eased their weary limbs and festering wounds in the fresh water of the river.

In the early afternoon, they watched as a little boat rowed furiously towards them against the strong current. When it arrived, two Europeans leaped ashore, greeted the group and asked for M. Picard, saying that they were there on the orders of his old friends, MM. Artigue and Labouré. They had a large basket for his family, containing fresh bread, cheese, Madeira and filtered water, as well as dresses for the ladies and clothes for Picard. The delighted family eagerly shared these provisions with those who had shown them kindness during the march.

By 4 p.m. on July 13th, after more than three days in their lifeboats and a five-day desert march, the troop climbed aboard the boats sent by the English governor and started to sail towards Saint Louis. When they arrived at 6 p.m., it seemed that the entire colony had turned out to greet the euphoric survivors.[19]

Under oath

– Respect, above all, the rights of man; so that no one can say of us: 'The French have drunk the blood of their brothers, stuffed themselves with their flesh; the French were cannibals.'

The group of fifty-seven people, the first to have been put ashore by Lieutenant Espiaux on July 6th, found themselves stranded near Cap Mirick without supplies or water, listening to this admonitory declaration by their leader, Lieutenant Anglas de Praviel.

From the little hillock that Adjutant Petit climbed in order to take stock of their situation, he saw only an endless sweep of dunes, hypnotic like the sea, void of landmarks and dwellings, and offering no respite from the inhospitable and baking desert. Not only forbidding, it was fickle. When the desert wind whipped up, the battering, suffocating sand would dry up springs, efface paths and change every contour, so that what was there one day might disappear the next. Even the short, hot slog up to the vantage point made clear to the Adjutant that any attempt to walk on this shifting terrain would plunge their feet deep into the burning ground. Fortunately, the safest route south to their destination was along the coast where the sand was firm. It might not be the shortest way to reach Saint Louis, but it certainly seemed to be the best.[20]

In a heat that made de Praviel's head feel as if it were full of bubbling, boiling liquid, they proceeded with greater military organization than was possible with Espiaux's assorted band. They posted four armed men under a sergeant-major as an advance guard, four armed men under a corporal in the rear, two corporals on their left flank, and used the sea to protect them on their right.

By the evening of July 6th, without having eaten or drunk anything all day, and having slogged over the *Mottes d'Angel*, the high hills to the south of Cap Mirick, they found some deserted cabins, which, from the heads and feet of locusts scattered on the floor, they took to have been recently occupied by Moors. Sheltering from the wind that had been swirling up the sand and making the going tough, they rested there until, in the coolest part of the night, they set off again, hoping to find edible roots or plants and some sign of fresh water. Unsuccessful, they fell back on sea water as a last resort, but were checked by sudden outbreaks of vomiting and diarrhoea – reactions that doubtless saved some lives. Although sea water temporarily slakes the thirst, great quantities have a dehydrating effect: the kidneys are unable to cope with such large amounts of salt, and delirium and death follow in a matter of hours. As a safer alternative, several members of the troop chose to drink their own urine, but this, naturally enough, was hardly plentiful. In any case, those who tried it were revolted and soon gave up.

By July 8th, hollowed by hunger, their skin cracked, their lips chapped, their tongues black and pasted to the roofs of their mouths, the castaways were more than half-wishing to be rounded up and taken as slaves by the Moors; at least then they would be given water.[21] On the following day, July 9th, their fourth day of deprivation, a corporal's wife fell exhausted onto the sand and died. The only witness to the fatality was her husband, who had stayed behind with her when she had collapsed and several people suspected him of having run her through with his sabre in order to put her out of her misery. Alarmed by the woman's death – most probably caused by the murderous climate and lack

of water – fear spread among the frazzled troop as they stag-
gered to a salt-water pond where they spent the first part
of that night. At about 3 a.m., when it would have been
wise for them to move off, half the group were unable to
summon the requisite strength. Praviel, paralysed with
exhaustion, beseeched a sailor to shoot him through the
head, but his entreaty was flatly refused.

Portendick was where Espiaux had put ashore and was,
for Anglas de Praviel and his troop, more than one-third of
the distance between Cap Mirick and Saint Louis. The
trading post had been in the possession of the English since
1808 and so both groups of castaways hoped to find some
sympathetic signs of European life. Instead they found the
settlement, or what was left of it, deserted. The sight of
the sand-covered remains of the Longboat, the Pinnace and
the Senegal Boat, with scattered traces of clothing or abandoned objects close by, led de Praviel and his frightened
group to suspect the worst – that their comrades had been
taken into captivity by hostile tribesmen.

During the next day, these wasted men looked on as one
of their number started to dig into the sand. Thinking he
was searching for water, they gathered round, only to watch
him climb into the hole that he had hollowed out for his
own grave. Glancing from person to person, he implored
his comrades to take his life. Refusing his desperate, half-
crazed pleas, they began to move on. Hanging back, one
sailor, who had previously lent the man a jacket, climbed
down into the grave and, believing the man to be dead,
started to ransack his corpse, looking for anything of value.
The victim, still alive, started to cry out in terror, summoning
another straggler to his aid.

Their senses numbed, incapable of speech and their minds
increasingly succumbing to fantasy, they struggled desperately to respect the oath they had taken as five or six of
their number died, providing them with a possible source
of sustenance. Now desperate for fluids, several men stopped

the circulation in the end of a finger, pricked the skin and sucked the oozing blood. Even the liquid from their numerous blisters offered some relief.

In the coolest part of the night, Adjutant Petit took three soldiers to explore some huts. Perhaps taken for raiders, or simply tired fools drawn into an obvious trap, they were surprised by a band of about thirty Moors brandishing swords. Eventually encircling the entire troop, the Moors grabbed the shirts and uniforms hanging in tatters from the backs of the castaways. Then they led them off to a stagnant, moss-covered pool from which the troop gulped great quantities of stinking water – only to throw it up within seconds. Conducted to the Moors' camp, they found that the women and children delighted in taunting the weary band while the two officers, Praviel and Petit, were summoned to meet the Chief. In broken English, he put several questions to them:

– What country?
– France.
– Where from?
– France.
– Here how?
– A storm wrecked our ship.
– Where?
– A day's journey would take you there.
– What carry?[22]

Praviel tried to communicate the purpose of their voyage and expressed their urgent desire to reach Saint Louis as soon as possible, offering the Chief rewards of tobacco, guns and powder if he would guide them. Pleased by the proposition, the Moor ordered a small portion of dried fish to be distributed, the first real food the castaways had eaten in six days. He then arranged for goatskins to be filled with water and prepared everybody for immediate departure. They marched all day on the 11th, until, in the late evening, they arrived at some huts inhabited by Moors belonging to the same tribe as their guides, and were subjected to the same cruel and insulting behaviour that had greeted them in the middle of the previous night. Exhausted, they were allowed to rest for only two hours before resuming their march.

They had not travelled far, when, out of nowhere, sprang a large band of bellowing Moors. They pulled up a little distance from the troop and told the castaways in English not to be afraid, that their argument was with the Moors who were guiding them. The bigger, better-armed troop clearly fancied themselves the rightful proprietors of the unfortunates, perhaps to guide them, perhaps to enslave them, perhaps to trade them. The dispute swung in the favour of the new arrivals, who, before dispatching the outnumbered guides, cut off the vanquished Chief's beard as a sign of contempt.

– You belong to me, declared the imperious Hammet, leader of the new band. The castaways were rounded up and led to a camp where they were left for two days. The Moorish women, every bit as cruel as those in the first camps, exacerbated the sufferings of the Europeans, taunting them sadistically and flinging fistfuls of sand at their running sores. As they slept, the blisters covering their sunburned bodies rubbed against the ground and burst. To clean their wounds, they went down to the sea's edge and attempted, against fierce, stinging pain, to wash them in salt water.

On the fourth day of their captivity, they sighted *The Argus* tacking offshore, but as the castaways frantically signalled to the brig, it distanced itself, obviously mistaking them for Moors. During the next two days they found no water, but their captors gave them milk mixed with camel's urine. This common source of nourishment for the nomadic desert tribes, who spend up to a week without solid food, was at least preferable to the putrid water they had been obliged to drink.[23]

On their sixth day with the Moors, they encountered

the camel loaded with provisions that had been sent in the direction of Portendick by the Irishman, Kearney. They were considerably sustained by these supplies and, three days later, the swarthy figure of Kearney himself, in magnificent Arab robes and mounted on a large camel, came into view, carrying a letter:

> My dear Anglas, the person who brings you this letter is an English officer whose large and generous soul exposes him to all the dangers and inconveniences of a trip towards the place where you disembarked . . . He knows the country, its language and customs perfectly . . . follow his advice carefully . . . The rest of us aboard the longboat and those from the other boats arrived here yesterday; we found a most generous welcome. Our ills are already eased, and we wait for the complete happiness that our reunion with you and those with you will bring . . . Your friend, Espiaux.

Kearney distributed portions of rice, which some impatient sailors, to their subsequent discomfort, ate raw. Despite their terrible indigestion, the lesson appeared lost on them as they proceeded to devour the tough, raw meat of a bullock they had killed, suffering immediate diarrhoea and vomiting. The less desperate or impetuous cooked their ox, following the Moorish example of making a hollow in the ground and starting a fire. The skinned and gutted animal was thrown into this heated pit and covered with sand, over which another fire was lit.

Still almost a hundred kilometres from Saint Louis, the castaways sighted *The Argus* once more and Kearney fired several shots to attract attention. This time the brig put out a boat, but the breakers proved too strong for it to reach the shore. Risking their necks, Hammet, his brother and the Irishman plunged into the waves, managing to scramble aboard the boat. They rowed out to the ship and braved the pounding waves to return with biscuits and bottles of brandy.

While food and water were no longer a problem, the conditions remained grim. Shoes that had been toughened in the intense heat cracked and disintegrated into the burning sand so that fired, blistered feet were further scorched and torn. The blinding reflection of the sun off the desert provoked pounding headaches and seared eyes. Mouths were parched white as frost. Tongues cleaved to hard palates as the baked air resisted their attempts to breathe. Yet after a further march, when the palm trees of Saint Louis at last came into view, the troop became delirious.

It was 7 p.m. on July 22nd, sixteen days after the castaways had been put ashore in the desert, when Praviel arrived in the tiny village of Guet N'Dar on the banks of the Senegal. A hideous sight in the underpants given to him by Kearney, his legs swollen from sunburn and insect bites, his body scarred and emaciated, his skin broiled, he looked like someone about to be ferried over the Styx, as he climbed into a canoe to cross the river to Saint Louis.[24]

5

The Raft

AT 11 a.m. on July 5th, as the boats pulled away from the half-submerged raft, there were 147 people on board. Among the officers and N.C.O.s who huddled self-protectively in the centre, were the surgeon Henri Savigny, the geographical engineer Alexandre Corréard, and Jean Griffon du Bellay, Secretary to Governor Schmaltz. The most senior naval man on board, Midshipman Coudein, lay with a wounded left leg perched on a barrel in an attempt to keep it as much out of the salt water as possible. Even though precious flour had been jettisoned to lessen the weight of the makeshift platform, many people clinging to the structure were submerged to their waists, and everybody was swamped by the repeated batterings from waves and spray. As the boats disappeared into the distance, the belief that they had been heartlessly sacrificed, cold-bloodedly abandoned, numbed every soul on board. Slowly, dismay gave way to anger, fuelling threats of vengeance hurled into the void.

Unable to obtain the Governor's permission to assign his twelve workmen places alongside him in a boat, Alexandre Corréard realized that duty compelled him to stay with his men and so he had joined them on the raft. Looking out on the desolate expanse of ocean, this young man, who had behaved honourably, reflected on the cutting of the ropes attaching the makeshift structure to the towing boats. That arm, hacking like an executioner, performed an act of the most extreme cowardice. If that was the kind of leadership that the Bourbon Restoration gave the French, then it was clearly in the interests of France – and, indeed, of humanity itself – to overthrow this regime. Looking out at the friendless sea and lowering sky, Corréard determined to stay alive in order to record and accuse. In a perfectly human way, he may have regretted his decision to take a place on this impossible platform, and perhaps he now questioned his decision to flee to Senegal, instead of staying at home where an important political struggle was simmering.

The leaders immediately set about searching for the compass, charts and anchor that Lieutenant Reynaud had promised were on board. None was found. The lack of a compass was a particularly serious want, but Corréard remembered seeing one in the hands of the workshop foreman who was on board. Happily, the man did have one; but, as he handed over the tiny instrument to Coudein, it slipped, fell between the wooden supports and was lost in the sea.

The 146 men and one woman crammed onto the raft could hardly have been a more diverse group. The Navy had indeed been favoured in the evacuation of the frigate, as there were only about twenty sailors on board. Otherwise there was a butcher, a baker from Rochefort, an armourer, an artillery sergeant and captain, a master cannoneer, a barrel maker, a helmsman, domestics of the staff officers on *The Medusa*, members of the *Société philanthropique* and, among the soldiers from the Africa Battalion, men from Italy, Arabia, Guadeloupe, San Domingo, India, Asia, America, Poland and Ireland – an explosive grab-bag of mercenaries, captives and ex-convicts, all furious with the French leadership.

Midshipman Coudein's father, the captain of a man-of-war,

who had witnessed Napoleon's capitulation to the *Bellerophon*, had recently been retired to make way for men like Chaumareys. Coudein's scorn for the captain of *The Medusa* was clearly shared by most of the leaders on the raft, but was at odds with the Secretary to the Governor, Griffon du Bellay, who displayed a surprising loyalty to the commanders of the expedition. One of the first to crack, Griffon du Bellay threw himself overboard during the first day. Saved by Savigny, he attempted suicide again, but found it impossible to release his frightened grip on the raft.

Several days before their departure from France, Coudein had suffered a severe bruising to his left leg, which had not healed and the effect of sea water washing over the painful abrasion almost made him faint with pain. His condition made him unable to move, and the 'strong and courageous' Savigny took the initiative, becoming the *de facto* leader. Born in the bloody year of 1793, Jean-Baptiste Henri Savigny passed his medical exams in Rochefort at nineteen and went to sea for the first time in October 1812. For the following three-and-a-half years he served on four different ships before being assigned to *The Medusa* as a surgeon, second-class. When he sailed for Senegal, his sweetheart in La Rochelle had given him a belt ribbon as a love token and talisman. This he intertwined with Republican colours, thus declaring his political sympathy with the likes of Alexandre Corréard.

As a gentle breeze was blowing, Savigny supervised the erection of a small mast and sail. While this enabled the raft to move, without a compass to guide them and a rudder to steer them they remained at the mercy of the winds and currents. The fact that this mast was erected under the supervision of a surgeon, while there were engineers and carpenters on board, suggests the degree to which Savigny had taken charge. He proposed their first meal of sodden biscuit, made somewhat palatable by soaking it in a little wine. Having distributed and consumed this uninviting mixture, the biscuits were gone and the raft was left without food. The human body can survive for up to fifty days without solids, so this was not, in itself, alarming, but in the sweltering heat it would be necessary to satisfy the need for liquid, and the remaining water and wine would not last long, shared among everyone on board. All through the rest of that first day, this combustible bunch fed off their need for revenge. Having someone to blame, someone to attack, made them eager for survival and provoked lively exchanges about how best to achieve it.[1]

As night fell the wind freshened, the sea rose and clouds and darkness obscured the horizon. Savigny, along with some other resolute individuals, began lashing ropes to the raft with which people might attach themselves for extra safety. As the sea smashed over the platform, everyone struggled to secure themselves. They were bucked back and forth by the agitated ocean, and bodies fastened to the ropes were flung overboard and buffeted, banging back against the raft. Through the pitch-black, broken only by the white-capped waves, the desperate leaders thought they glimpsed a distant light. They signalled by igniting some gunpowder and firing shots from a pistol they had hung up, out of harm's way, near the top of the mast. There was no response and, as the light disappeared, they were left to conclude that it could only have been some distant breaker catching a streak of moonlight as it pierced the rumbling cloud.[2]

The first sight the breaking day afforded was that of squealing people who had been trapped and mangled between the masts and spars laid and lashed together to form the deck of the raft. The salt water that swamped the deck at each scoop and pitch of the craft drenched their lacerations, causing them excruciating pain. Slowly, their shrieks and moans diminished as they lost consciousness and died of their wounds, or slipped off the platform and perished in the sea. The deck was still too crowded to permit a clear view of what had happened and so, before the next distribution of drink, a roll call was taken. Although the number was approximate, for in such a throng anyone could easily call out twice in order to secure a double portion, the total revealed that about a dozen people had already been lost.

With day's calm came the heat and a thirst hardly alleviated by the meagre ration. A baker and two apprentices could bear the situation no longer and committed suicide by hurling themselves into the sea. A tightly packed mass on a vulnerable structure, under a suffocating expanse of sky, sparked flashpoints of panic, charging the heavy atmosphere till it became as electric as the breaking of a tropical storm. By nightfall, people began to hallucinate and bawl out as fear overpowered them. The wind whipped the sea into a frenzy more furious than that of the night before, and again people clutched at the raft while struggling to protect their limbs from being crushed between the heaving spars of its deck. Mountainous waves curved above the platform in a manner that reminded Corréard of his native town of Serres, overhung on its steep mountainside by a threatening arc of rock. In the misadventure of his attempt to flee from a country overwhelmed by calamitous circumstances, that giant wave of rock, now so far away, might never be seen again.

The raft was now running before the wind, easing the force and frequency of the waves drenching those on board. This meant, however, that the vulnerable stern was taking the full force of the storm, sending men surging forward. As the prow was likewise fragile, the overcrowding in the middle of the raft resulted in the crushing or trampling to death of several people in the stampede from port to starboard as the mass attempted to counterbalance the lateral pitch of the craft. When the sea calmed, a group of terrified soldiers, thinking their end was upon them, decided to drown their last moments in drink. They broke open the wine cask lashed near the centre of the raft, and gorged themselves on a liquid swiftly mixing with the salt water that sloshed in through the hole they had gouged. Soon oblivious to the increasing undesirability of the mix, these famished men became easily intoxicated. Already crazed by the onslaughts of the angry sea, they became hell-bent on slaughtering everybody and smashing the raft in an orgy of destruction.

An enormous Asian made for the edge and began to hack at the cords holding the raft together. Raising his hatchet and swiping viciously at an officer who tried to stop him, he was run through with a sabre and pushed into the sea. Immediately the drunken band elbowed towards the leaders who had placed themselves, in relative security, around the base of the mast. A soldier lifted his sabre to attack an officer, but was cut down with repeated blows. Such a firm response repulsed the attack, and the rioters, still wildly swinging their swords and bayonets, regrouped in the stern, where one of them, pretending to rest, slyly set about cutting the fastenings of the raft in order to sink the structure and kill everybody on board. A leader, getting wind of what was going on, rushed at him. Another soldier pulled his knife to intervene and slashed at the officer's coat in his attempt to cut him down. The leader swirled round, grabbing both men, and hurled them into the sea. This clash triggered a riot in which the drunken soldiers started to chop the shrouds and stays, toppling the mast across the thigh of Captain Dupont of the Africa Battalion, who tumbled, senseless, to the deck. The drunks fell on him and heaved him into the sea, from which he was rescued by the other leaders, who then laid him across a barrel. From that perch he was dragged by the rioters, who, according to Savigny and Corréard, were intent on settling some score by gouging out his eyes. Such relentless and murderous frenzy forced the leaders to counterattack, slashing or clubbing the drunken mob into submission.

Corréard had slumped into a kind of trance, when the

noise of this brawl roused him and he assembled with his
workmen in the bow. Far from protected in their rear, they
were attacked by both the mob on board and by those who,
having fallen off into the sea, tried to scramble onto the raft
again. A traitor among Corréard's workforce, a carpenter
named Dominique, had sided with the mutineers.
Nevertheless, finding that this renegade had been thrown
into the waves, Corréard plunged in to save him. When they
were back on board, the traitor's wounds were treated, after
which he once again sided with the rebels – a choice that
cost him his life.

Seeing the only woman on the raft thrown overboard
with her husband, Corréard and the foreman, Touche-
Lavillette, roped themselves together and plunged into the
sea to save them. Back on deck, husband and wife collapsed
into each other's arms as, once again, the tanked-up mutineers attacked and the leaders counter-attacked till the raft
was strewn with dead and bludgeoned bodies.

Corréard heard the woman he had saved calling out to
Our Lady of Laux. Like the mountainous waves that peaked
above them, this invocation took him back to his native
region, where a church dedicated to Our Lady of Laux was
a place of pilgrimage where the lame and paralysed sought
miraculous cures. He was particularly pleased to have saved
a woman from his part of the country, which, it transpired,
she had left twenty-four years before. A sutler selling provisions to the soldiers, she had since travelled with the *Grande
Armée* through many campaigns and battles.

After a short period of relative calm during which many
of the soldiers fell on their knees and asked to be pardoned,
a furious band of drunkards, brandishing knives and sabres,
attacked the raft's leaders. Rioters without weapons went at
their victims with their teeth and several people were
savagely bitten, among them Savigny, who was also hit by
a sword in his right arm, depriving him of the use of two
fingers for some time. One of Corréard's workmen was

seized by a frenzied soldier who chomped at his Achilles
tendon, while three others slashed at him with their knives
and smashed him with the butt of a rifle. Lavillette saved
the man from certain death. Other leaders rescued
Lieutenant Lozach, whose assailants, in their stupor, had
mistaken him for Lieutenant Anglas de Praviel, an officer,
they claimed, who had been harsh with them prior to the
departure of the expedition and whom they had become
obsessed with killing. Throughout the conflict, amid the dark
tangle of wet, bloodied bodies, Coudein remained incapac-
itated on his barrel, protectively nursing a young sailor only
twelve years old. Suddenly, the Midshipman was seized and
flung, along with the barrel and the boy, into the waves.
Despite his wounded leg and the heavy swell, Coudein struggled to save them both, dragging himself and the boy back
onto the raft.

The riot quelled, Savigny fell into a profound torpor. He
was hardly aware of his sabre wounds, but his ratcheting
stomach pains were insupportable, his vision was blurred,
his legs would hardly support him and he was dimly aware
that he was finding it difficult to think. He heard people
around him crying desperately for a little chicken or some
bread. Some, thinking themselves still on board *The Medusa*,
asked to be allowed to sleep in their hammocks. Several
cried out to imaginary boats to save them. Some assumed
they were moored in pretty harbours with well-provisioned
towns embracing them. Corréard was rambling on the Italian
hills when Griffon du Bellay interrupted his reverie:

– I remember, we were abandoned by the boats, but don't
worry, I'm writing to the Governor and within a few hours
we'll be saved.

To which the drifting Corréard replied:

– Have you a pigeon to carry your request swiftly?

Horror, half-dreams and hallucinations were merging the
real with the imaginary so that existence on the raft became
an impossible kaleidoscope of fact and fiction. In the grip

of such delirium, the day had no need to accept what the night sanctioned.[3]

The naturalist, Gaulthier, had led an expedition to explore the Senegal River in 1795. Moored in the delta in terrible heat, the men on board his ship succumbed to a kind of delirium, threw themselves overboard and perished. Although some contemporary doctors thought that this behaviour, accompanying a condition known as calenture, was caused by sunstroke, others – pointing out its appearance at night – argued that such derangement was the result of the continual build-up of hot air trapped inside the hull of a ship. Oppressed by the excessive temperatures of the stifled spaces between decks, sailors in the tropics became dangerously overheated, hallucinated fantastic objects on the surface of the water and fell victim to a fever and frenzied delirium in the hours of darkness. They awoke babbling, with flashing eyes and menacing gestures; fantasizing the fields and forests of homes a world away, they would throw themselves overboard into the sea. Although there were no confined spaces on the raft, there was certainly congestion. During windless afternoons, when the platform lay baking in the searing July sun, the air became sufficiently incandescent to provoke tropical fever.[4]

As dawn broke on the third day, those left alive were jolted by the scene of utter desolation. The raft was a butcher's block. Strewn out, heaped up, sixty people had somehow been murdered or killed or had committed suicide during the night's fighting. The remaining two barrels of water and two barrels of wine had been slung into the waves, leaving only one last cask of wine on board. Into another day of drifting, the survivors were in a wretched state, their clothes slashed and ripped and their bodies smeared with the blood of battle and blistered red by the sun. Summoning up unguessed-at resources of determination, the leaders repaired and re-erected their mast, trying to position the sail so that onshore breezes would, despite the contrary currents, speed them to the coast. But they made little headway and merely zigzagged across the longitude on which they had been wrecked – steadily, but not swiftly, moving south.

A small ration of wine was distributed over the carnage of the second night's battle. Hunger was champing at them, and so, using sharp or pointed decorations from their uniforms, they made hooks with which to fish. They even bent bayonets to make hooks large enough to catch sharks, but, despite the attractive trail of blood pooling from the raft, they were unable to hook one. Indeed, the entire venture failed as the current swirled the improvised fishing lines beneath the raft, where they snagged.

Without a successful catch, and with no food left on board, the men became desperate. Some took to eating the leather harnesses and scabbards of their sabres or their ammunition pouches. Others ate fabric or portions of their hats that were covered with grease or scum. In other shipwrecks, or in similar situations of deprivation, such resources had often been consumed. The crew of the English ship *Fattysalam* had, in 1761, eaten the buttons or leather from belts and cartridge cases. Captain Bligh and the few faithful from *The Bounty* had resorted to raw sea birds. On board the raft, one sailor, pining for food, steeled himself to eat excrement, but, lifting it to his mouth, found he was unable to persist.

Those still just about alive studied the heaps of dead human bodies strewn across the deck. There was a resource, a heap of nutriment lying at their feet, carcasses of meat that certain writers had likened to veal or pork. One such authority had asked what difference it made to a 'lump of clay, whether it be devoured by worms, by animals, or by its fellow creatures'. Taking the precaution of counselling his readers against the dangers of developing a taste for human meat, which had once happened after a famine in India, the German explorer von Langsdorff had asserted that when

survival was at stake, such as in famines, sieges and shipwrecks, the gravity of the situation sanctioned the breaking
of any taboo. In the Old Testament, the Israelites under siege
were told that they would eat the fruit of their own bodies,
'the flesh of thy sons and daughters'. Von Langsdorff reminds
his readers that in the Third Book of Herodotus, when the
Persian army under King Cambyses was crossing the desert
to Ethiopia and ran out of food, the King ordered the killing
of every tenth man in order to feed the rest. While such
extermination was the act of a ruler who held human life
cheap, there had been sufficient examples of expedient
cannibalism for it to become, for shipwrecked men, a custom
of the sea. In 1710, when the ship's carpenter of the wrecked
Nottingham Galley died and 'his Skin, Head, Hands, Feet and
Bowels' had been buried in the sea, his body was quartered
and eaten. In 1727, a similar fate awaited those who perished
on board the stricken *Luxborough Galley*. On some occa-
sions the desperation of starving men had even driven them
to murder. In 1759, the crew of *The Dolphin* had cast lots
and an unlucky passenger was shot through the brain. His
head was flung overboard, while the rest of his body kept
the crew alive.

In 1766, after the wreck of *The Tiger*, a slave was killed
and smoked. When the American sloop *Peggy* was stricken
in a storm during her return from the Azores and supplies
dwindled, two pigeons and the ship's cat were killed, cooked
and served. The Captain received the cat's head and 'devoured
it with greater relish than he had ever enjoyed from tasting
food'. In the days that followed, the survivors consumed
candles and oil, tobacco and leather, until those supplies ran
out. In a complete reversal of European suppositions about
cannibalism being a habit of the African tribes, the sailors
pulled a black man from steerage, shot him through the
head and began to cut him up. They were about to fry up
his bowels for supper, when 'one of the foremast men . . .
was so ravenously impatient that, tearing the Negro's liver

from the body, he devoured it raw'. Having pickled all but
the head and fingers, the rest of the body kept these men
alive for the following nine days, at which time lots were
drawn for a fresh execution. The unlucky straw fell to one
David Flat, who remained brave and chose the same executioner as had killed the black. Mercifully, rescue arrived
before he was shot.

Although in their narrative Savigny and Corréard
approach the moment with great dollops of remorse, at sea,
in times of extreme peril, cannibalism appears to have been
considered a legitimate and accepted means of survival. So,
on the third day of drifting helplessly, some of those left
alive on board the raft set upon the dead bodies strewn
about and started hacking off limbs and eagerly chomping
on raw human flesh. They incised and pulled away the skin
from a shoulder, or stomach or thigh, and ate off the body,
slicing or scooping out the brownish-purple flesh.

During the third night the sea was calmer and it was
possible for the survivors to get some fitful rest. The water
washing over the raft swelled up to their knees and it was
necessary to doze standing up, crushed against one another
for protection. When dawn broke on the fourth day, they
found ten or twelve more dead bodies scattered about the
raft. It was an unsettling awakening for the survivors, who
realized that they too must soon meet the same fate. Slowly,
they consigned the bodies to the deep, saving only one,
who, as Savigny and Corréard put it, would 'nourish those
who, only a short while before, had clasped his hands in
friendship'.[5]

Pangs of hunger plagued those who had not yet
succumbed to the ready supply of human flesh and, towards
evening on the fourth day, when a shoal of tiny flying fish
landed on the raft, those with sufficient energy trapped a
huge quantity, which they gutted and placed in an empty
barrel. Somewhat bucked by their sudden good fortune,
they managed to rig up a makeshift oven and cook the

catch, which they immediately devoured. The fish were tiny and ultimately unsatisfying, so some took advantage of the fire to grill human flesh, rendering it less odious. It was at this point on the fourth day that Savigny and Corréard and the other leaders first tasted one of their late companions. From then on, they were forced to continue their cannibal diet, but it was never again possible to cook the flesh because there was nothing left on board the raft with which to start a fire. Instead, they decided to cut the flesh into slices and hang it up on the stays to dry, making its eventual consumption a less nauseating prospect.

Satisfied by their meal and exhausted, everyone attempted to fall asleep, gingerly trying not to rub or pummel their ulcerated wounds. Hardly had their immense fatigue overcome their chafing pain than another riot broke out. According to Savigny and Corréard, some Spanish, black and Italian soldiers attacked the leaders in an attempt to finish them off, rabid for Lieutenant Anglas de Praviel, whom they could not believe was not on board. They started to scale the mast, intent on capturing some money that had been hung on high to keep it safe for when the raft was washed ashore. Again there was butchery. Again the battle-worn sutler was flung overboard and again she was recovered. At length, the trouble-makers were overthrown, stabbed to death and discarded, leaving – out of the original 147 souls that had been crushed aboard the raft – a group of just thirty survivors.

There was a belief that frequent submersion could rehydrate the body by virtue of the absorbent nature of the skin: the efficacy of wearing clothes drenched in sea water, an idea handed down from James Lind, the man wrongly credited with finding the cure for scurvy, was widely upheld. The problem on the raft, however, was that too-frequent submergence combined with the drying vigour of the tropical sun created serious problems. Frequent dowsing in sea water refreshed the body to a certain extent, but also

removed the grease from the skin and, as the sea water evaporated, salt crystals acted as irritants, provoking boils, excori-
ations and ulcers. Their bodies, covered with pustules,
became so sore that each movement proved agonizing, and
by the fifth day the sea water had scoured the sun-blistered
skin from the feet and legs of those left alive.[6]

The survivors, in their increasingly deplorable state, calculated that they had enough wine left for four days, after
which, without liquid and at the end of their tether, death
would swiftly follow. Such calculations were made futile
when, on their seventh shadowless day afloat, two soldiers
snuck behind the remaining wine cask, drilled a hole and
started drinking. This crime was judged, by common
consent, to be capital and the sentence was executed at once.

The twelve-year-old cabin boy, Léon, whom Coudein
had already rescued from death by drowning, perished in
the Midshipman's arms. This left only twenty-seven souls
alive, fifteen of whom, from all appearances, were likely to
be lost in the following hours.

Gravely wounded or critically ill, those left alive had lost
their sense of time and much of their reason. A council of
the inner circle of leaders was held at which they discussed
the state of their supplies and considered putting those closest
to death on half-rations. With a sinister logic, they perceived
that this would condemn the weakest to a slow but certain
end; at the same time, it would consume the raft's dwin-
dling resources. Working under such a rationale, they agreed
on an even tougher and more desperate solution. Amidst
intense despair at the horror of what they had consented
to do, they decided to throw the weakest overboard and
thus secure, for those remaining, at least six more days of
precious wine. Certain that they would all perish unless such
hard-hearted measures were adopted, their instincts for self-
preservation made them resolve to eliminate those too weak
to resist. But who among them was willing to be the callous
executioner? Who would be able to carry out such an

inhuman act? Savigny and Corréard record that three sailors and a soldier 'took upon themselves this cruel execution'. There was no command recorded, no drawing of lots. Perhaps there was a question of rank, but by that stage, after the innumerable sufferings, the violence, the degradations and indignities that had so deformed their sensibilities, any one of those who remained might have been capable of such an act.

Among the victims was the lone woman, whose thigh had been broken between the masts and spars of the raft's deck. Also murdered was her husband, who had been severely wounded in the head. Using the pathos of this sutler's story, Savigny and Corréard, aware that they were recording a new depth of abasement, interjected an appeal into their narrative: 'Readers, who shudder at the cry of outraged humanity, recollect, at least, that it was other men, fellow countrymen and comrades, who had placed us in this abominable situation.'[7]

The fifteen survivors of this cull next agreed to throw their sidearms into the sea, so as to avoid the crazed quarrels likely to erupt between such crippled spirits. They kept one sabre and a few tools, and were soon diverted by an unexpected visitor. A familiar sight in a meadow on a summer's day in France, a common white butterfly flittered above this shambles, before settling on the mast. It signalled the proximity of land and the overjoyed but broken men scrambled to scour the horizon. Then more butterflies arrived, sending the men's spirits soaring and fluttering with hope. Soon afterwards a gull was sighted, as if to confirm that land must be close, and so they prayed for a new storm that would carry them in and dash them onto the nearby shore. When other gulls arrived, the famished men attempted to snare one – but without success. Such gentle evidence of a world beyond the blood-stained frontiers of their raft brought them up sharp. But, despite their self-disgust, they were so cheered by these sightings that they set about constructing a new raised platform near the mast. On this they would make a shelter.

Their efforts considerably improved their living conditions and alleviated some pain. Hunger had diminished since the first few days, though their heads still ached from the dazzle of the sun and their thirst was brutal: their tongues were swollen, their lips were cracked. Some wet their mouths with urine cooled in small tin containers. Griffon du Bellay downed ten or twelve cupfuls in succession, but another man found that he could not touch the stuff. It was a widespread but mistaken belief that urine is poisonous and that its consumption could do permanent damage. In fact, with its high proportion of water, it is a valuable source of ingestible liquid. Those left on the raft, heartened by the promise of nearing land, diverted themselves with comparative tastings. Savigny observed that certain people produced decidedly tasty urine, whereas the output of others was bitter and unpalatable.[8]

When a lemon was miraculously found along with a few cloves of garlic, the disputes over rights of apportionment became savage and almost ended in further killing. Two vials of teeth-cleaning liquid were also found, and drops containing cinnamon and cloves eased parched tongues and slaked chronic thirst, if only for a few seconds. Some tried putting pewter in their mouths, which gave a sensation of coolness and kept the saliva moving. Sipping their meagre wine ration through a quill had a more restorative effect than drinking it outright, which only intoxicated these broken men and made them feisty.

By the tenth day, when it seemed that the slightest upset might make anyone among them snap, and a general testiness was building towards a full-scale brawl, several sharks, each about ten metres long, and perhaps already partly sated by the bodies thrown from the raft, surrounded the platform. Watching the sleek backs moving in so close, the men half-wished that the sharks would do their worst and finish them off. Some even defied them by lying on the submerged part of the raft in a painful attempt to refresh themselves. But while the sharks, surprisingly, did not attack, these men were stung all over by *medusae* or Portuguese men-of-war, giant jellyfish whose stinging filaments can reach up to fifteen metres long. The agony of their sting lasted only a few hours, but induced vomiting, fever and fearful stomach cramps.

By July 16th, their eleventh day on board the raft, the survivors knew themselves to be close to death. Branded by the white-hot heat, skin blistered into huge ulcers, these wild-eyed, bearded spectres nonetheless summoned up their last reserves of strength to build a smaller raft out of the slats and supports at the edges of their platform. Oars were made from barrel staves and the plan was that eight of them would row for shore. A sailor went aboard to test the structure, but it sank immediately and so they resigned themselves to their raft and to inevitable death. Prostrated by the heat, chafed and inflamed by the salt water, blinded by the screaming light, emaciated, hallucinating and wasted, they passed the night of July 16th in a state of self-recrimination and terror. They mumbled in their delirium about the sad state of France. Lavillette observed that in the good old days he had been afraid only in the heat of battle, whereas now he was surrounded by Frenchmen, who threatened him all the time. Others craved the chance to take on the Bourbon enemies of liberty. Still others longed for a death that would deliver them from the oppressions of the new regime. Savigny suggested that, with one of the tools left on board, they carve their names and some indication of their misadventure on a piece of wood and fix it to the mast, in the hope that after their deaths it would be found and the contents communicated to their families and friends at home.[9]

In the early morning of July 17th, while they were consuming their small ration of wine, a sail was sighted. Thrilled out of their delirium, the men struggled to attract the ship's attention. It was so distant that they could make out only the tops of the masts of what they slowly recognized to be a brig.

They fastened different-coloured handkerchiefs to some straightened hoops from a cask and a man was helped up onto the mast to signal. For half an hour their stomachs were tight with an agony of expectation. Some imagined the ship was moving closer, others that it was sailing away, until, at last, it did indeed disappear from sight. Their excitement collapsed into a fathomless despair. It had been, like the fastening of the towropes to the raft all that hell ago, a false hope and now there was nothing left but to resign themselves to death.

Two hours later, the master-gunner, wanting to go forward to take some air, poked his head out of their shelter. Flying French colours and sailing straight towards them was *The Argus*. Tears erupted and rolled down burned and blistered cheeks. Desiccated bodies throbbed with unbelieving exultation. The brig hove to and put out a boat to investigate. For those on the raft, the sight of a well-kempt and kitted crew clustered on the bulwarks, waving their hats and handkerchiefs, was like the most fantastic mirage. When the boat lay to beside the raft, the officer, zealous and tender, lifted the most badly burned and ulcerated of the survivors on board, placing Alexandre Corréard, who was in the most urgent need, beside him. As they were gently carried aboard *The Argus*, these skeletal figures presented a most pitiable and frightening sight. They were hardly able to move, their eyes were sunken, their beards had matted, and their flesh had shrunk against their skulls as if in readiness for death.

They were given a good hot broth and their wounds were dressed attentively. The surgeon, during the two days that the survivors remained on board, put them on a strict diet to gradually readapt their bodies to normal fare. But delirium persisted. One army officer who wanted to throw himself overboard in search of his lost wallet had to be restrained. Those who managed to sneak behind the doctor's back to gorge themselves were rewarded with excruciating cramps.

The Argus had given up her search for *The Medusa* and was heading back to Saint Louis when she was first detected by the survivors on the raft. After the brig disappeared from their sight, a change of wind made Captain Parnajon resolve to continue his search for the wreck, a decision that led to the discovery of the raft, which had drifted south to a point about ninety nautical miles from the wreck and thirty-two nautical miles off Portendick.

Under a favourable breeze, they sailed for Saint Louis, where they dropped anchor at three o'clock on the afternoon of July 19th. In his report to Governor Schmaltz, written in the roads of Saint Louis, Parnajon noted that:

> I found on this raft fifteen people . . . These unfortunates had been obliged to fight and kill a large number of their comrades who had revolted in order to seize the provisions . . . Others had been taken by the sea, or died of hunger or madness. Those that I rescued had fed themselves on human flesh for several days, and, at the moment when I found them, the ropes which held the mast were covered with morsels of this flesh which they had hung up to dry. The raft was also covered with scraps which further attested to the food which these men were obliged to consume; they had been sustained by a little wine which they handled as carefully as possible; they still had several bottles when I found them.

Of the 147 people abandoned on the raft two weeks earlier, fifteen were left alive: Dupont, the infantry captain; the aptly named l'Heureux, a lieutenant in the infantry; Lozach and Clairet, second lieutenants; Griffon du Bellay; Midshipman Coudein; Sergeant-Major Charlot; Courtade, a master-gunner; Lavillette, the workshop foreman; Coste, a sailor; Thomas, a helmsman; François, a male nurse; Jean-Charles, a black soldier; Corréard, the engineer; and Savigny, the surgeon. Of these fifteen who had the exceptional stamina and indomitable will to survive, five would be dead within the next few months.[10]

6

Tea and Pastries in Senegal

AFTER cutting loose from the raft, the Governor's and Captain's Barges managed to stay close to each other. Governor Schmaltz had stashed on board twenty-three kilos of biscuits, eighteen bottles of wine, two bottles of eau-de-vie and sixty bottles of water. Captain Chaumareys was less lavishly provisioned: for the twenty-eight people in his barge, there were only eighteen bottles of water, a dozen bottles of Madeira, a sack of biscuits and some overripe pears.

As they pulled away from the raft, freed of immediate and crippling responsibility, they profited from a north-north-westerly breeze speeding them in the direction of Portendick and Saint Louis. They sailed briskly through the day in the knowledge that if they made good time, their provisions would last until they reached Senegal.

By July 8th, as the tropical sun burned down upon them and the ocean's glare dazzled their eyes, Midshipman Sander Rang was on the point of putting into shore when he calculated that, as they could be only about thirty-five nautical miles from Saint Louis, they would do best to continue by sea. At ten o'clock that evening, a French brig and a French corvette were sighted. The barges hoisted their main sails,

sent up flares, cried, '*Vive le Roi*' and '*Vive la France*', and
made in the direction of the lights on board the ships with
all possible speed. At length, they were hailed from the deck
of *The Echo* and astonished the watch by replying that they
were boats from *The Medusa*. The surprised officer demanded
the whereabouts of the frigate, and Rang replied that Captain
Chaumareys would explain anon.

The twenty-eight people from the Captain's Barge were
already aboard *The Echo* when the Governor's Barge drew
alongside. Desiring nothing but rest and sleep, they were
given a good supper before settling down for the night,
thankful to be aboard a ship from their convoy, safely
anchored off Saint Louis in Senegal.[1]

The French connection with this part of West Africa
dated from the end of the fourteenth century, when
merchants from Dieppe were active along the coast. During
the first third of the fifteenth century, Portuguese explorers
profited from the imperialist ambitions of the Papacy; under
obligation to convert the heathen population, whose goods
they were authorized to steal, they were also granted permanent rights of possession over the territories they discovered and were busy charting the mouth of the Senegal River.
By the end of the century, the Spanish, likewise benefiting
from papal endorsement, were exploiting the region. The
Dutch came later to barter and plunder, eventually losing
their foothold to the French, who in the seventeenth century
came to dominate trade in the area. They eventually
attempted to secure the delta of the Senegal River by
building a giant, ill-designed and vulnerable mud fort on
the island of Saint Louis. In 1758, during the Seven Years
War, the English obtained control of Senegal and kept it
until 1783, after which the colony reverted to France, with
England continuing to enjoy commercial rights. Along
the coast a series of trading posts had been established on the
Île d'Arguin, at Portendick, Saint Louis, Galam and on the Île
de Gorée. At all of these posts, gum was traded, and at Saint

Louis and Gorée there was a thriving traffic in human beings.[2]

In 1800, with the capture of Gorée, the English demonstrated their considerable commercial interest in the area. Benefiting from Napoleon's indifference to French colonial holdings, they took Saint Louis in July 1809 without a struggle. So when, on July 9th, 1816, Governor-designate Schmaltz went ashore, he came under the jurisdiction of the English governor, Thomas Brereton, until such time as the British government, in accordance with the recent Treaties of Paris in March 1814 and November 1815, sanctioned the handing back of the settlements of Senegal and Gorée to the French.

Though they were to appear dilatory in giving up the colony, the English were quick to react to the hardships endured by the French colonists. A British officer, Major John Peddie, whose compassion for the victims was considerable, noted 'that every attention within the means of this Garrison was immediately afforded'.[3] Governor Brereton wrote to Schmaltz on July 9th: 'A most ready and prompt compliance shall be given to your wishes in affording every bit of assistance in my power and I have ordered two craft ... best suited to the purpose. They will be dispatched without delay.'[4] Representatives of both governments sent men and ships to search for survivors, although Schmaltz's initiatives seemed, in comparison with those of the English, bafflingly sluggish.

The first group of castaways, including Brédif and the Picards, arrived in Saint Louis on July 13th and were greeted by the English governor on horseback, accompanied by Kearney and several officers. Dismounting, Colonel Brereton, in marked contrast to his French counterpart, seemed most affected by their sufferings, and those in the worst condition were at once admitted to the English hospital.

Although many French merchants and all the French

administrators had been forced to leave Saint Louis in 1809, there were still some tradesmen in the colony and the successive waves of survivors were welcomed by these compatriots, as well as by a host of deeply sympathetic English families. Most of Picard's children lodged with M. Artigue, his old friend from his previous stays in the colony. Charlotte and her sister, Caroline, however, were billeted with a kindly English couple, the Kingsleys, who occupied one of the fifty European-style bungalows in the centre of the island of Saint Louis. These dwellings had meagre gardens and terraced roofs, and housed the 500 resident merchants and administrators. There were also 2,000 free blacks and mulattos along with 7,500 slaves on the island, which was just over three kilometres long, and, at its maximum, a kilometre wide. The French fort stood in the middle of the island, flanked by large, unpaved roads that proved unpleasant thoroughfares when the wind blew, carrying sand off the Sahara. At the northern end of the island, inland from the mangroves, there was a hospital, a church and a store for gunpowder. In the southern part, amid the palm trees and baobabs, stood the natives' badly constructed straw huts, largely blackened by smoke.[5]

Upon arrival, the sisters were taken to be washed and treated with ointment by two of the Kingsleys' black servants. They were given clothes and linen of a smoothness and whiteness that were shocking against their frazzled skins. Throughout their recent ordeal Charlotte had been kept alive by her exceptional fortitude, but once saved and finding herself in the luxury of European-style surroundings, she feared a complete breakdown. Having gone beyond the limits of all she had ever known or could imagine, the sheer comfort of white linen appeared oddly terrifying. When her hostess invited her to join the family in the drawing room, Charlotte struggled to summon up hidden reserves of strength in order to negotiate this difficult return to civilization. The young lady, who only days before had drunk muddy, putrid water from a soldier's greasy cap, was taking tea and pastries in the company of late enemies who were offering her – in conspicuous contrast to her own leaders – the most gentle welcome.

M. Picard's understandable outburst over the cowardice of the commanders of the expedition had been reported to Schmaltz and was most probably the cause of the Governor-designate's neglect of the family. When Picard asked for supplies, Schmaltz refused. Unable to obtain anything from his leader or from M. Durécu, the prosperous merchant who was currently financing and supplying the French expedition, Picard was eventually obliged to borrow money in order to rent a small apartment in which to lodge his entire family, all of whom had, miraculously, survived the desert trek. If he had made enemies among the nastiest and most powerful of the survivors from *The Medusa*, Picard luckily still possessed a group of old friends from his previous visits. Furthermore, blacks from the surrounding countryside came to offer help, carrying donations from their simple harvest. Thus, living cheaply on native dishes, the Picards were discovered by the kindly Major Peddie, who immediately instructed the Mayor of Saint Louis to grant the family the rations expected by English officers.[6]

Although the various accounts do not agree on the details and the extent to which the English were of assistance, neither are they unanimous concerning the actions of the French merchants. Brédif, who praised the English officers for their kindness and attention, also writes that he was received with 'tender hospitality' by M. Durécu and his nephews, noting that 'it was with great simplicity and without ostentation' that Durécu helped the victims of the shipwreck. Charlotte Picard, on the other hand, suggests that Durécu was an opportunist who, it was rumoured, was taking 100 per cent profit on all the loans he made. Yet, because he was Schmaltz's chum, he was awarded the *Légion d'honneur.* This portrait of Durécu as a calculating profiteer is upheld by Savigny and Corréard, who suggest that the Governor had entered into a kind of business pact with Durécu, a pact that would lead to some very sinister dealings.

Whereas Major Peddie's actions and attitude are universally praised, the conduct of Colonel Brereton is frequently questioned. Savigny and Corréard are incensed by his apparent procrastination in handing over the colony. As the gum harvest was imminent, a hold-up in the transfer would guarantee the English merchants that year's profit from the lucrative trade.[7] Gaspar Mollien, Savigny and Corréard record that any kindness shown by Brereton was short-lived. As early as July 17th, before the raft had even been found, or all the desert castaways accounted for, many French soldiers, sailors and officers were obliged to embark for their settlement at Cap Vert. Schmaltz would follow, while those too sick to travel would remain in Saint Louis until they regained their health. However guilty the French governor-designate was of sluggishness or hard-heartedness, the situation in which he found himself was obviously uncomfortable and logistically problematic.

Describing Cap Vert, Geoffrey de Villeneuve wrote of its 'perpetual greenness', of the 'singular vigour of its productions' which 'proclaims an earth fertilized by several centuries of vegetal decay, and by the two volcanoes of which we see traces everywhere'. Cotton and indigo were cultivated, there was game in the forests and fish in the sea. Cornette de Vénancourt, in his survey of the area, noted 'papaya, guava, citrus fruits, manioc, sugar cane and cows'. Clearly, it was a potentially rich peninsula for the proposed agricultural establishments sponsored by the *Société philanthropique*. Despite the breathless heat of early August, the explorer Gaspar Mollien set about, with the help of the sometime stowaway Rabaroust, planting seeds of lettuce, carrots, celeriac and melons.

Dakar was the largest of the six villages on the peninsula,

and a provisional camp for the Army and Navy was established there by Vénancourt. Dysentery was endemic and excessive drinking reduced many to a stupor. People were dying daily. Chaumareys attempted to manage the growing disorder between the soldiers and sailors, but it was Schmaltz, arriving on 26th July, who solved the problem. He separated the feuding members of the different services by containing the sailors on board *The Argus* and *The Echo*.[8] Meanwhile, Schmaltz installed himself comfortably on the nearby Île de Gorée, which lies in the lee of the cape. It was an island where Europeans who became sick while living in Senegal went to regain their health.[9]

When, with the permission of the English governor, the raft survivors were disembarked at Saint Louis on July 19th, Lieutenant Reynaud – whom Savigny and Corréard accused as the person who had cut them adrift – was on the quay to shake their wretched hands. The crazed survivors were terrified that they would be put to death for murder and cannibalism. In the most wretched condition, Alexandre Corréard begged to be thrown into the sea. With their coming ashore, Brédif writes that those already arrived in the colony became aware of 'the terrible butchery' that had occurred, how large numbers of men had been carried off by the breakers and how the survivors had been found with 'pieces of human flesh hanging above them and urine bottled' – their only food and drink. 'What horror,' he observes, 'caused by the incompetence of a single man.' The government had appointed Captain Chaumareys in scandalous disregard of sound judgement.[10]

To those who had never been pushed to such extremes, the men who had been on board the raft were frightening beings who had transgressed all civilized standards in order to survive. They had lived beyond what was deemed acceptable and now appeared as strangers among friends. Their notions of what might or might not be permissible were blurred and, while dining with a merchant one evening, one of the survivors blithely commented that the liver of the pig they were eating was not half as tasty as the liver he had torn from a man on the raft. When he embraced Savigny and Coudein at Governor Schmaltz's, Sander Rang records that they seemed like figures risen from the tomb; indeed, he notes that letters had already been dispatched to France reporting their certain loss.[11]

Towards midnight on July 19th, the same day on which *The Argus* arrived, Lieutenant Anglas de Praviel reached the colony in 'a state of utter destitution'. The weakness of his voice making him difficult to understand, Praviel announced the arrival of the second group of castaways.[12] The very next day, July 20th, Kummer and Rogery, the two men who had been washed ashore at Portendick in the same group as Brédif and Charlotte Picard, and who had wandered separately off into the desert and been given up for lost, were led into Saint Louis by some Moors.

Soon after leaving his party early in their march, Kummer had found the camp of Prince Muhammed, the son of King Zaide of the Trazas tribe of Moors. He had boldly stridden into the midst of their encampment and, in the few words of Arabic that he knew, passed himself off as the son of a Muslim woman. The Moors seemed overjoyed to welcome him, quizzed him about recent events in France, enquired as to why the trading posts on Arguin Island and Portendick had fallen into disuse, and asked him to lead them to the place where his boat had come ashore.

While they were resting by a pond, another group from the same tribe arrived with Rogery, who declared that he had not been treated well. The women and, above all, the children had pestered him and robbed him of almost everything he carried or wore. After a short rest, the Frenchmen were conducted to the camp of King Zaide. They negotiated a fee for their safe conduct to Saint Louis and were able to observe the customs and pursuits of their hosts –

the polygamy of the King, the fair treatment and education of black slaves, and the trade in salt, furs, feathers and skins.

The King put a stop to the tormenting of Rogery, who, without the pretended traces of Muslim blood, had been made to feel less welcome than his friend. Zaide exhibited considerable knowledge about recent European events and pressed them for information about the *Cent-Jours*. He treated the two Frenchmen with much kindness and sent them off on their journey to rejoin their countrymen.[13]

The victims from the raft were, according to Brédif, being badly cared for in the English hospital. De Praviel visited them on July 23rd and found Corréard still in the most desperate state. He also noted that the raft survivors were given preference over his own troop from the desert, who had arrived during the previous days. The least healthy among the desert marchers were packed in a single room and given a ration of biscuit and bacon, while those from the raft were given the English soldier's ration of white bread, meat, rice, sugar, coffee, Madeira and rum. Despite this largesse, the survivors from the raft protested that such a ration was unsuited to the restoration of their health and, while the English surgeon and Governor Brereton proved deaf to their complaints, Major Peddie and some other English officers showed them considerable kindness, inviting the four healthiest officers to dine with them daily and even offering them a good Champagne d'Épernay.[14]

Corréard, who remained in the hospital longest, was left on what he described as a hard bed with dirty sheets. He was in excruciating pain from the sores, the sickness and the bayonet and knife wounds he had sustained on board the raft, and he passed endless days and often sleepless nights brooding on his misfortunes:

Nothing relieves me; on the contrary, the length of the nights, the continuation of my sufferings, the sight of those of my companions in misfortune, the disgusting filth by which I am surrounded, the inattention of the army nurse who is always drunk or negligent, the insupportable hardness of a wretched bed, scarcely sheltered from the inclement air, all bode an inevitable death.

Indeed, it was at the English hospital that those who had survived the ordeal of the raft – Second Lieutenants Lozach and Clairet, Sergeant-Major Charlot, the black soldier Jean-Charles, and Courtade, the master-gunner – would soon die.

Having received no news from the French at Cap Vert, Corréard was becoming anxious to join them, but Major Peddie dissuaded him from going to a camp where dysentery was rampant. The Major had come bearing gifts, and had shed tears at the sight of Corréard's sufferings. He professed himself honour-bound to reciprocate a little of the kindness that he and his comrades had received at the hands of their late enemies during the Napoleonic Wars. It was to Peddie and three other English officers, who exhibited much kindness towards him, that Corréard claimed he owed his life. Not once, during all this period of suffering, did Madame or Mademoiselle Schmaltz care to visit the hospital.[15]

The Argus had returned with the survivors of the raft on board, but without sighting *The Medusa*, so another salvage expedition was dispatched on July 26th. This attempt was made by a far-from-seaworthy schooner owned by Durécu. There were other ships available that were more suited to the task, but Schmaltz liked to deal exclusively with Durécu, whose ill-equipped vessel was forced to return after encountering adverse weather. Setting off once again, she was again forced to put back to port after her sails were all but destroyed in a gale. She set sail for a third time and at this attempt found *The Medusa* on August 26th, fifty-two days after the frigate had been abandoned.

The ghostly hull was broken and she had slumped on her port side. On board, like some weird Gothic vision from a contemporary poem, were three cagey, skeletal figures crouched in different parts of the deck among the scattered debris. They had only brandy left to drink – and just days, if not hours later, would have been dead. Indeed, a fourth had died only a short while before the arrival of the schooner and had been committed to the sea. Of the other thirteen who had been left on board on July 5th, the crew of the schooner learned that for forty-two days they had survived with an ample supply of biscuit, bacon, prunes, wine and brandy, but that when these had begun to dwindle, twelve of them had constructed a raft and set sail. This rudderless craft was eventually found washed up on the shore by some of King Zaide's men, without trace of survivors. One of the five remaining men tried to make for the shore on a chicken coop, but sank a short distance from the frigate. The four other men preferred to stay safely on board rather than offering themselves to the 'sea-monsters which are found in great numbers on the coasts of Africa'. These four fed themselves on salt pork, tallow and the remaining brandy until all but the liquor ran out and one of them died. At the time of their eventual rescue, despite their weakened state, the three remaining appeared ferocious, brandishing knives at one another and charily guarding their self-apportioned and broken domains.[16] When the schooner had salvaged what it could from *The Medusa*, these wild survivors were taken on to Saint Louis.

The first day that Corréard was able to get up from bed and take a short walk in the town, he called on the family of the French governor. He was appalled to discover their attitude towards the schooner's expedition. Their only concern seemed to be the recovery of valuables and provisions from the wreck, no one caring a fig for the possible survival of the men on board. Already disgusted by their indifference, Corréard became irate when he learned that he would not be able to recover any of his own engineering instruments, on which his livelihood depended. Later, when the schooner arrived in Saint Louis, it was declared that what it had recovered from the wreck was a 'prize'. Lieutenant Reynaud was among these 'pillagers' and carried off several trunks as Saint Louis was turned into a week-long market fair. Everything was up for sale, including the French flag that had been transformed into tablecloths and napkins. Blacks bought signal flags to make aprons and cloaks. Even vases belonging to Chaumareys were on offer, and the Captain himself later noticed them gracing the house of the Governor. There were furniture, tackle and instruments for sale – even clothes belonging to people who were still alive. Thereafter the various other merchants in Saint Louis were authorized to plunder the wreck in a fifty-fifty split with Schmaltz.[17]

But even before the finding of the wreck, the first moves in the discovery and exposure of the scandal of *The Medusa* began. On July 29th, *The Echo* set sail for France. She carried a letter from Schmaltz to the Minister of the Navy, Vicomte DuBouchage, stating that he was left with only half the complement of his garrison. On board were fifty-five survivors of the tragedy, among them the valorous Lieutenant Espiaux, Ensign Lapeyrère, Midshipman Coudein and Henri Savigny.

In complete contrast to the disorder that had endangered his outward voyage, Savigny recorded that in all his time in the Navy he had never beheld such a well-kept and soundly run ship. Cornette de Vénancourt was in command, a man of skill and rigour; his navigation to Senegal had been exemplary and Governor Schmaltz praised his 'zeal after the loss of *The Medusa*'. In a report of the *Société philanthropique*, written at the end of July, Vénancourt was likewise singled out for his aid in exploring Cap Vert after the delegates, from *The Medusa*, had lost all their possessions in the wreck.[18]

Vénancourt was also an ambitious man. He took obvious

satisfaction in tactful criticism of Chaumareys's handling of the convoy. Considering their respective careers in the Navy, while Chaumareys had spent the last twenty years resting on the laurels of his fictitious heroism during the Quiberon campaign and steadily forgetting his maritime skills, Vénancourt had been sailing. Appointed captain of a frigate in 1815, after nine years as a lieutenant and twenty-five years at sea, Vénancourt had demonstrated the flair and courage needed to bring a ship full of mutineers to heel during the *Cent-Jours*. Clearly, with such a long and distinguished career, superior qualities of seamanship and Royalist sympathies, it dismayed him to think that the bungling Chaumareys had been allowed to steer a large number of people to dereliction and death. During the thirty-four-day voyage home, when he found out about the manuscript that Savigny was writing as a kind of therapeutic rite of passage back to civilization, Vénancourt realized that the misjudgements and resulting horrors catalogued by the account could do nothing but demonstrate to the government that it had plainly appointed the wrong leader.[19]

Towards the end of the day on September 2nd, 1816, a telegraph arrived at the Ministry of the Navy in Paris from Vice-Admiral Saint-Haouen in Brest, alerting the authorities that *The Echo* had arrived in his port carrying news of the wreck of *The Medusa*. Two days later, Saint-Haouen telegraphed the Ministry to say that he had asked for reports from those officers from *The Medusa* who had arrived on board *The Echo* and would dispatch them forthwith.

The Captain of *The Echo* also presented a neutral and non-accusatory verbal report to Saint-Haouen. Furthermore, on his own initiative, Vénancourt sent *The Echo*'s log direct to the Minister of the Navy, Vicomte DuBouchage. He also asked Savigny for a copy of the narrative that the surgeon had written during the voyage. At that stage, without the input of the politically agitated Corréard, the text was mildly accusatory, but not insistently anti-Royalist. It was therefore not offensive to Vénancourt, nor would it be anything but an embarrassment to his minister. It would, moreover, prove useful in Vénancourt's desire to underline the innate superiority of his own seamanship – a fact that, once established, might serve him well, both in regard to future appointments and in his solicitation for the *Légion d'honneur*. By the time Savigny set out for Paris, on September 11th, to deliver his narrative to the Ministry, Vénancourt had already dispatched a copy to a friend, who passed it on to Councillor Forestier, who was supposed, in turn, to hand it on to Vicomte DuBouchage. Realizing the volatility of the document (and presumably for reasons of political inclination), Forestier gave it not to his Royalist minister as was intended, but to the man who, over the previous months, had desperately been trying to save the Restoration from hardening into a dangerous and unacceptable resurrection of the *ancien régime*: the Minister of Police and the King's favourite, Elie Decazes.[20]

7

Sex and the Street

JUST as the news of the wreck of *The Medusa* was beginning to break, Théodore Géricault fled France for Italy. If, in the emotional turmoil of flight, he was much aware of the shocking news item, it is — like the exact date of his departure — unrecorded. But, as the laudatory letter of recommendation from his teacher, Pierre-Narcisse Guérin, to an unknown Florentine is dated September 20th, it is safe to say that the news of the shipwreck and the horrors of the raft, which were shocking France, could not altogether have escaped the attention of a smart young man. Certainly Géricault was not yet ready to register the metaphorical potential of the catastrophe; for the artist to understand the personal and political resonances of the wreck, he would first need to experience both the feeling and the fact of loss. The former would result from his determination to try to put an impossible liaison behind him. The latter would shake his premature return to France.[1]

It is certainly possible that his aunt Alexandrine — a married woman with two children, a position in society to maintain and much to lose — might have found the strain of a quasi-incestuous affair too great. Whoever initiated the separation, Géricault's aesthetic education provided an

130

excellent pretext. The year that he spent in Italy is signifi-
cant for the understanding of his emotional dilemma as well
as his awakening engagement with a new kind of subject
matter.

Neoclassicism had been popular for more than thirty years
and, though it had served the ideals of the Revolution, the
reality of what was happening in France could best be
perceived in the streets, rather than in the detached idealism
on show at the Salon. In Italy, it was not in the museums
and among the classical ruins that Géricault was to find his
revolutionary voice, but on the street corner, in the piazza;
it was there that he began to become a painter of modern
life who treated scenes and events that revealed truths about
his world.

The close friends who had planned to accompany
Géricault on the journey were, for one reason or another,
delayed and unable to join him. He travelled part of the
way with a fabulously wealthy Polish nobleman who had
served in the Imperial Army. It was perhaps through this
connection that Géricault came to be invited to the opera
in Florence, where he was accorded a place of honour next
to the Duchesse de Narbonne-Pelet, wife of the French
minister to the King of Naples. Such dazzling evenings did
not belie the fact that Géricault was feeling very much
alone. In a letter to the painter Pierre-Joseph Dedreux-
Dorcy of October 18th, he urged his close friend from
Guérin's studio to make haste to join him, rounding up as
many good companions as he could muster, for 'you can't
have too many old friends around when you're abroad'. This
need for friendship and distraction was not only a question
of homesickness, but was also a reflection of his sorrow in
having left Alexandrine.

Restlessly moving on to Rome in mid-November after
a short, unhappy stay in Florence, Géricault hoped to divert
himself with some friendly faces, but once again he found
himself to be 'far from consolation'. Despite his exhilaration

at the sight of the Sistine Chapel, he wrote that, generally, 'things appear in their ugliest light'. Wherever he went, whatever he saw, the melancholy within tarnished his vision. Dejection dominated his voyage and, as he candidly confessed in a letter of November 27th, 'My heart is never easy for it is too full of memories.'[2]

Rome was, along with Naples, cardinal to the artist's study of antiquity. However, early on in his Roman stay, Géricault wondered if one year was not a sufficient period of study, rather than the five-year span accorded to the *pensionnaires* of the French Academy. His observation registers an intimation of the declining importance of the study of the classical for a painter who was searching to take issue with modern life.[3]

Géricault rented a studio in the Ludovisi quarter, near the Piazza Barberini. He visited that master of clarity and order, Jean-Auguste-Dominique-Ingres, the Provençal painter François Granet, and met the English architect Charles Cockerell, who would prove to be a good friend to him during his later visits to England. He saw, in fact, quite a number of old friends and yet remained, to all intents and purposes, depressed. His watercolour sketches of modern Italian life were vivid and accurate, but the poses of his Italian peasants remained academic.

There were, however, two events that seem to have provoked Géricault's increasing feeling for the scent of the street. The first was an execution that he witnessed, of which he produced a series of pencil, pen and ink sketches. Some of these demonstrate Géricault's continuing attachment to classical models. Others capture the more spontaneous clumsiness of the sinister event, such as the moment in which menacingly hooded executioners, wishing to preserve their privileged anonymity, conduct their victim to a terrible end. It is a theme that would recur in Géricault's work in numerous guises: the following year, in the abduction of the magistrate, Fualdès; then at the hanging of the

Cato Street conspirators in London; and finally, in the violent seizure of innocent human beings in his drawings for a large projected canvas inspired by events in Senegal, *The Slave Trade*.

The other spectacle that seized Géricault's attention during his stay in Rome was the climax to the Roman Carnival, the race of the riderless horses down the Via del Corso from the Piazza del Popolo. In Géricault's masterly small painting, a study for an unrealized larger canvas, the horses strain with unbridled energy against the classical confines of the ordered public space. Dramatically backlit, and symptomatic of the release of anarchic and subversive energy during Carnival, the horses rear against the restraining stable boys, while the shadowy rabble behind, a looming political force, can be seen dimly to echo their desire for freedom. The small painting captures more than a spectacle, or a contest; it hints at a barbarous eruption in a civilized space.

In addition to that important painting – the most robust and vital that Géricault produced during these unhappy months – was a series of drawings thrashing out themes of tortured eroticism. Prior to his departure, he had in fact begun to sketch these sometimes personal, sometimes mythological explorations of violent or delighted sex. There are numerous extant drawings in this vein and there were, most probably, many more. In the mid-1850s, the painter Paul Huet discovered that some Norman relatives of Géricault possessed, among other works, a stash of several hundred drawings that they would not permit visitors to see. Huet assumed that as these were most probably of an erotic nature, they would eventually be destroyed. If Huet's estimate of the number is accurate, such a bulk of material argues the persistence and strength of Géricault's sexual dilemma.[4]

Some of the erotic drawings that the artist made in 1816–17 explore fantasies of violence and cruelty, perhaps reflecting his feelings of guilt and conflict about his ill-starred affair. A man of twenty-five, at the height of his sexual powers and recoiling from a passionate and forbidden relationship, was perhaps somewhat terrified of the extreme intensity of the drives that seemed to saturate his being; a dialogue with these urges, using the stock, sexually charged figures of mythology such as satyrs and centaurs, would help him to thrash out and objectify his lust.[5] Among the sketches that have survived, there is also evidence of erotic delight and physical exuberance. Embraces are often ecstatic, clearly the work of a man who knows the intensity of physical passion and who is reliving his rapture in a time of deprivation.

Géricault managed to conceal much of his soul-searching beneath the refinements of a young man of his class. During a reasonably happy interlude in Naples during April and May 1817, the elegant young artist was praised for his 'very pleasing ways' and 'most considerate manners'.[6] He made sketches and watercolours of the classical ruins at Herculaneum and Paestum, and then returned to Rome for the rest of the summer, being held up by brigands on the way.

Despite his urge to get back to Paris after 'a year of sadness', Géricault did manage a few days sketching in the Uffizi in Florence on his way home. Then he pressed on to Paris, arriving in early November 1817. Charles Clément, Géricault's biographer, characterized the Italian episode as 'a real exile' and Géricault's contemporary, Louis Batissier, speaks of the period as one of 'heartaches'. It is more than likely that he prematurely terminated his Italian trip expressly to return to the arms of Alexandrine.[7]

If Géricault had left France as the story of the wreck of *The Medusa* was breaking, he returned just as the full complexity of the drama was unfolding, with the publication of Savigny's and Corréard's immediately best-selling book, *The Shipwreck of the Frigate, The Medusa*. In France, it had been a year of political upset and intrigue, marked by a struggle for justice and the beginnings of a serious and far-reaching investigation into the ill-fated expedition to Senegal. Once again, just over a year after the scandal broke, the wreck was very much on everybody's mind.

Géricault, however, was distracted by urgent personal matters. Although an apt vehicle for the development of his career was on everybody's lips, he was still not quite ready to take the wreck of *The Medusa* on board. He had tried to make a break with Alexandrine. It had proved impossible. He had begun to sever himself from an impersonal, obsolete and anodyne Classicism. That seemed possible. Without having met, Stendhal had been in Naples when Géricault was there; a few years later, in his book *Racine et Shakespeare*, Stendhal was to discuss the Classical, which he categorized as outmoded, and the Romantic, which he dubbed modern and fascinating. Summarizing Stendhal's argument, Isaiah Berlin has since noted that Romanticism 'is a matter of understanding the forces which move in your own life';[8] during Géricault's time in Italy, sex and the scope of the street had been tugging at his soul.

8

Breaking News and
Stifling Scandal

WHEN Elie Decazes, Minister of Police and favourite of
Louis XVIII, witnessed the dangerous abuses of the measures that had been introduced to stabilize France, when he
perceived that the *ultras* would press on as far as civil war
in order to destroy the constitutional charter, reclaim their
old possessions, and return the balance of power to that of
the *ancien régime*, he realized that the present government,
the so-called *chambre introuvable*, with its ultra-Royalist
majority, must be dissolved.[1] Ruthless in his attempts to
discredit the *ultras*, Decazes formed a close alliance with the
King, with whom he shared the findings of his police spies.
But the problem remained that if the right was significantly
diminished, it would be difficult to check resurgence of the
left. Decazes was walking a tightrope and, by early 1816, his
course of action had become apparent: he needed to 'royalize
the nation and nationalize the Royalists'.[2]

Throughout the cold, dull and agriculturally unproduc-
tive summer of 1816, Decazes was tireless in placing before
the King persuasive justifications for the dissolution of the
chambre introuvable. He demonstrated the divisive contempt
that the *ultras* entertained for the soldiers of France.[3] He

emphasized the ardour of ultra-Royalism in the south, arguing that such passion was a tinderbox to insurrection. Backed by the Russian ambassador, and supported by the other Allies, who feared that an *ultra* triumph would result in France reneging on her war debts, Decazes argued that it was essential to dissolve the Chamber in order to demonstrate stability and regain the confidence of the country's recent enemies. Richelieu, the head of the government, detested meddlesome foreigners, and Decazes cleverly persuaded him that the follies of the *chambre introuvable* were delaying the liberation of France from its Allied occupiers.[4]

Decazes shrewdly realized that the 'policy of the King must have two grand objectives: firstly, the liberation of French territory and the re-establishment of order and Royal authority; and secondly, the consolidation of a Constitutional Monarchy by the alliance of the throne with the notion of liberty'.[5] By mid-August, Louis was, at last, in agreement about the need to dissolve the Chamber. It was a dangerous moment, particularly for the King; the Minister of Police may have engineered the Ordinance of Dissolution, but the King had to sign it. In so doing, Louis was taking a daring initiative against members of his own family and particularly against his *ultra* brother, the Duc d'Artois. He was, in fact, putting himself in opposition to the court and the first Royalist assembly elected since the Revolution.[6]

Throughout July and August, while these political deliberations were taking place, the King, government and people of France remained blissfully ignorant of the fact that the expedition to repossess and colonize Senegal had gone disastrously wrong. It was not until three days before the King issued the Ordinance of September 5th dissolving the *chambre introuvable* that DuBouchage at the Ministry of the Navy received a telegraph informing the government of the wreck of *The Medusa*.

At Brest, Vice-Admiral Saint-Haouen began to put together a dossier of reports. It included two letters written

by Captain Chaumareys, both dated July 29th, the day of
The Echo's departure from Saint Louis. In the first of these
letters, Chaumareys blamed the wreck on unsatisfactory
maps and noted that the strong currents off the West African
coast made for a treacherously shifting sandy seabed. In the
second letter, in which he neglected to mention the castaways in the desert, Chaumareys spoke of the finding of the
raft, although he chose not to mention the number of casu-
alties involved.[7]

However, a collective report by those officers of _The
Medusa_ who had returned on board _The Echo_, including
Lieutenant Espiaux and Ensigns Maudet and Lapeyrére,
revealed some alarming facts: firstly, that Chaumareys had
failed to take a sounding an hour before the disaster;
secondly, that at that time _The Medusa_ had been sailing
south-south-east; thirdly, that the raft had been abandoned
because it was judged that the efforts of the boats towing
the platform were proving ineffective; and fourthly, that as
a number of men had refused to leave the frigate,
Chaumareys, its captain, could not have been the last to
leave his ship. The dossier also contained a report by
Midshipman Coudein, the most senior member of the Navy
on board the raft. Although this report was objective and
even non-accusatory, it did hang huge question marks over
the motives prompting certain decisions.

Cornette de Vénancourt, in his testimony before Saint-
Haouen, merely supported the assertion that the maps of
the area were poor; his decision to supplement this bland
verbal account by sending _The Echo_'s log and Savigny's narrative to DuBouchage was calculated to embarrass the
Minister, who had entrusted the safety of French people
and a great French enterprise to a moth-eaten émigré. While
Vénancourt's intention had not been to provoke a scandal,
within days the country would have its first indications of
some alarming facts surrounding this avoidable catastrophe.[8]

That the news of _The Medusa_, particularly embarrassing

to the *ultras*, should surface at a time when the King had, at last, signed the Ordinance dissolving the *chambre introuvable* was, for Decazes, impeccable timing. If neo-conservatives were a dangerous element in the delicate equation of constitutional monarchy, then the scandal of the wreck of *The Medusa*, captained by an unsympathetic and sycophantic Royalist, provided a devastating instance of the danger of entrusting the affairs of state to such fossils. To confront the nation with proof of the fatal ineptitude of the likes of Hugues Duroy de Chaumareys afforded Decazes an unprecedented public-relations opportunity.

The first announcement of the loss of *The Medusa* was a brief mention in *La Quotidienne* on Friday, September 6th, four days after the arrival of *The Echo* at Brest. There was, at that stage, no hint of any scandal. But on September 5th, the day the King signed the Ordinance, a telegraph had been received at the Ministry of the Navy, declaring that 'of the 150 men, soldiers and sailors who were put on the raft, 135 perished' and that news appeared in the *Journal des débats* on Sunday, September 8th, the day on which the text of the Ordinance was published.[9]

That night Richelieu was at the opera, and the crowd in the stalls cheered the President of the Council; this was just the first of many signs of enthusiasm that greeted the Ordinance, an act seen as a deliverance and understood as a strategy to consolidate the throne. In the King's statement, Louis had reasserted his commitment to the *charte*, and the *Bourse* reacted favourably, with government shares immediately increasing in value. Abroad, the news was hailed as a step towards an era of peace and prosperity. At home, the left was thrilled; Royer-Collard, the liberal deputy, wanted to erect a statue to the great Decazes.

There were, of course, large portions of the population who were mortified by the act. On the subject of the dissolution of the *chambre introuvable* the Vicomte Chateaubriand was acid: 'This ministerial measure, they say, will save the legitimate Monarchy. Dissolving the only assembly since 1789 that has shown purely Royalist sentiments is, to my mind, a strange manner of saving the Monarchy.' But whatever the eventual consequences of Decazes's '*coup d'état*', in the short term the measure was greeted by a majority of the population with relief and enthusiasm.[10]

By contrast, the news of the raft published in the *Journal des débats* on September 8th, provoked immediate concern and the Ministry of the Navy was besieged by anxious demands for further details. By September 11th, however, some more alarming aspects of the drama began to come to light; *La Quotidienne* gave brief details of the wreck, commenting that the circumstances of the disaster 'were unheard of in the history of the French navy' and that only fifteen people had been rescued from the raft. These would, had they not been saved, 'have finished by devouring each other as their unfortunate companions had done'.[11] The revelation of cannibalism added a new and sinister note to the tragedy.

It was on that same day that Henri Savigny, still suffering from his wounds and with his arm still in a sling, arrived in Paris to deliver his report to the Ministry of the Navy. But the copy that Vénancourt had requested had already found its way to Councillor Forestier, an adept courtier who wanted to further himself. Forestier slipped the unofficial report to his good friend, Decazes, the architect of the downfall of the right, a man who was effectively altering the course of French history and who was perhaps powerful enough to oversee Forestier's possible appointment as nothing less than Minister of the Navy.

Thus Decazes found himself in possession of political dynamite. While the papers were merely carrying the brief facts of the shipwreck, Decazes had in his hands a scoop, an eyewitness account that would horrify the nation. To leak the full story of the atrocity to the press, in all its unmitigated horror, would provide devastating proof of the wisdom of everything that he had been arguing. The ensuing outrage would inevitably galvanize the country into understanding the dangers and risks of allowing the extreme right to remain in control. Something as compelling as the *Medusa* scandal would prove more tangible, would impinge more acutely on the public's imagination, than the mere political act of dissolving a chamber. It would provide the living and dying proof of misguided leadership. It would give a popular and immediately comprehensible justification for a politically necessary action. As with the *ultra* violence in the south, the horrors of abandoning compatriots, of armed revolt on the raft, of cannibalism would affirm what Decazes had been abstractly propounding. France, it would be seen, would fare better in the hands of men such as Espiaux or Vénancourt – men who had profited from the time between 1789 and the present – than it would under the incompetent old guard. The realization that an émigré, appointed as commander of the Senegal expedition, was responsible for substantial loss of life, for the most horrific of crimes, for the loss of His Majesty's property and money, and for endangering His Majesty's colonial enterprise at a time when France was in search of international respect, could prove enormously damaging to the right.

Decazes, wishing to leave nothing to chance in the wake of his constitutional coup, and perhaps fearful of a right-wing backlash, understood that some devastatingly anti-right propaganda had come into his hands. He leaked Savigny's report to the Secretary-General at his ministry, who just happened to be one of the co-directors of the *Journal des débats* and who, in turn, published it in his newspaper on Friday, September 13th.[12]

Newspapers, at that time, were not sold on the streets, but rather by subscription and the sales figures were therefore not large. However, the *Journal des débats*, a moderately Royalist publication with faith in the *charte*, attempted to appeal to a broad base of the population and had, along

141

with the liberal *Constitutionnel*, the largest print run. Although the sales were small, the readership was in fact much greater, as many people devoured these publications in reading rooms and cafés, where a single copy of a paper would be passed from person to person.

Papers tended to deliver the news straight, publishing editorial articles only once or twice a week, and so an eyewitness account which reported events that DuBouchage would obviously be keen to keep under wraps was guaranteed to provoke a stir.[13] What is more, Savigny's report was lengthy, occupying four and a half columns, more than half of the September 13th issue. The article was prefaced by a brief editorial statement vouching for the reliability of the eyewitness source and describing the event as being as 'sinister as it is inexplicable'.

Savigny records the promise, made by the officers, to tow the raft. He judiciously claims that he is far from accusing these men of not having acted honourably, but rather states that a string of circumstances doubtlessly forced them to abandon their plan, nonetheless adding that the incident merits 'scrupulous examination'. What is more, Savigny provides a focus for that examination when he fixes on the actions of Lieutenant Reynaud, second-in-command of *The Medusa* and captain of the Governor's Barge: 'seeing that his efforts had become futile, having towed us alone for a moment, he cut the cable attached to the raft'. Savigny goes on to give a brief but thorough account of the appalling events that resulted from this action. Writing of the cramped conditions of the victims on board the raft, he speaks of limbs being trapped in the gaps between support struts, of subsequent death, of the mutinies, of the deteriorating health of the victims, of cannibalism, and of the awful decision to execute the weak in order to prolong the life of those whose chances for survival seemed less unlikely. The report was signed, 'On board the corvette, *Echo*, 22nd August, 1816. Savigny, Surgeon'. It appeared, with that ubiquitous lack of newspaperly decorum, above the results of the latest draws of the Royal Lottery, the healthy stock-exchange rates and the list of plays currently being presented in the capital.[14]

This bolt from the blue redounded heavily on Savigny, who was at once summoned to the Ministry of the Navy, where he was asked to prove that he was innocent of offering for publication the report that was scandalizing the country. Savigny went immediately to the Editor of the *Journal des débats*, asking him to confirm that he had not obtained the report from Savigny's own hands. DuBouchage remained unsatisfied by the disclaimer offered by the paper and asked for further proof. A second, signed statement was duly provided, declaring, more explicitly, that it was not from the hand of Henri Savigny that the *Journal* had received the report, but from the office of the Minister of Police.[15] Although this satisfied the Minister vis-à-vis Savigny, it petrified DuBouchage, who at once understood what Decazes was about. The Minister of Police sought to expose the tragedy as a political misdeed, and he wanted heads to roll.

DuBouchage hit back; in an article carried by both the right-wing *Quotidienne* and the liberal, or Bonapartist, *Constitutionnel* on Sunday, September 15th, the Minister questioned the veracity of the diverse reports about the tragedy that had appeared in different newspapers. He asked:

> how can one describe one's feelings while reading the *Journal des débats* of the 13th of this month . . . in which one can't help but notice a certain malign insinuation which makes one doubt the exactitude of the facts? The author of this article should have thought that, above all, he would be answerable for his opinions at the Court Martial which will deliberate this affair . . . How, in short, can the author be a witness if he has already gone public as an accuser?[16]

Savigny, in turn, made a public declaration in *Le Moniteur universel* that was picked up and, surprisingly, printed as a reply to DuBouchage in the *ultra La Quotidienne*. The surgeon confessed to be astonished by the publication of his report in the *Journal*, claiming that, as he had arrived in Paris at 11 a.m. on the 11th and spent only a few minutes at his lodgings before being conveyed to the Ministry of the Navy, where he handed over all the papers at his disposal, it would have been impossible for him to have made contact with the Editor of the *Journal des débats*, to whom he categorically denied having given the report. 'After all the evils that have beset me,' he continued, 'nothing could have been worse than to be seen to have failed in my duty. I would have thought that such misfortune would have given me the sympathy of people rather than provoking a severe reprimand from my superiors.'[17]

DuBouchage knew that, under the stringent censorship laws, newspapers were effectively controlled by the Minister of Police and so the secrecy he so urgently sought was unlikely to be respected. Indeed, on the front page of its September 22nd issue, in pride of place, *La Quotidienne* reprinted a private letter reporting on the sailors, troops and colonists who had been forced to trudge through the desert. It suggested that the establishment of a colony on Cap Vert had been delayed by one year because of the loss of essential instruments. Both *Le Constitutionnel* and the *Journal des débats* carried this item in much the same form the following day. Clearly, it was in the interests of Decazes to keep the story alive outside the secret confines of a ministerial investigation and an *in camera* court martial.[18]

A Board of Inquiry had begun to sit on September 17th at Brest under Vice-Admiral Saint-Haouen. The Minister of the Navy, meanwhile, solicited the opinion of Admiral de Rosily on some uncertainties relating to the wreck. A reply came back from this Director of the Hydrographic Service on September 25th, confirming that Chaumareys had been mistaken in sighting Cap Blanc in the late afternoon of July 1st, because at midnight *The Echo* estimated herself to be twelve minutes north of the cape. At the same time, Admiral de Rosily conceded that the route outlined in his *Nautical Description of the African Coast* was dangerous. However, as the current Director-General of the *Dépôt de Paris*, which had issued the maps for the expedition, de Rosily felt less comfortable about accepting Vénancourt's assessment that the Bellin map was not the best available, as it placed the coast between Cap Blanc and Saint Louis fifty kilometres to the east of where, in fact, it was to be found.

The next official step was the Commission of Rochefort, convened by Rear-Admiral Maurville. It started to sit on November 7th in order to determine the time at which Cap Blanc had been sighted, the route that had been set by Chaumareys after that sighting, and what attempts had been made at salvage and rescue. By the end of the three-and-a-half-week investigation, it was clear that Chaumareys had indeed been guilty of negligence. Cap Blanc had not been doubled during the late afternoon or early evening of July 1st, but at around 2 a.m. on the morning of July 2nd. *The Medusa* had been a good deal farther north than had been supposed and thus, when, at 7.30 a.m. on the morning of July 2nd, she veered south-south-east in the direction of Portendick – assuming that she had cleared the dangerous shoal – she ploughed straight onto the Arguin sand bank.[19] The day before the Rochefort Commission concluded its investigations, on December 1st, 1816, Hugues Duroy de Chaumareys, a passenger on board *The Loire*, left Senegal for France. The tragedy that had resulted from the quality of his leadership had already become an international sensation.

Decazes bribed the London *Times* 10,000 francs a month to plant articles under the names of their own correspondents. When the Foreign Secretary, Viscount Castlereagh, asked Sir Charles Stuart, the British ambassador in Paris, to verify this surprising fact, he received the reply that 'most of our public prints are now in the pay of M. Decazes'.

Whether as a result of such interference, or merely by virtue of its nose for news, the paper translated and printed Savigny's report on September 17th. The previous day, *The Times* had already picked up the morsel about cannibalism that had appeared in *La Quotidienne* on the 11th.[20] Not only did these items astound British readers, but copies of the papers eventually arrived for the English administrators in Senegal, where Savigny's frank tale shocked Colonel Schmaltz and Lieutenant Reynaud into issuing a strong refutation. Their fears were compounded when a French schooner, *The Flore*, arrived from Bordeaux with letters on board informing the colonists about the 'big sensation' that their misadventure had caused in France.

Schmaltz and Reynaud drew up a report, which was conveyed to Corréard who was still in hospital. Corréard read the report and, finding it to be untrue, refused to sign his acceptance of the facts as it presented them. Several times underlings were sent to change his mind. On one occasion Schmaltz went himself to exert maximum pressure on the frail patient. Corréard still refused to sign. Kummer, Corréard's friend, was dispatched to persuade the invalid to approve the document, saying that without his signature he would not be permitted to return to France; such coercion, Corréard and Savigny observe, testifies to the urgent need felt by Schmaltz and Reynaud to suppress the truth. Their document claimed that the towrope had broken. It maintained that the words 'We're abandoning them' were never spoken. It protested that Savigny's report was a defamation of the officers, who had done everything in their power to save him. Understandably, Corréard refused to sign.

At the bottom of the document, Corréard was surprised to see the signature of one of his companions in misfortune, Griffon du Bellay, whom Savigny himself had saved from drowning. Subsequently it came to light that the Secretary had signed the document when he had been in a weak and confused state. Shortly after the appearance of the first edition

of Savigny's and Corréard's book, Griffon du Bellay wrote
to the surgeon to beg his pardon for having acted on the
'first impulse of a weak and exaggerated imagination'. While
Corréard remained unyielding, the Governor's persistence
and intimidation succeeded with other victims from the raft
who were still in a delirious state. Captain Dupont, Lieutenant
l'Heureux, Sergeant-Major Charlot, the workshop foreman
Touche-Lavillette and Jean-Charles, the black soldier, all
signed – some to gain favour with the Governor, others too
weak to realize what they were doing. They blamed Savigny
for the horrors that had taken place on the raft; it was,
according to their statement, he alone who had incited
violence. Touche-Lavillette subsequently signed a disclaimer
on the very day that Savigny's and Corréard's book appeared,
becoming one of the four survivors to repudiate what he
claims he had been encouraged to affirm while in a state of
'mental derangement'.[21]

By the end of November 1816, Corréard was just about
well enough to make the journey home to France. On the
23rd and 24th he was visited by Majors Peddie and
Campbell, the two English officers who had shown him
much kindness over the previous months. Under the auspices
of the Royal Society in London, Peddie and Campbell were
about to set off to explore the scientific aspects and commercial prospects of the interior of the continent – continuing,
in effect, the work of the great explorer Mungo Park. Despite
strained relations between the English and the French in
Senegal during that unusually tempestuous autumn, the
expedition stimulated a degree of cooperation. For whatever motive, Schmaltz promised 'every assistance in his
power'. Kummer, Corréard's associate in the *Société philanthropique*, joined the team and his 'Journal of an Expedition
into the Interior of Africa', written in perfect script and
embellished with meticulous botanical and zoological pencil
and watercolour drawings, survived the expedition. Sadly,
Major Peddie did not.[22]

The English major felt concerned for Corréard and generously gave him 300 francs for his journey home, along with some sound advice that Savigny and Corréard used to advantage in their narrative: 'Without pretending to guess how your Navy Minister will act towards you, I nevertheless think myself justified in presuming that you will obtain no relief from him; a Minister who has committed a fault will never suffer it to be mentioned.' Guided by such thinking, Peddie advised Corréard not to return to Paris, but to go to London, where he would find 'a number of philanthropists' who would help him. This kindly advice provokes an upsurge of patriotism in Corréard and Savigny, permitting them to contrast what they have done for their country, what they feel about France and how they expect Frenchmen to act, with the malignity of the leaders of their expedition, who 'have nothing French about them but their dress'. The touching episode also gave the authors the pretext for citing (in a footnote in the earliest editions, and thereafter in the body of their text) some of the seven or eight other doubtful commands 'who do no more honour' to the 'choice or discernment' of DuBouchage 'than the expedition to Senegal has done'. They despair that 'we have seen titles pass for knowledge, repose for experience, and protection for merit'.[23]

It was, in fact, only through the intervention of English doctors that Corréard was able to escape from Senegal and save his life. It was the certificate that Corréard had been given at the English hospital that made it impossible for Schmaltz, who had not yet taken over as Governor and who therefore remained under English jurisdiction, to refuse Corréard's passage home. On November 28th, Corréard embarked on a coastal cutter that was to carry him out to *The Loire*, anchored in the roads. Weakened by five months of suffering, and exhibiting an intense psychosomatic revulsion to being on board a boat, Corréard was immediately seized by fever and vomiting. Becalmed, the cutter drifted

under the noonday sun and Corréard, in his delirium, over-
heard a fellow passenger, who was nodding in his direction,
say: 'There's someone who won't reach France.' After many
hours drifting in the burning heat, a life-saving breeze blew
up and the cutter was able to join the ship.

As it set sail on December 1st under the command of
Gicquel des Touches, the cumbrous store ship was carrying
a number of other survivors from *The Medusa*, including its
captain, Hugues Duroy de Chaumareys, returning to France
to give an account of his expedition. Also on board was the
English governor, Thomas Brereton, returning to England
for reasons of health and carrying with him a menagerie of
rare and beautiful animals, which, during the storms suffered
between the Azores and Cap Finisterre, were nearly all
crushed by chests that had been inadequately secured
between decks.

On board, des Touches found the attitude of Chaumareys
very strange; he records that *The Medusa*'s captain spent no
time preparing his defence for the forthcoming court
martial, could not understand how controversial – if not
despicable – his actions had been, and seemed rather pleased
to have come out of it all as well as possible. Corréard, who
encountered Chaumareys strolling on the quarter-deck, likewise found his attitude odd and inconsistent. The Captain
seemed dead set on establishing his innocence and shifting
the blame onto Governor Schmaltz, whom he accused of
stirring things up between himself and his second-in-
command. He also recalled the unsympathetic attitude of
his officers and insisted on his own qualities as a mariner,
though his evidence was restricted to the very earliest years
of his career. He praised the younger officers from
Napoleon's navy, saying that he differed from them only in
politics, lamenting the fact that France was full of 'young
Jacobins', and blaming the wreck of *The Medusa* on such
men. So many of Chaumareys's attitudes and actions seem
peculiar. He was either so dim as to be oblivious to the

gravity of his errors and omissions, or he had, indeed, been unhinged by the events of early July 1816. It seems crazy, but Chaumareys thought that the case of *The Medusa* would demonstrate beyond all doubt that all the King's ships should be commanded by officers from the *ancien régime*. Arriving in France, Chaumareys wrote to DuBouchage asking for 'several months holiday in order to restore my health which is in a terrible state'. By way of reply he was arrested.[24]

With violet-coloured, scorbutic scars covering his body, Corréard was admitted to the officers' ward of the Navy hospital in Rochefort. Savigny visited him each day and it was perhaps during this time that they planned to collaborate on a more extended account of their sufferings. Certainly, the frustrations of the ensuing months would provide them with a powerful incentive to produce such a text. What is more, Corréard had not yet benefited, as Savigny had done, from the therapeutic effect of externalizing his misfortune. He told his companion in suffering about Schmaltz's trumped-up document and showed him his written refutation. Savigny immediately set about procuring similar disclaimers from the survivors François and Coudein. While his verbal report to Saint-Haouen had seemed to excuse those who dropped the towropes, passing over the thorny question of responsibility, Coudein's written testimony spoke of Savigny's 'prudence' being 'of the greatest service . . . in suggesting to us the means by which to maintain good order'. With these three certificates and an intention to further clear himself of any blame, Savigny sought permission to go to Paris in order to alert the Minister about the mendacity of Schmaltz's plotting. He waited many weeks for a reply, eventually receiving a negative response in May 1817. The combination of the interminable delay followed by a blunt refusal so angered Savigny that he quit the Navy.[25]

When he at last felt that his condition had somewhat improved, Corréard likewise wished to make for Paris. First, he needed to clothe himself, for he had disembarked from his ill-fated voyage almost naked; and so, using the little that was left of Major Peddie's gift, he equipped himself for his journey. All too recently returned from the hot tropics and suffering from a lesion to his right ankle and from gouty rheumatic pains that were particularly susceptible to cold and damp, he set out in the depths of the French winter, on foot. After walking for three days, he had nearly covered one-third of his route when he was overcome by fever. He called on the mayor of a small village just outside Poitiers, where he unsuccessfully sought lodgings, forcing him to slog on a couple of miles to an inn where he could rest. The following day, February 4th, suffering great pains in his chest and spitting blood, he reached Poitiers, where he fainted in the street. Fortunately, the mayor of that city was more sympathetic to Corréard's situation and lodged him with a compassionate landlord, by whom he was treated as something of a celebrity. Corréard rested and then completed his journey to Paris by coach.

Arriving in the capital, Corréard felt it his first duty to express his gratitude for the help he had received from the English officers in Senegal and thus addressed a letter to the British ambassador. The inclusion of this letter of March 4th, 1817 in Savigny's and Corréard's narrative stresses the fact that the survivors of the wreck received their most generous succour from the English – contrasting, by implication, the worth of Peddie and Campbell and the 'wisdom of the government that appointed them' with the insufficiencies of France. Corréard's next step was to seek employment at the offices of the Minister of the Navy. On being refused, he was advised instead to make an application for a situation in the colonies, and spent the next three frustrating months attempting to obtain compensation for his losses on *The Medusa* and in fruitless requests for such employment.[26]

The court martial of Chaumareys, which had started just

before Corréard set out for Paris, was a largely perfunctory affair. There were no surprising testimonies or unexpected revelations, but there was drama in the attitude of those who tried him, the sentence they pronounced and the effect that it had on the evolution of the public's understanding of the *Medusa* scandal. When the news had first broken, liberal elements of the government had made political capital out of the affair; it was now the turn of the conservatives in the Navy hierarchy to minimize the penalties for those whose incompetence had resulted in the disaster.

The court martial began on January 22nd at Rochefort under the presidency of Rear-Admiral La Tullaye, in the presence of seven captains and with Le Carlier d'Herlye acting as the King's Prosecutor. Twenty-three witnesses were summoned, culminating in the interrogation of Captain Chaumareys, whose testimony began with a demonstration of his capacity for error; when he was called to testify on February 3rd, he managed to miscalculate his age by three years, claiming to be fifty-one instead of his actual fifty-four.

Chaumareys attempted to justify his actions. He blamed the delays caused by the shortages in the shipyard at Rochefort and the different capacities of the ships in the convoy. Orders were to reach Senegal as swiftly as possible, and he had been acting under the pressure of Schmaltz's impatience. Elements considered as vital evidence in naval trials, such as log books and charts, had been lost in the wreck. Chaumareys was thereby guilty of a breach of discipline, for a captain is responsible for removing his log when he abandons his ship. As the officers on board *The Medusa* had also lost their diaries and watch reports, the log of *The Echo* – kept with precision and not without wry editorial comment by Cornette de Vénancourt – was a vital document in the trial. Vénancourt's log clearly states that at 11 p.m. on July 1st he had not yet sighted Cap Blanc because it was still eighteen nautical miles off his port bow.

Vénancourt records that he doubled the cape at 3 a.m. on July 2nd. Chaumareys was altogether less decided. In his written report of July 29th, he had claimed an unmistakable sighting of Cap Blanc in the afternoon of July 1st. He now stated that this sighting occurred at 8 p.m.

The log of *The Echo* was likewise useful in establishing other errors. While Vénancourt kept setting off flares and hoisting more lights throughout the night of July 1st–2nd, Lieutenant Reynaud, the officer of the watch on board *The Medusa*, had made no attempt to keep in contact with the corvette. During that night Vénancourt also recorded that he took soundings every hour. At 8 a.m. on July 2nd, finding a depth of sixty-one fathoms, Vénancourt took the precaution of steering farther west. At 10.30 a.m., finding the depth increased to ninety fathoms, he set a course west-south-west, which he kept until he reached a latitude of nineteen degrees north. By contrast, Chaumareys showed a cavalier attitude towards soundings: it emerged that those he recorded in his report of July 29th, as having been taken at 9 and 10 a.m. on July 2nd, were never done. Throughout his various statements and accounts, Chaumareys also revealed considerable confusion over the exact location of the wreck: before the court, this captain, who had been appointed by a minister of the Crown to lead this all-important convoy, indicated no fewer than three different points at which *The Medusa* ran aground.

During the court martial, the testimony of the officers of *The Medusa* established four important points: firstly, that Chaumareys refused to take a sounding one hour before the catastrophe because it would slow the ship down; secondly, that *The Medusa* was sailing south-south-east at that time; thirdly, that the raft was released because the efforts of the boats towing it were judged to be ineffective; fourthly, that as a number of men had voluntarily stayed on board the frigate, the Captain was not the last to leave his ship. In conclusion, the prosecutor added the following points: that

Cap Blanc had not been accurately identified and the course of *The Medusa* had been determined according to this mistake; and that the abandoning of the raft was not the sole fault of the Captain. He insisted that, in violation of all rules and usages, the Captain had not been the last to leave his ship. As the legal consequence of this final fault was capital, La Tullaye, as early as January 23rd, took the precaution of writing to DuBouchage to secure a stay of execution. The Minister and the King responded favourably to the arguments that the Captain had not acted with evil intentions, noting that, in the past, he had served the Bourbons well.

Chaumareys had lied to save his skin when he had been brought before the Revolutionary Tribunal after the Royalist attempt at Quiberon. He had denied being an émigré, denied his nobility and denied having participated in a military capacity in the Quiberon uprising. His lies earned him a stay of execution and allowed him the chance to escape and flee to England. At Rochefort, it is doubtful that he deliberately falsified the facts; it seems more likely that his testimony was born of confusion, ignorance and incompetence – all, in this instance, damning. However, once again it appeared that Chaumareys was to escape the death penalty. The Captain showed skill in his defence, maintaining that he stayed on board *The Medusa* until he was beseeched to take command in a large lifeboat. Chaumareys had gone to the aid of the raft; he claimed that when those on board the platform saw him take command of the towing operation, heart-warming cries of '*Vive le roi*' resounded. He spoke candidly about the abandoning of the raft, citing the impossibility of the task and the necessity of saving those in the lifeboats. On the advice of his defence counsel, Chaumareys added that when he left *The Medusa* he was aware of the Navy rule that he, as Captain, should be the last to leave his ship, but that he was also aware of the ruling of 1765, Article 1285, stating that in each situation an officer should behave so as to best serve his calling. 'It was,' he claimed, 'this last article that motivated me.'[27]

The trial to examine and pass judgement on the facts established at the court martial began on a grey, rainy February 24th, on the Admiral's ship anchored in the Charente. The King's Prosecutor, Le Carlier d'Herlye, presented his summary of the case on February 28th. On the separation of the convoy near Finisterre, Chaumareys was held to be not guilty as he had been acting on orders to reach Senegal as speedily as possible. The Prosecutor acknowledged the gross errors in the maps used by the expedition, but observed that this had no bearing on the Captain's negligence in respect of soundings. Chaumareys was thus guilty of the shipwreck of *The Medusa* through arrogance. However, he was not guilty of the loss of the frigate, as everything in his power had been done to save her. Nonetheless, he would have to be declared 'incapable of serving' in the Navy, according to Article 39 of the Penal Code. Next, Le Carlier d'Herlye tackled the evacuation and the abandoning of the ship, which could result in the death sentence. Surprisingly, the attitude of the Prosecutor appeared lenient. Suggesting that Chaumareys's actions resulted from an error of judgement, rather than from treachery or cowardice, the Prosecutor recommended that he be held in a military prison for five years, rather than pressing the court for the ultimate punishment. On the subject of abandoning the raft, Le Carlier d'Herlye asked whether it and the lifeboats should be treated as an entity under a single captain or as separate entities. Favouring the latter, it was clear that if force of circumstances made it necessary to abandon any one of the boats or the raft, then Chaumareys would not be accountable. Finally, to cap such remarkable tolerance, Le Carlier d'Herlye gave a glowing report of the behaviour of Captain Chaumareys after his arrival in Senegal.

On March 3rd, after lengthy deliberations, the President

pronounced judgement. At 11.30 that night, the Captain of
The Medusa was led into a large cabin on board the Admiral's
ship, where, standing hat in hand by the light of low-burning
candles, he received the astonishingly lenient judgement.
Hugues Duroy de Chaumareys was condemned by a
majority of five out of eight to be removed from the list
of officers and never allowed to serve again; to be imprisoned for three years; and to pay the costs of the trial. In
the crowded confines of the Admiral's quarters, braid
surrounded by braid, how could Chaumareys have fared
badly?[28]

The puzzlingly light sentence caused much controversy.
The old guard thought it too severe and claimed that the
Prosecutor had been too indulgent towards the other officers. Those of a less conservative frame of mind wondered
if there had not been some interference from above; during
the exploratory court martial and subsequent trial, rumours
had been circulating in the naval community in Rochefort
that DuBouchage had bribed the principal witnesses so that
they would not prove too vehement in their condemnation
of the Captain.

In a letter to his minister, La Tullaye pleaded that the
condemned man should not be forced to pay the costs of
the case, as his family would be ruined. On March 6th,
Chaumareys himself intervened, petitioning the King that
to be struck off the list of officers and condemned to three
years in prison was penalty enough, without being stripped
of his decorations. DuBouchage, in his turn, successfully
petitioned the King for a choice of open prison and relief
from the costs of the case. Thus, on September 11th, 1817,
Hugues Duroy de Chaumareys was committed to the prison
of Ham, from which, during the following month, he petitioned to be transferred to the prison of Mont-de-Marsan,
closer to his family home.

While Chaumareys continued to seek the restitution of
his medals and a pension for his family (neither of which

was granted), the leniency of his sentence was considered outrageous in many quarters. Those who had suffered enormously in the aftermath of the wreck were appalled. They felt that the full horror of *The Medusa* must not be left to drift into oblivion, like its captain. To add to the slew of inhuman horrors – which, thanks to the opportunism of the ambitious Elie Decazes, had already become the talk of the town – there was the new affront of Chaumareys's farcically inappropriate sentence. Those who had paid with their health, their sanity and their careers felt cheated. Alarming facts had already come to light, gossip was rife, liberals and Bonapartists were eager to seize any opportunity for discrediting the monarchy, and the inhabitants of France, not to mention the appalled public of all sea-faring nations, deserved to know more.

Superficially, the French political situation appeared to have calmed. The elections of October 1816 had returned a more moderate Chamber. The hope that it should be composed of 'men who love the King with passion and respect the *charte* with sincerity', as Decazes had urged in a handbill, had been largely realized. Out of 238 deputies, 146 members in the new Chamber supported the government, whereas only ninety-two *ultras* had been elected. Elie Decazes had limited *ultra* extremism and the militant left had not, as yet, grouped itself into a palpable menace to the monarchy. However, while Decazes was feeling confident that all the steps he had taken to secure a working acceptance of the *charte* were coming to fruition, the *ultras* were out for his blood and left-wing elements were not, in point of fact, rallying around a monarchy that was attempting to accommodate them, but rather were preparing, in one way or another and with varying timeframes, for its overthrow. It was into this political ferment that Alexandre Corréard arrived in Paris in that frustrating and humiliating spring of 1817, and it was into this buzz that Théodore Géricault returned from Italy later in the year to find, like Corréard, that Paris had once again become a politically exciting city.[29]

In order to emerge from his troubles with something positive, Corréard sought the *Légion d'honneur*, but his request seems to have been lost or blocked – perhaps deliberately – among the mass of paperwork at the Ministry of the Navy. At length, he received a communication from DuBouchage, dated June 4th, notifying him that all his applications would most probably come to nothing. Despite the support for him of twelve deputies, the authorities refused to be of any assistance in Corréard's attempts to secure a position as an engineer.

He had meanwhile learned that a Councillor of State had indeed recommended him for the *Légion d'honneur*, but that the Minister of the Navy himself had refused to put the request before the King. Corréard rightly felt it unjust that a victim of official incompetence should be blocked from receiving from his King some assuaging sign of 'justice and benevolence'. The indifferent Lieutenant Reynaud, the executioner himself, had been given command of the transport vessel *The Gironde*, while, by contrast, Corréard was still finding it difficult to walk and Savigny's fevers and pains made it impossible for him to work for two weeks out of every month. Having lost all his 'resources in the course of duty', Corréard felt 'disgusted' by the official attitude and, above all, 'forgotten'.[30] He had watched the men in braid, comfortably installed in their well-provisioned boats, pull away. He had been plunged into the abyss, but had returned to the world a wiser man; should his health permit, he was ready to take it on.

The wreck of *The Medusa*, as a news story and as a pretext for political change, was still affective. On March 12th, the *Journal des débats* carried the result of the trial of Chaumareys. On June 22nd, DuBouchage was forced to resign from the government. Having largely purged his ministry of liberal or Bonapartist sympathizers, he now provided Decazes, through his injudicious appointment of a particularly inept émigré, with a tangible pretext for purging him. Decazes had never liked DuBouchage, so along with other unsympathetic elements in the government, DuBouchage was replaced.

Comte Matthieu Molé, the new Minister of the Navy, had served Napoleon as Minister of Justice and had even accepted a post during the *Cent-Jours*. Molé immediately set about reversing the backward-looking policy of his predecessor. A Royal Ordinance appeared in the *Journal de débats* on October 22nd, announcing a reduction in Navy personnel. From November 1st, 1817 there would be six rear-admirals, twelve commodores, sixty captains of warships, 300 lieutenants and 400 ensigns. Although several esteemed émigrés were able to hold on to their commissions, the largest number of men retired were those who had been reappointed during the Restoration after years of inactivity. Rear-Admiral La Tullaye, who had served under Louis XVI and had proved a lenient President of Chaumareys's court martial, was among those dispatched. The misadventure of the prestigious expedition to Senegal thus played its part in curtailing the careers of nine admirals and 173 captains.[31]

While the Navy thus benefited from the tragedy, Corréard and Savigny were continuing to smart for their pains and suffer for their losses. As the gruesome complexities of the ordeal had not been adequately articulated, the affair had never altogether slipped from the public's interest. A letter, written by Mlle Schmaltz, that was circulating in Paris fuelled the disgust of survivors. In it, according to Savigny and Corréard, the young lady 'confessed that the sight of the shipwrecked persons inspired her with a degree of horror . . . "It was really impossible for me," she wrote, "to endure the presence of these men, without feeling a sentiment of indignation."' It was such a lack of compassion, along with the Navy cover-up, that finally convinced Savigny and Corréard to bring before the public the ugly sweep of their scandalous saga. In their narrative, they analysed the source of Mlle Schmaltz's repugnant aversion and exploited it politically with a honey-tongued irony:

> She could say to herself, 'these men have in their hands the fate of my father. If they speak, if they utter complaints . . . if they are listened to (and how should they not be listened to in a country, where a charter, the noble present of our august Monarch, causes justice and the law to reign), instead of being the daughter of a governor, I am but a wretched orphan; instead of these honours, with which it gives me so much pleasure to be surrounded, I fall into the degradation, and the oblivion which generally await the unhappy family of a great criminal.'[32]

The conditions for exposing governmental faults were, however, difficult. Censorship and secrecy had become important and controversial political tools of the Restoration. Etienne Pasquier, the *Garde des Sceaux*, the French equivalent of Lord Chancellor, observed that it was indispensable to maintain surveillance on newspapers and periodicals 'in a country emerging from a long period of political torment'. Opponents of current repression, such as the Baron Martin de Gray, maintained rather that 'the manifestation of thought is the vital driving force of free and representative government' and that it is 'to police tribunals that you hand over the limits of thought, you give them the right to say to human intelligence: "You can't go any further"'. Decazes, supporting the law of censorship – which was, to all intents and purposes, an extension of his laws of autumn 1815 – skilfully smoothed over the debate by claiming that the purpose of censorship was to 'maintain a complete and just equality, to consign the past to oblivion, to extinguish hatred, to make power loved and respected, which is the aim of the government'.[33] It was against the backdrop of this discussion about governmental control of politically inflammatory material that the bombshell, *The Shipwreck of the Frigate, The Medusa* was first published. Although decidedly less politicized than later editions, it was not calculated to 'consign the past to oblivion, to extinguish hatred' or 'to make power loved and respected'.

Registered at the *Bibliographie de la France* on November 1st, 1817, this first edition was the only one that carried Savigny's name before Corréard's and it is the simplest and shortest of all the versions, the one that most closely resembled the original text that Savigny had written on board *The Echo*. The book was available at a cost of three francs from five shops in the capital, including that of its printer, François Hoquet, and that of the renowned legal and children's bookseller, Alexis Eymery. Books at this boom time in French publishing were brought out by printers or booksellers, and Savigny's and Corréard's text was published by three people who owned establishments in the Palais Royal, that vital hub of Parisian life.[34]

That *The Shipwreck* would become a rallying point for the liberal cause was clear from the extensive review that appeared in the liberal *Mercure de France*, of which Alexis Eymery was an administrator. The moderate *Journal des débats* likewise carried an excellent review in which we read that:

Nothing is more terrible than this tale, we tremble at each page, shudder at every line. The secret passages of Anne Radcliffe, and all the imaginary horrors of our melodramas and tragedies are nothing compared with the real horrors of this awful catastrophe . . .

Savigny and Corréard:

. . . survived by a miracle! But intrigue and persecution awaited them ashore and it is more difficult to escape from the injustice of man than the fury of the sea.

Everyone will read the tale that they are publishing; it is an historical piece that will give rise to stringent reflection and must find a place in all libraries.[35]

Le Journal du commerce, the rebaptized *Constitutionnel* that had been repressed for its pro-Bonaparte stance in July 1817, carried a large, two-column review of *The Shipwreck* on November 29th, placed significantly under 'Domestic News' rather than 'Book Reviews'. It claimed that there had been no event 'so deplorable' as the wreck of *The Medusa* and spoke of a Subscription Fund being set up for the survivors by Etienne Jay, who had first announced the fact at the end of his lengthy review of *The Shipwreck* in the *Mercure.*

When *Le Journal du commerce* published a list of initial subscribers, it was obvious that sympathy for the ill-treated victims of government incompetence came from all levels of society and all walks of life: a member of the *Académie Française,* a lawyer, a doctor, the Duc de Berry, the Duc d'Orléans, the proprietor and regulars of a café in the rue St Denis all gave. Sums ranged from the 500 francs given by the liberal banker Laffitte to the touching two francs given by 'Mlle Caroline B., orphan'.[36]

The disaster was reaching far and wide and stirring the hearts of people. The scandal and the issues surrounding the wreck of *The Medusa* played into the hands of the ever-strengthening liberal faction – Republican ideologues, reeling from the collapse of the Empire, the fiasco of the *Cent-Jours* and the repressive measures of the *ultras* in the regressive *chambre introuvable.* Slowly they were organizing an offensive with far-reaching consequences, and the magnitude of the *Medusa* scandals would play a part in their story.

Théodore Géricault,
possible likeness of
Alexandrine-Modeste Caruel

Alexandre Colin, *Portrait of
Géricault in 1816*

Théodore Géricault,
*Le Chasseur de
la Garde*

PLAN DU RADEAU DE LA MÉDUSE,
au moment de son abandon.

A. Corréard Ingénieur del.¹

Alexandre Corréard, *Plan of the Raft of The Medusa*

Anon., *The Frigate,
The Medusa*

Yole 17 hommes longueur 20 pieds	**SKIFF**
Canot du Capitaine 28 h— 24	**CAPTAIN'S BARGE** Rang and Chaumareys
Canot du Sénégal *Comdé Mr Maudet enseigne* 25 h— 24	**SENEGAL BOAT** Maudet
Chaloupe du Sénégal *Comdé Espiaux lieut* 88 h— 30	**LONGBOAT** Espiaux
Canot majo Comdé *Mr Lapeyrère enseigne* 49 h— 27 5	**PINNACE** Lapeyrère
Grand Canot Comdé *Mr Reynaud 1er lieutenant 33 ou 38 — 27 5* *le gouverneur sa famille*	**GOVERNOR'S BARGE** Reynaud and Schmaltz
Radeau Commandé par *Coudein célèbre aujourd'hui 147 hommes* *enseigne* long 40 a 42 large 22 a 24	**THE RAFT** Coudein, Corréard and Savigny

Anon., sketch on ms report showing order of the boats towing the raft

Anon., *Shipwreck of the Frigate, The Medusa*

Léon Antoine Morel–Fatio, *The Abandoning of the Raft of The Medusa*

Anon., *The Finding of the Raft by The Argus*

Anon., *Saint Louis in Senegal*

Théodore Géricault, *An Execution at Rome*

Théodore Géricault, *The Race of the Riderless Horses*

Sébastian Cœuré, *Fualdès Being Dragged and Shoved into the Maison Bancal*

Théodore Géricault, *Fualdès Being Dragged and Shoved into the Maison Bancal*

Théodore Géricault, *Studies of a Dancing Couple and a Centaur Abducting a Nymp.*

Théodore Géricault, *The Embrace*

Théodore Géricault, *The Kiss*

Théodore Géricault, *Lovers Reclining*

Théodore Géricault, *Anatomical Fragments*

Théodore Géricault, *The Severed Heads*

Théodore Géricault, *Study for Cannibalism*

Théodore Géricault, *Drawing for the Mutiny on the Raft*

Théodore Géricault, *The Raft of the Medusa*

Théodore Géricault, *Study for the Figure of Corréard*

C. Motte, *Valade the Police Commissioner Confronting Corréard in Prison*

Anon., *The Shape and Dimension of the Places for the Slaves
in the English Slave-Ship, Brookes*

Alexandre Corréard,
Posthumous Study of Géricault

Théodore Géricault,
Study for the Slave Trade

Théodore Géricault, *The Shipwreck*

9

The Fualdès Affair
and the Love Affair

ON March 20th, 1817, a body was found in the waters of
the River Aveyron in southern France. It was soon identified as Antoine-Bernardin Fualdès, a magistrate and criminal prosecutor from Rodez, who had served the Revolution
and the Empire and who had come out of retirement during
the *Cent-Jours*. The previous evening, Fualdès had left his
house with a substantial I.O.U. tucked in the pocket of his
frock-coat and was on his way to redeem the debt. He was
followed into a rough part of Rodez, where, at about 8
p.m., he was ambushed at the corner of the rue
Hebdomadiers, gagged with a handkerchief and bundled off
into a gambling den, aptly named 'The Crooked House', a
notorious haunt of smugglers and prostitutes. After the assassins had forced their hostage to sign letters of exchange for
the I.O.U., Fualdès was stretched out on a table. Sawing
with a blunt knife, his murderer opened a transversal section
across his neck from the right to the left carotid arteries.
Posted by the assassins at the corner of the street outside,
hurdy-gurdy players ground out their eerie melodies, oblit-
erating the screams of the victim. The murderer smeared
the body of the ex-magistrate with a little of the blood he
had let, while the rest dripped steadily into a bucket. When

full, this was given to a pig to drink. The animal, having gorged itself, subsequently died. At around ten o'clock in the evening, the bloody body of the hapless Fualdès was placed on two poles, wrapped in a sheet, covered with wool, tied and then carried to the river by four individuals, who dumped the corpse into the Aveyron and hence, they thought, into oblivion.

That is the gist of the official account of the crime as presented by the Public Prosecutor in Rodez. Despite lengthy trials and an eventual verdict, the truth behind the murder of Antoine-Bernardin Fualdès has, until recently, remained an enigma. Certainly, it had all the ingredients of a very murky mystery: the roughness of the isolated, inward-looking town of Rodez, which was torn by the furious political quarrels that had afflicted France over the previous decades; the probability that the murder was the work of an avenging ultra-Royalist gang; the rumours, lies and faked convictions; above all, the barbarity of the crime itself, made to seem even more vicious by the official verdict that the murder was carried out by men who were among the victim's best friends.[1] It was also obvious from the start that the authorities in Paris, anxious about their judicial hold on the volatile south, took a special interest in the case.

After hearing hundreds of witnesses, confessions and denials, a verdict was returned in early September, which was annulled by the Appeal Court in Montpellier a month later. A retrial opened in the spring of 1818, one year after the crime had been committed. By that time the Fualdès affair had become a media sensation, with reporters from the large Parisian papers in attendance.

Considering Fualdès's lengthy career serving the Revolution, it was obvious that he would be a prime target for Royalist revenge. The Comte François Régis La Bourdonnaye, *ultra* deputy for Maine-et-Loire, listed a thousand heads that should tumble; Fualdès was on that list.[2]

The intrigue surrounding the murder of Fualdès was, like

the *Medusa* scandal, testimony to the running sores that plagued France after a quarter of a century of revolution and civil and foreign war. But, while the *Medusa* scandal was brought before the public in order to discredit the ultra-Royalists, the truth behind the Fualdès affair was hushed up in order to suppress evidence of civil strife.

The falsification of the Fualdès verdict was, to a large extent, made possible by the volley of lies, contradictions and hysterical accusations that tumbled from the mouth of a celebrity-seeking woman named Clarisse Manzon. Just as Corréard decided to expose the *Medusa* scandal in print, so the mysterious and highly strung Clarisse Manzon published her version of the events in Rodez. She was the quintessential publicity-seeker who understood that if you say something sufficiently shocking, however ill advised or stupid, people will lap it up. The thirty-two-year-old Clarisse soon achieved her aim of making Rodez 'famous from Gibraltar to Archangel'.[3]

Unlike the *Medusa* investigation, which was conducted *in camera*, the Fualdès case was a civilian affair, providing flamboyant copy for an avid press. *La Quotidienne* observed that 'no one thinks of greeting a friend without asking for the news from Rodez'.[4] Indeed, as the trial became the preoccupation of salons throughout Europe, it attracted the attention of writers, painters and printmakers and a mini-industry grew up around the spurious proceedings. In Paris, along the quays of the Seine, booksellers hawked numerous images and lithographs treating the murky affair.[5]

Théodore Géricault's interest in the Fualdès murder, and his subsequent obsession with the *Medusa* scandal, reflect his developing absorption with crime and catastrophe – with the violent and shocking phenomena that were the staple of broadsheets, with their starkly embellished wood-cuts dramatizing sinister events. Such publications fascinated the public and fed popular literature with tasty morsels suitable to the Gothic novel, a genre that has been described

165

as a 'literature of cannibals that feeds on bits of human flesh'.[6]

In the second half of 1817, the Fualdès affair had somewhat eclipsed the wreck of *The Medusa* as the talk of the town, but, with the publication of *The Shipwreck of the Frigate, The Medusa,* once again the maritime atrocity seized the public's imagination. The sheer scale of the loss, the mortifying tale of selfishness, cowardice, cannibalism and murder – to which must be added the resolve and courage of the authors in getting their version of events into print – was simply staggering: Savigny's and Corréard's narrative exposed nothing less than the government's failure in its duty to its subjects.

On his arrival in Paris in late 1817, Géricault would seem to have had time neither for the top stories of the day nor for painting. The months in Italy had only exacerbated his desire for his aunt and mistress, and he rapidly fell into the arms of Alexandrine-Modeste, the woman he had left France to forget. In his private sketches he now expressed more intimate and personal evocations of loving. Mythology had once provided a way to sublimate the sexual dilemma of his life; now he was producing works that expressed the intensity of coitus or those gentle moments of tender intimacy either before or after.

These drawings and washes are celebrations of sex in which the woman is active, and not, as is so often the case, a displayed object to delight the male voyeur.[7] The passionate hug of the woman on top in *The Embrace* reveals someone who clamours for, and enjoys, sex. These are not titillating scenes, not confessions of psychological and physiological distress, but celebrations of the power and pleasure of physical union. Wash drawings such as *The Kiss* express the sheer exuberance of tender-hearted love-making, the sensual and spiritual rapture experienced by reunited lovers. Géricault revels in the plump form of his beloved. Their union was obviously intense and, as with all true love, supremely precious. Catastrophically, it was to prove short-lived.

For all their elation at being reunited, something occurred that crushed them. After more than a year apart, they had plunged feverishly back into their affair. Within two months, Alexandrine was pregnant with Géricault's child. It would soon no longer be possible to conceal their intimacy. Within a matter of months the pregnancy would be obvious to Alexandrine's husband and her position in society, as a wife and mother, would be in jeopardy.

In the early decades of the nineteenth century, the upper classes of French society became obsessed by the subject of adultery. Alexandre Dumas dated this fixation from the 1804 *Code Civil*, which abolished primogeniture, the right of the first-born to inherit. Fathers, stewards of a family's fortune who were suddenly obliged to acknowledge all the children produced by their wives, naturally became anxious over the question of paternity; bastards, under the *Code Napoleon*, were entitled to the same privileges as legitimate children. When such concerns were brought to bear on marriages complicated by decades of difference between husband and wife, anxiety increased. The divorce law under Napoleon had allowed a husband to get rid of his wife for adultery, but, in 1816, the *chambre introuvable* abolished divorce. In the case of Géricault and his aunt, the kindred nature of the relationship did make it easier to contain the problem within the family – the preferred course, when the guilty woman and her lover (if he was a bachelor) faced imprisonment for a period of up to two years.[8]

By April 1818, with his aunt's womb swelling into scandal, Géricault had begun to play with the macabre subject of murder. After he had made a series of preliminary sketches, however, the Fualdès affair, already treated so well by the popular engravers of the day, appeared to him somehow wanting. Instinctively, Géricault was searching for a contemporary event of sufficient scale, energy and universality to make a lasting impression. It was during this period, while his child was growing towards an uncertain life, that

Géricault became interested in, and fixed on, a much grander tale of murder. It was a story whose themes touched the deep and searching questions that the French were asking about their national identity, and it presented a particularly striking example of man's inhumanity to man.

The period between the breaking of the *Medusa* story and the publication of Savigny's and Corréard's book, with its upsetting, in-depth revelations, had been a difficult time for Géricault. In early 1818, as a result of the calamitous twist in his secret relationship, he developed an even deeper engagement with suffering, which would, in one way or another, transform him into someone who, for the rest of his short existence, would wrestle with questions of life and death. Géricault was facing the inevitable loss of his loved one, along with the probable loss of his child. At this time, he decided to abandon the Fualdès murder for the horrors that followed the catastrophic loss of *The Medusa*.

10

Trips to the Morgue

I wander aimlessly now and always go astray. Vainly, I search for
any support. Nothing is solid, everything escapes me, everything
deceives me . . . If anything is certain upon earth, it is our pain.
Suffering is real and pleasures are nothing but imaginary.

No exact date can be placed on the letter from which these
lines are taken, but it seems likely, as Géricault also writes
of the 'terrible difficulties' into which he has 'rashly thrown
himself', that it was written during the bewildering months
after the discovery of Alexandrine's pregnancy.[1] Apart from
his self-reproach, there would have been a feeling of help-
lessness at not being able to be with and console his beloved
as her condition became increasingly evident.

While the pregnancy remained invisible, and seven
months to the day before Alexandrine gave birth to
Géricault's child, her husband – either by a cruel irony or
by way of reaffirming and consolidating their marriage –
added his wife's maiden name to his own; henceforth he
would be known as Jean-Baptiste Caruel de Saint-Martin,
to which, in 1819, he would add the title of Baron. As he
was preoccupied by business, over fifty and already blessed
with two male heirs, we can guess that sexual relations
between Jean-Baptiste and his wife were rare or non-
existent, otherwise there would have been an obvious (if
deceitful) solution to Alexandrine's dilemma. How culpable

169

and forlorn she must have felt disclosing her condition to her generous husband; how awkward before her two children. Whether confined in the Château du Grand-Chesnay or sequestered in the depths of the country, how alone she must have felt without the comforting presence of her nephew. Would she have dared to admit the identity of the father? Would such a treacherous relationship prove more, or less, insulting to her husband than some chance dalliance?

As there is no record of subsequent visits made by Géricault, either to the Château du Grand-Chesnay or to the Caruels' Parisian establishments, it does suggest a permanent rupture, signalling the fact that the painter was indeed known to have been Alexandrine's lover. In light of the pregnancy, Caruel, the astute businessman, could not have failed to consider the intense relationship between his wife and nephew that had developed over the previous years and reflect upon its possible consequence. It was certainly not uncommon for women in upper-middle-class families, often married to much older men, to help a younger male in the advancement of a career – such intimate collaboration often plunging the pair into an emotional relationship that led to the young man's initiation into the pleasures of sex.

During the early part of the pregnancy, the *Medusa* scandal was once again in the news with the February 28th publication of Corréard's and Savigny's entirely reworked second edition of *The Shipwreck of the Frigate, The Medusa*. With the addition of Brédif's notes, and some further observations on West Africa, it was a much-amplified text, embellished by a plan of the raft drawn by Corréard and a portrait of King Zaide somewhat surprisingly providing a frontispiece. The short, four-month interval between the first two editions suggests that the public's appetite was keen, and Corréard's name placed before Savigny's on the title page established the fact that the text had, by this second edition, become Corréard's baby.[2]

At five a.m. on August 21st, 1818, a son was born to

Alexandrine-Modeste Caruel at the house of the celebrated obstetrician, Dr Danyau, at 14 rue Pavée Saint-André-des-Arts. In violation of Article 312 of the Civil Code declaring that any child born into a marriage, even one sired by a third party, was legally considered to be the husband's, the boy was taken away and registered as being 'of unknown parents' at the *Mairie*, of what had been at that time the 11th *arrondissement*.

Such declarations of anonymity were not uncommon; with the 30,000 or so abandoned children and the 70,000 illegitimate births registered in Paris each year, about one in three children was the fruit of an extra-marital liaison. It was Dr Danyau who registered the infant at the *Mairie* and, seemingly under instruction from the father, gave him the name 'Georges-Hippolyte' – Georges, in honour of Géricault's father, who had been consoling in a time of crisis, and Hippolyte, a Greek name meaning 'I release the horses'. The unrecognized Georges-Hippolyte was first cared for by Danyau and was then sent to a nurse at the home of a Monsieur Dubois in Normandy, where he spent his childhood.[3]

As the pregnancy was coming to its term, Géricault had begun work on some studies to help him bring before the Salon public some as-yet-unchosen moment from the *Medusa* saga. To capitalize on the interest generated by the enlarged second edition of *The Shipwreck*, Henri Savigny, in May 1818, published his *Observations on the Effects of Hunger and Thirst Experienced After the Wreck of the King's Frigate, The Medusa, in 1816*. This was a study of calenture, the delirium and fever that attacks sailors in the tropics. Although Savigny presented the work as a thesis at the Faculty of Medicine in Paris, it was hardly an original piece. It copied whole passages from a study of the phenomenon, which had been published by Fournier de Pescay in 1812, and it added little to Pescay's more recently published work on the subject of March 1818.[4] Savigny's thesis was, however, useful to Géricault who, from the outset, craved facts about the catastrophe and assembled a file full of related documents. There were the first two editions of *The Shipwreck* and clippings from the newspapers, to which he added Savigny's treatise on calenture. The painter supplemented these printed sources by securing interviews with certain survivors of the raft, and by making a series of gruesome anatomical studies.[5] There was a modernity in his profound factual, intellectual and emotional engagement with his subject, and such a depth of research had, at the same time, a palliative effect: Géricault was somewhat distracted from his own misfortunes through immersion in these horrific events. At last, a subject of sufficient size and pertinence had presented itself to him and it could not have come at a more welcome moment.

Géricault was drawn to several particular episodes on the raft: the mutiny of the soldiers and sailors against their leaders; the cannibalism; the sighting of *The Argus*; the approach of its lifeboat; and the moment of rescue. The actual abandoning of the raft proved unsuitable: the problem of realizing a dramatic composition with a glut of 147 people crushed onto a small platform was simply too great. A similar excess of incident, albeit cunningly disposed, is apparent in an advanced sketch for the *Mutiny*, which also provides ample proof that Géricault was keen to make maximum use of Corréard's and Savigny's account: the broaching of the barrels, the jettisoning of the casks, the ropes used to keep people from being washed away, the leader at the base of the mast repelling a hatchet attack, the axe-wielding mutineer who was plunged into the sea, the vulnerable stern, and the supplication of the frightened souls on board. Géricault soon came to understand, however, that the writhing turbulence of this scene also worked against the most profound message that could be extracted from the catastrophe.

A small seascape produced around this time reflects the

artist's preoccupation with cataclysm. This gloomy marine disaster was Géricault's *The Deluge*, which reveals, in the foreground of the sombre scene, scattered people hopelessly clinging to the small, barren rocks of a reef. A black block of cloud filling the top third of the canvas, bearing down on the shipwrecked victims like the wrath of God, perhaps expresses the plight of its tormented maker.

Géricault took himself out of circulation in order to work. He installed himself at no. 232 faubourg du Roule on the outskirts of Paris with the sole purpose of focusing on the *Medusa*. The list of welcome visitors was short: his close friend Dedreux-Dorcy, his pupil Jamar, his disciples Montfort and Leroux, and those survivors of the raft whose brains he wished to pick. Géricault shaved off his hair so as to strengthen his resolve not to enter society. He slept in a room off the studio and arranged for his meals to be brought to him. Most importantly, he had chosen a location only a short walk from the Hôpital Beaujon where he could go to observe human suffering and from which he would obtain severed body parts for private study.[6]

The hospital near Géricault's new and temporary work space had been founded in 1784 by Nicolas Beaujon as a hospice for orphans and the poor of the parish. Becoming a hospital in 1795, it slowly grew until, by 1816, the authorities crammed 140 beds into a space originally intended for eighty. During the Allied occupation at the beginning of the Restoration, typhus resulted in a death rate of nearly one in every four patients, but conditions began to improve in 1818, when the hospital was provided with facilities for washing laundry and supplying water to each floor. Although the mortality rate was in decline, there remained a steady supply of dismembered limbs and dead bodies for student study.

Géricault's interest in corpses and human fragments was not merely anatomical, but also pathological. The *Medusa* project compelled him to observe the effects of deprivation

173

and violence, and he made arrangements with the interns and nurses at the Beaujon to allow him to follow the phases of suffering on site, as well as to provide him with amputated limbs for studio study.[7] Because exhumation and dissection were, from October 1813, forbidden outside the Faculty of Medicine, Géricault may have had to come by his limbs and heads in a roundabout way. It is quite possible that Henri Savigny, through his medical connections, was instrumental in helping the painter to obtain some of the amputated limbs.

The conditions that Géricault encountered on his visits to the dissecting theatre would give him some insight into the state of the raft after the carnage of the mutinies. Hector Berlioz, who at that time was a young medical student, vividly described the scene:

> this human charnel house, scattered members, grimacing heads, skulls half open, the bloody cesspool in which we trod, the revolting odour . . . filled me with such fright that, jumping through the window of the amphitheatre, I escaped as fast as I could and ran panting to my place, as if death and its dreadful cortège were hot on my heels.[8]

Unlike Berlioz, Géricault felt compelled to accept such pursuit, inviting death into his studio.

The city also provided Géricault with an extensive site in which to study human misery. Pre-Haussmann Paris remained a densely packed warren of pest-ridden streets in which ordure, offal and assorted rubbish were scattered by scavenging dogs, splattered by cart wheels and further mired by the horses that circulated through the entrails of the city.[9] An anonymous English visitor noted that the 'climate of the French metropolis is bad, unpleasant and unhealthy. It is subject to frequent and sudden falls of rain', so that the city was known – even by the French themselves – as the 'chamber-pot of France'. This situation was compounded by the:

injudicious manner in which the drains are laid on for conveying the rain-water and filth of every description, which gradually amasses, from the roofs and gutters of the houses, and which, instead of being carried down, as in England, to the ground, project from the house to the distance of three or four feet, and consequently inundate the passenger who walks under them.

These dense, unhealthy spaces were littered with amputees, men whose lives had been saved on countless Napoleonic battle-fields by the celebrated seventeen-second disarticulations performed by Dominique Larrey. Swifter and less dangerous than full amputation, the success rate was significantly better and resulted in the large number of cripples who now mooched out an uneasy and impoverished existence in the capital. In these fetid streets Géricault was surrounded by much evidence of abandonment and disease and produced, during 1818–19, poignant and provocative lithographs that formed an elegy for the Napoleonic adventure: *The Retreat from Russia*, *The Cart of the Wounded* and *The Swiss Sentry at the Louvre*. As with the artist's work on the *Medusa*, all of these explore different forms of betrayal, attest to the burgeoning of Géricault's political consciousness and disclose the morbidity of his mood. His familiarity with the city's streets, his trips to the nearby Beaujon, as well as to the Hôpital Bicêtre and the Morgue, all contributed to his researches for *The Raft of the Medusa*.[10]

The Paris Morgue stood on the south bank of the Île-de-la-Cité, near the Pont-Neuf, only a stone's throw from where Georges-Hippolyte was born. A gaunt, free-standing rectangular structure, it was visited by people of fashion, come to meditate on the transitoriness of life or to gloat over the wages of sin. Just across the road stood the *Académie Suisse*, an informal studio where many of Géricault's friends came to draw. On the testimony of the regulars, it seems that Géricault worked opposite in the Morgue for long hours, on and off, over a period of a year. The function of the Morgue was to receive the unidentified cadavers that came under the jurisdiction of the police. Inside, the clothes they had been wearing when found were hung above the anonymous corpses in order to offer some clue to identification. Stillborn babies and miscarriages were displayed for a period of three days, during which they could be reclaimed by relatives; a particularly poignant sight, perhaps, for one who had so recently been forced to give up his infant son to an anonymous nurse.[11]

On occasion, Géricault's friends, Charles-Émile Champmartin and Alexandre Colin, joined the artist in his noxious studio to paint severed limbs and heads. In the *Anatomical Fragments* now in Montpellier, Géricault presents a tangle of limbs that recalls the human debris strewn about the raft. An intimation of cannibalism is suggested by the section cut above the shoulder, like a choice offering on a butcher's block. The cut of the joint is presented as something potentially edible and lit in a manner that recalls those Dutch still lifes that celebrate a brace of pheasants or a rib of beef. Eugène Delacroix, sounding the Romantic artist's understanding of what Géricault was attempting to achieve, called these studies 'the best argument for Beauty as it ought to be understood', revealing as they do the transfiguration by art of what was odious in nature.[12]

After a two-day period of rigor mortis, which sets in six to twelve hours after death, the effect of the stiffening lactic acid wears off and the body softens and putrefies. Géricault kept cadavers and fragments for weeks, and his closest friends, along with those few visitors who had not been on the raft, became afraid of infection.[13] By contrast, Géricault himself did not hesitate to handle these toxic fragments, and touching and smelling death brought him closer to the world of those abandoned by Chaumareys and Schmaltz. If he was not about to eat the flesh that he brought home, he was prey to its odours, and the sense of smell accounts for much of what we 'taste'. Géricault felt the flesh becoming limp, he smelt the putrefaction, he all but tasted the meat. If not directly related to his sketches for the *Medusa* project, for which he used live models, these studies of severed limbs undoubtedly enhanced his sense of living and dying on the raft.[14]

Installed in the new studio, shaven-headed after discarding the thick locks of an earlier, happier self, Géricault set to work. The soft, blushing, elegant figure had been transformed: Lebrun would no longer come upon an embarrassed, vain young dandy with hair in curling papers. The shaving of his head, a practical preparation for settling down to work undisturbed, was also perhaps an impetuous act of purification, a renouncing of sex.

Deprived of love, Géricault became a man of compassion. He dedicated himself to painting the cruelties of modern life. Amid the acrid relics littering his studio at Saint-Philippe du Roule, Géricault set out on his own short and fatal voyage. In the wake of separation and loss, he seemed to be saying, 'I'll sorrow with the sorrowful – I'll repent among the dead. I will set myself adrift on a difficult sea.'

11

The Raft of the Medusa

As the winter of 1819 wore on, Géricault was hard at work, intent on finishing his painting for the Salon, which would open in August of that year. He had won a gold medal with his debut in 1812, exhibited three works in 1814, but missed the exhibition in 1817 because he had been in Italy. It was high time to make his mark. The Salon, organized by the administrators of the royal museums, was supremely important to painters; with an embryonic art market and with non-official or privately mounted exhibitions a rarity, it was their only established forum.

The 1819 Salon would not only be larger than its predecessors, it would be coupled with an Industrial Fair, proclaiming that France was emerging from the ravages of instability and beginning to embrace the modern age. The return of a good deal of Napoleonic plunder to its rightful owners had left gaping spaces in the Louvre's collection, now waiting to be filled with the best in modern French painting. The artists attracting the most official interest were those history painters who turned their backs on the large battle scenes that had been so popular during the Empire, in order to flatter the restored monarchy with illustrations from the lives of French kings.[1]

The Raft of the Medusa

Ignoring this trend and having discarded other ideas, Géricault finally settled on the most poignant moment in Corréard's and Savigny's scandalous narrative, a moment of hope that would evaporate, leaving the enfeebled survivors in despair. Apart from their inherent technical difficulties, episodes such as acts of mutiny or cannibalism might have compromised the painting's polemical meaning by provoking awkward questions about the culpability of Corréard and Savigny, who were, after all, his new friends. What had been their motives in giving an exhaustive account that repeatedly apportioned blame while praising and flattering its two authors? Had they, in order to survive, and in refusing the role of victim, been guilty of actions that were as cowardly or egotistical as the leaders whom they accused?[2] In choosing to paint the first sighting of *The Argus*, when the brig remained too distant to notice the raft, Géricault subtly reminded spectators of the culpability of the leaders of the expedition. By freezing that moment, the painter presented his public with a scene of great suspense. The unsaved were fixed at a point before the happy ending – before, at the eleventh hour, rescue miraculously arrived.

On a political level, the image is a stern indictment. Géricault's decision to include, on the extreme right-hand side of his canvas, the blue, white and red of a uniform trailing off the raft into the water, acts – with its echo of the Revolutionary *tricolore* – like a requiem for Republican French values. On another level, if the almost-imperceptible *Argus* were to be read as a religious or spiritual metaphor, it suggests that salvation might simply not be forthcoming. The artist's search for a composition capable of conveying far-reaching meanings precluded any off-putting scene of Gothic horror, such as that surrounding him in his studio. Géricault sought a potent image, and not realism in all its awful excess.

Montfort, Géricault's young assistant, recalled the painter's complete need of quiet as he worked: 'when I made a bit of noise with my chair, in the midst of the absolute silence in the studio . . . Géricault, who was standing on a table in order to paint the top of his canvas, reproached me gently with a knowing smile, which let me know that the noise of a mouse was enough to stop him from painting.' Géricault's pupil Jamar was, for that reason, obliged to wear slippers. Concentration was intense and the hours were long; the artist would start early, so as to benefit from the morning light, and work on uninterrupted through the day until nightfall.[3] Even when he left the studio that he had littered with death, Géricault found himself attracted to the pallor of suffering. One day in Sèvres, he encountered his friend, Théodore Lebrun, who had succumbed to jaundice. Lebrun recalled that:

> I had much trouble finding a lodging; my cadaverous face frightened all the inn-keepers; none of them wanted me to die at their place . . . one afternoon, I saw Géricault approaching with one of his friends . . . suddenly he recognized me and seized me in his arms: 'Ah, my friend, you are really beautiful'. I frightened myself, children ran away, taking me for dead – but I was beautiful to the painter who was looking everywhere for the colour of death. He pressed me to visit him and to pose for the *Medusa*.[4]

Among the people who came to model for Géricault was the young painter Eugène Delacroix, who posed for the man face down in the centre foreground of the picture. Delacroix remembered that *The Raft of the Medusa* had a terrifying effect in its unfinished state, and recalled that the 'impression it gave me was so strong that, as I left the studio, I broke into a run, and kept running like a fool all the way back . . . to the far end of the faubourg Saint-Germain'.[5] Generally, Géricault used professionals such as the popular model, Joseph, who sat for the figure of Jean-Charles, the black man signalling. He also made numerous studies of survivors, such as the ship's carpenter Lavillette, and Savigny and Corréard.[6] They came to the studio to provide the artist with eyewitness accounts and they came to pose. Corréard, as a recognizable figure, first appears in the sketches for the scene of false hope that Géricault finally selected for his painting.

Since September 1818, Corréard had been running a bookshop in the Palais Royal that had become a meeting place for political activists. The publication of *The Shipwreck* had made him a celebrity, and unlike the retiring Savigny, who wished to put his difficult past behind him, Corréard capitalized on his success and went so far as to call his book-shop 'At the Victim of the Shipwreck of The Medusa'. Corréard was trading on his misfortune as well as making a political point, alerting the authorities of his desire to disseminate what they considered to be sedition.

Corréard exerted a considerable influence on the painter. Certainly, they became friends and even collaborators, when Géricault produced engravings for the third edition of *The Shipwreck*; with additions such as an account of Corréard's trial, a list of the 'Subscribers to the *Medusa* Shipwreck Fund' and a seven-page indifferent Ode, this fell somewhere between a self-promoting gripe and a de-luxe collector's edition. Although it was unlikely that Corréard could radi-cally influence Géricault, he had by now a reputation to maintain. Elements of his narrative had already been contested by other survivors of the raft, and Corréard could not afford to have his authority further questioned. His credentials as an agitator needed to remain secure. If the scandal was, once again, to be brought to the public's atten-tion, and particularly in such a prominent place as the Salon, would it not be in Corréard's interest that certain elements be sanitized so as to avoid embarrassing speculation about those actions that enabled him and Savigny to survive? Would it not be in his best interest that Géricault's painting stress the culpability of the leaders rather than the horrors of the raft? Corréard's cause would be served by a painting that made a grandly political statement, rather than one that presented a vision of bloody and controversial massacre or cannibalism.

In the finished *Raft of the Medusa*, Géricault placed Corréard in pride of place, positioning him almost centrally, on the line of the canvas's all-powerful golden section, with his side-lit face carrying the charged expression of one who has something to broadcast. He is looking at the swathed head of Savigny, his co-author, as if saying, 'There you have it. What we see in the distance is not a rescue vessel, it's nothing but a part of the same state machinery that is responsible for our present plight.' His gesture is not one of exuberance at having glimpsed hope, but alarmist and accusatory. His outstretched arm against the dawn light takes the eye along the line from the dead son outstretched in his father's arms to the controversially placed black signaller at the apex of all their hope. Although this signaller is given a position of importance, Corréard pulls the eye as the key figure in the composition. The painting does not present Corréard as victim, but Corréard as messenger, Corréard the polemicist, the saviour who would take up arms against a sea of troubles.

On April 21st, 1819, still smarting from the lack of sympathy shown to him and his fellow sufferers, Corréard presented a report to the Chambers of the Peers and Deputies, attacking the inexperienced and unworthy men who, to his mind, had caused the tragedy of *The Medusa*. He sought justice on behalf of the victims of the shipwreck who, nearly three years after the tragedy, were still struggling against official indifference, exhaustion and pain. Corréard pleaded for even the smallest display of compassion from the authorities. Insisting on nothing for himself, and in the name of national honour, he beseeched the members of the

Chambers, those 'moral guardians' of France, to observe the rights set out in the *charte* and adequately punish the guilty parties.

He attacked the ex-Minister of the Navy, Vicomte DuBouchage, whose pride had prevented him from adequately pursuing and punishing his appointees. Corréard accused DuBouchage of concealing crime and encouraging it by impunity, having tried Chaumareys only for the loss of his ship. He further accused DuBouchage of having imperilled the lives of Frenchmen and other ships of His Majesty by placing them under the command of like-minded incompetents.

Corréard urged the members of the Chambers to consider whether Captain Chaumareys had been adequately tried for the two major crimes he had committed: the abandoning of his ship and the abandoning of the raft. Often citing the letter of the law and before proceeding to the capital crimes, Corréard lists the various misdemeanours of the Captain and the other officers: Chaumareys for allowing the convoy to break up; Chaumareys and the Officers of the Watch for abandoning a fifteen-year-old ship's apprentice who had fallen overboard on June 23rd, 1816; the officer commanding the boat that put in to shore at Santa Cruz on June 29th, who refused to rescue six French prisoners; Chaumareys for having failed to recognize Cap Blanc. He then accused Chaumareys for having lost *The Medusa*, and again for not being the last to leave his ship, but rather for disembarking when there were still sixty-four men on board – which, according to Article 35 of the law of August 22nd, 1790, carried the death penalty. All of *The Medusa*'s officers are accused of having abandoned the '152' people on board the raft; this 'in the name of all the laws of humanity and Articles 36 and 37 under Heading 2 of the aforementioned law', which clearly stated that 'All officers entrusted with commanding a convoy found guilty of having voluntarily abandoned it will be condemned to death'. Corréard also chided Chaumareys for not having sent *The Argus*, *The Loire* and *The Echo* to search for the raft as soon as he reached Saint Louis.

Corréard also attacked Colonel Schmaltz for various crimes and misdemeanours: for having waited two days before liaising with the English governor over a possible search-and-rescue operation; for not accepting Colonel Brereton's offer of using all the ships at his disposal; for delaying the departure of *The Argus*; and for not punishing those who misappropriated government and personal property recovered from *The Medusa* two months after its wreck. He declared Schmaltz unworthy of representing the French government and stated that he should be indicted under clause no. 12 of Article 475 of the Penal Code, which condemns those who refuse or neglect to help the victims of a shipwreck or other accident. Most importantly, perhaps, Corréard openly questioned Schmaltz's behaviour in relation to one of the most far-reaching and unpleasant aspects of the whole recolonization of Senegal – the abominable trade in human beings that was becoming a burning issue for liberals in France, and which would unite Corréard and Géricault. Without swearing that such rumours were true, Corréard urged the Chambers to look into the possibility that Schmaltz was not only openly favouring, but actually profiting from, the slave trade.[7]

Corréard was still suffering physically from his ordeal, with painful scars covering his body, and he was not prepared to accept soft justice. Chaumareys had less than a year left in jail and Schmaltz was, by all accounts, active in the slave trade. Corréard was adamant that subsequent editions of *The Shipwreck* would contain a printed record of the catalogue of crimes that he had aired before the government and, henceforth, his attack would take on a larger target than mere reparation for past ills: it would begin to address this illegal trade in human flesh.

To place a black man in such a dominant position in his

finished *Medusa* composition suggests that Géricault sympathized with Corréard's political struggle and was listening to the debates in the liberal circle around him. To place a figure who, because of his colour, was generally considered to be sub-human at the summit of whatever hope *The Raft of the Medusa* may be said to express, was daringly, dangerously avant-garde.

Recent research shows that the three blacks in the finished painting were introduced at a late stage in the composition.[8] Their placing tells its own story. The one lying facedown, dead, over the haunch of the figure clambering from the deck, speaks of past despair. The second, placed significantly between Savigny and the political agitator Corréard, looks up hopefully to the third, who is signalling optimistically. A counterpoint to the story of voyagers abandoned by their leaders, these three blacks present the larger drama of a people passing from despair and victimization to hope for an enlightened future. The artist had become not only a witness to the malfunctioning French administration, but also an advocate for a fundamental shift in human rights.

While working on the painting, Géricault made short excursions out of Paris. In late March 1819 he made a trip to Le Havre to study the effects of clouds over water. He also went with Horace Vernet and a retired army officer on a short trip to visit English artists. The Channel crossing afforded Géricault further opportunity to study the sea and the clouds, and enabled him to experience the sensation of being on water.[9] Otherwise, the painter was mostly in his studio, hard at work on *The Raft of the Medusa*, which, as a result of his enforced isolation, he finished in the relatively short period of eight months. The painting was emerging darkly monochromatic. There was a lot of black, a colour that, Géricault observed, 'suits pain'.[10]

The large surface of the canvas may have been dark, but it revealed something surprising – even revolutionary. Traditionally, seascapes painted in Holland, France and

England presented distant scenes of disaster on small canvases in which any human drama was relegated to tiny, almost meaningless detail. In the powerful Northern Romantic work of Caspar David Friedrich and J.M.W. Turner, human incident was dramatically subordinated to the force and grandeur of nature, but in Géricault's large painting, however much we feel the presence of threatening elements, the work focuses on the survivors on the raft.

Géricault's major paintings bring the spectator right up to the action, revealing the artist's early and persistent understanding of the power of the close-up. In *The Raft*, such a procedure insists on the terrifying distance between the seemingly futile agitation of the survivors and the almost imperceptible fleck of *The Argus* on the horizon. This symbolically asserts the gulf between the peril of the abandoned and the distant attitude of the leaders of the expedition. *The Argus* is seen from either the stern or the bow, but it is impossible to say which, so those on the raft (and the spectator) have no way of knowing whether the ship is approaching or is about to disappear from sight. Furthermore, by making the ship a mere smudge, Géricault suggests that it may even be a delusion, a phantom of the delirious minds of these severely tested men.

When, in July 1819, Géricault thought he had finished his canvas, six men came to transport it to the foyer of the *Théâtre Italien* in the place Boieldieu, where paintings were being assembled for that year's Salon. Seeing the canvas with a refreshed critical vision once it had been removed from the familiar surroundings of his studio, Géricault realized that the bottom right-hand corner was disturbingly empty. Increased tension could be given to the painting by filling the space with a dead figure being dragged from the raft into the sea. He decided to reintroduce a figure that had appeared in a study for what may have been a scene of cannibalism.[11] He further modified his work by including another figure, lying dead on his back, at the extreme left.[12]

These additions to a raft already too populous to match the numbers given by the official reports, as well as by Corréard and Savigny, demonstrate how Géricault discarded journalistic verisimilitude. He placed his figures and structured his groupings in order to sweep from despair in the foreground to the false hope of the gesticulating black man on the barrel. Bolstered by his researches, which had secured an emotional depth and integrity, the painter here dared to depart from the literal truth in his expression of a more profound meaning.

When Corréard faced the finished picture, it must have made a tremendous impact on his sense of himself. He must have felt redeemed, honoured, rewarded. Here he was, in the middle of this vast painting, sending a wake-up call to France.

On September 18th, 1816, a worried Vicomte DuBouchage had written to Louis XVIII on the subject of the wreck of *The Medusa*: 'I bemoan the fact that the journalists revel in disclosing details of deplorable scenes, the picture of which must never be brought before the eyes of the public.'[13] When the generally lacklustre 1819 Salon opened on the Feast of St Louis, August 25th, nearly a year to the day after the birth of Géricault's son, there could be seen, hanging among the 1,600 items on show, *The Scene of the Shipwreck* – the compromise title devised by the Salon authorities in an attempt to deflect public attention from the true subject of Géricault's vast canvas. Ironically, in an exhibition intended as a political shop window for the recently restored monarchy, one of the most talked-about paintings was this very work, which, despite its neutralizing new title, obviously called into question the competency of the Bourbon administration.

The 1819 Salon saw the first stirrings of the debate between the old, neoclassical school, which had dominated French art for the previous thirty years, and the new

Romantic artists who had grown up during that period of turmoil. The quarrel would erupt dramatically in 1824 when the two schools would split into the Classical 'Homerians' and the younger Romantic 'Shakespearians'. It was an argument that involved questions of detachment versus immediacy, formality versus spontaneity, and it led eventually to a loss of confidence in Salon juries and the revolt against the Academy and official art that would so stimulate painting in nineteenth-century France. Géricault's gloomy shipwreck, painted on an unacceptably large canvas for its genre, provoked an early attack on the new school of painting, which appeared to reject 'good taste' for what was 'ugly'.[14]

Artistic affront to the establishment was a dangerous tactic and, although Géricault's private income allowed him to invest the time needed to produce a vast canvas, he could not ensure that the result would be accepted for exhibition. These Bourbons may have been more tolerant than their predecessors, but they faced a largely disgruntled population. Certainly, with its controversial subject matter, no Revolutionary or Napoleonic government would have admitted such a subversive painting as *The Scene of a Shipwreck*. In order to justify his selection, and sounding a decidedly pro-Romantic note, the Comte de Forbin, the courageous and perceptive Director of Museums and organizer of the Salon, wrote to the Comte de Pradel, Director-General of the Royal Household, that the 'arts are the enemy of restraint'.[15]

Hanging in the company of the large works commissioned by the monarchy, the Ministry of the Interior and the Duc d'Orléans and placed detrimentally high on the wall of the *Salon Carré* above the doorway to the *Grande Galerie* of the Louvre, was no. 510, Théodore Géricault's *Scene of a Shipwreck*. From the opening of the Salon, reaction to the work seemed to be largely unfavourable. Géricault swiftly understood that this had much to do with its positioning. With the aid of his friend Dedreux-Dorcy, the painter managed to have his enormous canvas rehung so that its baseline was only a little way from the floor. At this level, it took the spectator into what seemed like an extension of real space. Viewers were drawn into the upward thrust of the raft, an illusion that pulled them right on board. Not only was a moment of false hope frozen, but the viewer had been made part of it.[16] Hanging at this height, the impact of the scale of the figures was considerable and lent both drama and dignity to the suffering portrayed.

Louis XVIII maintained the custom, initiated by Napoleon, of the head of state visiting the Salon. With his health deteriorating, on August 28th he made his two-hour visit in a wheelchair and, accompanied by several people, including Elie Decazes (now Minister of the Interior), met Géricault. The King spent some considerable time studying *The Scene of a Shipwreck* and, in a celebrated witticism, demonstrated the scope and agility of his political acumen. Louis XVIII's remark to Géricault begins, as the French writer Jean Sagne has pointed out, with what seems like an accusation: 'Sir, you have made a shipwreck . . .', displacing the guilt that Géricault, Corréard and Savigny had heaped on the shoulders of the administration onto those of the painter. Expecting the sentence to keep up its accusatory tone, we are suddenly disarmed by the wit of its conclusion: '. . . which is not one for you'. As Sagne suggests, complimenting a work that dared to challenge the regime was a powerful demonstration of regal magnanimity. Perhaps, studying the painting in the company of his favourite, Elie Decazes, the King remembered how the catastrophe had, in their concerted effort to neutralize the *ultra* threat, played right into their hands.[17]

Once more, the wreck of *The Medusa* was the talk of the town. The ultra-Royalist *Quotidienne* recorded that Géricault's painting created a 'huge uproar' at the Salon. Surprisingly, the ex-Minister of the Navy, Vicomte DuBouchage, became enraged with the organizer, Comte

Forbin, not for accepting *The Scene of a Shipwreck* for Salon presentation, but rather for including the portrait by Jacques-Marie Legros of his nemesis, Alexandre Corréard – an exhibit which indeed confirms that Corréard had become something of a celebrity.[18]

Géricault, who until the late summer and early autumn of 1819, had been a relatively unknown artist, suddenly became 'the painter of the *Medusa*'.[19] Not only was there keen public interest in the subject matter, but the painting itself provoked a great degree of critical controversy. Its sombre, monochromatic effect was broadly disliked. *La Quotidienne*, in the first of its six articles covering the Salon, actually called the work by its real name – *The Raft of the Medusa* – and lamented the artist's use of monochrome, as did the critic of *l'Indépendant*. On the other hand, the critic in *Le moniteur universel* noted that 'The melange of red and gray tones produces a sinister effect which is in perfect accord with the spirit of the scene.'[20] The critic of the *Gazette de France*, calling it a 'monstrous painting', suggested that Géricault had sacrificed all the rules in order to catch man in the midst of a calamity that forced him to lose his dignity; there was 'nothing touching, nothing honourable'.[21] The critic of *l'Indépendant*, while admiring Géricault's draughtsmanship, found nothing of Corréard and Savigny in the work, which he would have thought to be the intention of the painter.[22] Meanwhile, aesthetes considered the 'majesty of the brushwork' belittled by the choice of subject.[23]

Géricault was upset by the generally unfavourable reaction to his masterpiece and irritated by the inanity of certain critics. Having painted a political work, he now became a victim of political and journalistic wrangling. He vented his exasperation in a letter:

> This year, our journalists have reached the heights of stupidity. Each painting is primarily judged according to the spirit in which it has been composed. Thus you hear

a liberal article praise a patriotic touch in a work . . . The
same painting judged by an *ultra* will then be nothing
other than a revolutionary composition governed by a
general tint of sedition. The faces portrayed will all have
an expression of hatred for the paternalistic government.
Finally, I was accused by a certain *Drapeau blanc* to have
slandered, by an expression on a face, the entire Ministry
of the Navy. The unfortunate people who write such
stupidities obviously haven't starved for 14 days, because
they would then know that neither poetry nor painting
are capable of rendering with sufficient horror all the
sufferings experienced by the people on the raft.[24]

It is obvious that as *The Medusa* was a *cause célèbre*, critics
would be likely to divide along party lines. Given the subject
matter, liberals took the pretext of the painting to recon-
sider the scandal of the shipwreck. To many of them, the
refined neutrality of the classicized figures and the disin-
fected conditions on the raft appeared as a wasted opportunity. In the *Courrier de Paris* a critic even asked, 'are they
Greeks or Romans?' The question is apposite: to deny the
brutality of the facts by using a lingering neoclassicism in
the treatment of the figures was to make a costume-drama
of a contemporary event and to compromise the political
message implied by the clash of the classes and races who
had been condemned to the raft. Yet to make a great and
important painting for the Salon, the language of
Michelangelo was still considered necessary, and so
Géricault's figures possess a muscular monumentality that
belies the painting's story. Nonetheless, the overall effect of
the canvas is darkly Romantic.[25]

Exhausted by pressures in his personal life and by his
punishing work on *The Raft of the Medusa*, as well as being
overwhelmingly discouraged by its reception at the Salon,
Géricault caved in to depression and retreated to the country.
On September 11th, he went to Machault and Féricy, near

Fontainebleau, with the liberal sociologist Auguste Brunet. Despite the sympathetic company and the late-summer splendours of the countryside, within two weeks Géricault retreated to his bed. He had become irritable and appeared to be suffering from persecution mania. By mid-October he was taken back to Paris to undergo treatment.

It was decided that there should be no prize awarded for history painting in the 1819 Salon. Géricault's masterpiece, along with works by thirty-two other artists, won a gold medal – an award that was eventually bequeathed to Alexandrine's second child, Géricault's godson, Paul. Meanwhile the canvas, having picked up an award but no buyer, was rolled up and stored in the obscurity of a fellow artist's studio.[26]

12

The Medusa Sails On

THREE days after Géricault was informed that he had won a gold medal at the Salon, Hugues Duroy de Chaumareys was released from prison and retired to his family domain, the Château de Lachenaud in Limousin. Meanwhile, Alexandre Corréard's call for justice before the Chambers had fallen on deaf ears and, even though the left would continue to cite the catastrophe as evidence of *ultra* misrule, the political potency of the scandal seemed to be on the ebb.

Across the Channel, however, the story was very much alive. Not only had *The Times* carried a version of Savigny's leaked article of September 1816, but two years later a full translation of Savigny's and Corréard's book was published. Savigny's name appeared first on this English edition, even though it was a translation of the second French edition, which had come under Corréard's control. The English publisher was the much-respected Henry Colburn, who was currently publishing the likes of Benjamin Franklin and Madame de Staël and acting as an agent for the collection of English donations to the *Medusa*'s Subscription Fund. The *Narrative of a Voyage to Senegal* proved a highly popular book. The part played by the late Major Peddie, whose kindness to Corréard when he had been hospitalized in Senegal stood in such heart-warming contrast to the callous indifference of the French leaders, endeared the saga to the British.[1]

The English relished a scandal that revealed weaknesses in French administration and a lack of discipline and moral fibre in their navy. French ineptitude reflected advantageously on English naval competence, and the gulf between the two forces was further highlighted by the impeccable behaviour following the shipwreck of the British frigate H.M.S. *Alceste* in February 1817. Returning home from the Far East with Lord Amherst, the British ambassador to the Emperor of China, on board, the frigate, negotiating the imperfectly charted Straits of Gaspar to the north of Java, 'struck with a horrid crash on a reef of sunken rocks, and remained immovable!' In complete contrast to the lack of adequate measures taken by Captain Chaumareys, the English captain, Murray Maxwell, had sailed through these Straits with 'the utmost precaution'. He had posted 'men looking out at the mast-heads, yard-arms and bowsprit end'. The 'officer of the watch, on whom the charge of the ship at such a time more particularly devolves', along with all the other officers on board, was vigilantly up on deck. In contrast to *The Medusa*, *The Alceste* was fortunately only five kilometres from the nearest island when she ran aground, and a raft was constructed to transport stores and baggage. A barge took the Ambassador ashore and then returned for members of the crew. During the ensuing days, while Lord Amherst made for nearby Java to summon help, food and water dwindled and the British were threatened by savage Malay pirates, who eventually set fire to the ship and harassed their camp on the island. The officers set an excellent example to those beneath them and, under 'all the depressing circumstances attending shipwreck; – of hunger, thirst and fatigue; and menaced by a ruthless foe, it was glorious to see the British spirit staunch and unsubdued'. Everybody survived the shipwreck, being rescued by H.M.S. *Ternate*, which had been sent from Java. Captain Maxwell was acquitted and praised by the subsequent court martial as having 'conducted himself in the most zealous and officer like manner'.

A book written from the notes kept by the ship's surgeon, John McLeod, was published in the same year that Savigny's and Corréard's *Narrative* first appeared in English, and the conduct of the British officers appeared exemplary beside that of Reynaud, Schmaltz and Chaumareys. So telling was the contrast between these eyewitness accounts that a volume, published in Dublin in 1822, brought together the story of *The Alceste* with a truncated version of the *Medusa* narrative. In some 'Observations' accompanying these texts, the editor states that the tales were placed together 'as they clearly point out the advantage to be derived from discipline, subordination and moral feeling, on the one hand; and hold forth, on the other, a lamentable picture of the vicious state to which men may be reduced, when uninfluenced by these'.[2]

With the hook of international rivalry, the sympathetic role played by the English, and all the horrific ingredients of the inhuman tale, it was not surprising that a Barnum-like figure called William Bullock would wish to bring Géricault's picture over to London as a topical attraction.[3] Apart from financial gain and the possibility that a triumph in London would eradicate the memory of a disappointing Salon showing, there was considerable interest for a French artist in coming to, and being shown in, London. Despite the enduring rivalry between England and France, a lively cultural exchange had been taking place during the Restoration. Peace meant that the English were, once again, able to visit and even take up residence in Paris. In fact, in the French capital, it was 'raining' Englishmen, ridiculed for their pot-bellied, red-faced roughness, and their ladies for their dreadful bonnets. The English were attracted to Paris for its relative cheapness, as well as for the French lifestyle and culture. The prostitutes and gambling dens of the Palais Royal welcomed the influx, which was so large and so prominent that a satiric sub-genre of fiction, the English in Paris, enjoyed enormous popularity.[4]

One reason for these growing ties between the two nations was the Anglophilia of Louis XVIII. He had been well treated in exile by the British, who believed that peace in Europe would be secured if the French monarchy could be restored. After the upheavals of the *Cent-Jours*, Louis kept a precautionary nest-egg in Coutts Bank in England and the French government turned to Barings of London, rather than its own banks, for a loan to help pay off its final indemnity to the Allies. At the same time, to the more liberal-minded French, London seemed a natural alternative to Paris; while the *ultras* were enjoying their domination of the *chambre introuvable* in the early part of the Second Restoration, the liberal Benjamin Constant had fled to London, as had the Duc d'Orléans.

To the French of the Restoration, Britain – with its industrial and naval supremacy – seemed progressive and powerful. But there was another side, a dark and unstable aspect to the country to which Géricault and his *Raft of the Medusa* came in 1820. The end of the Napoleonic Wars had plunged Britain into serious economic crisis, exacerbated by bad harvests and wildly fluctuating food prices. Around 400,000 demobilized soldiers were unemployed, factories that had lost their military customers faced ruin, government finances were strained under the huge debt incurred by the war, and the monarchy was enormously unpopular – all this placed Britain in a vulnerable and volatile state. There was open revolt and the spectre of revolution. What is more, it fell to the normally stable property owners, already protesting over excessive taxation, to pay the rates that financed Poor Relief. The government thus faced rebellion, not only from radicals and agitators who made their appeal to the working class, but also from the wealthier members of society. Recent

French history had provided a dangerous precedent, which prompted Lord Liverpool's Tory government to oppose reform, lest it lead to revolution. In 1811, George III had been declared unfit to govern and his politically incompetent and petulant son, George, became the Prince Regent. By the time this extravagant and narcissistic man was crowned George IV in 1820, he was detested.

Géricault embarked for England on April 10th, 1820. With life in Paris proving painful and disappointing, London offered a new horizon. Although Liverpool's reactionary government appeared to have successfully repressed revolt with the 'massacre' at Peterloo in August 1819, its extensive network of government spies, and its six 'Gagging Acts', there was still revolutionary ferment in the air, rendering London an intriguing destination for the increasingly politicized artist.[5]

William Bullock, who was to exhibit Géricault's masterpiece, had been in France in September 1819, and may have seen *The Raft of the Medusa* at the Salon. The entrepreneur undertook to handle all the arrangements for the London exhibition, elected to pay all costs, and offered Géricault one-third of the profits.[6] Originally a jeweller and goldsmith, Bullock had begun his working life as a collector when, based in Liverpool, he had purchased artefacts brought from such exotic places as West Africa by those arriving on the numerous trade ships. When, in 1809, he established his Liverpool Museum at 22 Piccadilly in London's West End, it rapidly became, according to *Bell's Weekly Messenger*, 'the most fashionable place of amusement in London'. Jane Austen, who visited the museum in April 1811, was singular in finding the crowds more exciting than the exhibits. The following year, a more spectacular home for Bullock's collection was built in the popular Egyptian style. Sited opposite the lower end of Bond Street, it cost £16,000 to construct and, although Bullock called his new establishment The London Museum, its flamboyant façade ensured that it became known in the capital simply as the Egyptian Hall. While Bullock's collection of nearly 15,000 items, which had been gathered during 'seventeen years of arduous research', was displayed with a certain scientific diligence, the showman in him guaranteed that sensational settings – such as a re-creation of Fingal's Cave, or a Pantherion, in which all known quadrupeds were stuffed and displayed against their natural habitat – would pull the crowds. Bullock's London Museum was conceived as a total entertainment experience, transporting the 'astonished visitor . . . from the crowded streets of the Metropolis to the centre of a tropical forest'. Special exhibitions proved spectacularly profitable. From the Prince Regent, for a sum of £2,500, Bullock astutely purchased the coach used by Napoleon in the Russian Campaign, which had been captured by the British at Waterloo. It proved an enormously popular exhibit, earning the entrepreneur about £35,000. Bullock also mounted a series of exhibitions of large paintings, beginning in 1816 with his presentation of Auguste Le Thière's neoclassical *Judgement of Brutus on His Sons*.

The lack of state or private patronage for history painting in England meant that there had been a tradition of commercial exhibitions in London during the previous half-century. In contrast to the exceptional presentation of the *Sabine Women Enforcing the Peace* mounted by its painter, Jacques-Louis David, as a commercial venture in Paris in 1800, London had seen many celebrated artists, such as John Singleton Copley, Benjamin West and James Ward, present their own large-scale works in exhibitions for which they made an admission charge.[7] Just prior to Géricault's arrival in the capital, Benjamin Robert Haydon 'engaged the great room upstairs at Bullock's Egyptian Hall, for a year from March 1st, 1820'. For £300 (a sum that he did not possess when he signed the contract), Haydon secured the space in which to show his *Christ's Entry into Jerusalem*. As the exhibition overlapped with Bullock's presentation of *The Raft of the Medusa*, the entrepreneur was praised by *The Literary Gazette* for creating the opportunity to compare French and English works.[8]

Shortly after Géricault's arrival in the English capital, he was joined by his friend Auguste Brunet and by the portraitist Jean-Baptiste Isabey. In fact, the latter crossed the Channel to escape the unwanted attentions of the French police, who suspected him of circulating seditious drawings. If one adds to this little nest of expatriate radicalism the fact that William Bullock, a member of several liberal scientific societies, was involved in anti-slavery activities, then Géricault's English adventure takes on a political as well as a personal and financial dimension. Abolitionists often cited African artefacts to help refute slave traders' arguments about the sub-humanity of their cargo, and Bullock's London Museum was a startling showcase for ethnic dexterity. The dates of the exhibition of *The Raft of the Medusa* may have been deliberately chosen to coincide with increased English concern over France's clandestine continuation of the slave trade in Senegal. The *ultra* magazine, *Le Conservateur littéraire*, certainly presented Géricault's trip as a political escapade, alleging that he wanted to produce 'a collection of portraits of the most illustrious radicals' and establish contact with 'fellow-Liberals' around Europe. It mockingly lamented the fact that the artist was too late to meet up with the insurgent Arthur Thistlewood.[9]

Thistlewood was the leader of the famed Cato Street Conspirators, who had plotted to blow up Lord Liverpool's Cabinet while it was dining. He had lived and fought in Revolutionary France, had a history of rebellious activity and imprisonment, and plotted the attack on the Cabinet as an attempt to revive the impetus towards a popular uprising. In the wake of the Peterloo Massacre, Thistlewood began to plot a series of nationwide uprisings to aid revolutionaries in Lancashire and South and West Yorkshire. One such revolt was timed to coincide with the annihilation of the Cabinet while they dined at the house of Lord Harrowby. The government, however, stole a march on Thistlewood, who was somewhat careless. Infiltrated and arrested by a government agent provocateur while they were plotting in a loft above a stable in London's Cato Street in February 1820, the conspirators were charged with high treason. They had effectively been framed: even the item in the press that announced the Cabinet dinner had been deliberately planted misinformation.[10]

The arrests caused a sensation, secured the government's position in the general election, and served to justify their 'Gagging Acts'. Thistlewood and four accomplices were put on trial for high treason and condemned to death. The plot and the trial were very much in the news when Géricault arrived in England and it is possible that he witnessed the execution of the conspirators at 8 a.m. on May 1st. Certainly the immediate, unfinished aspect of his sketch of the hanging suggests that it was done on the spot. It could, however, have been made during his following and much longer stay in London, when he was living in lodgings near Cato Street and became more deeply engaged with the problems of English life. Yet there was something in his darkness and despondency during his first weeks in London that could well have attracted him to the macabre spectacle of the hanging. As with the public execution he drew when he was homesick in Rome, as with his visits to the Morgue in Paris when his sentimental life had shattered, a hanging, followed by decapitation, would have fascinated his brooding soul.

Although Géricault was in London to see *The Raft* presented before a less hostile public, any excitement at the prospect of a more favourable reaction does not seem to have dislodged the depression that had settled over him six months earlier. Professional success and private happiness had eluded him at home, and on the streets of London, moving through the thick industrial air, he experienced a misery perhaps even more pronounced than that he had known in Paris. The image of death haunted him and he wrote his will, an act that his travelling companion, Nicolas Charlet, took as a prologue to a suicide attempt. With such fears in mind, when Charlet returned to their hotel late one night and found that Géricault had not gone out that day, he feared the worst. He rushed to Géricault's room, banged on the door, burst in and found his friend stretched out on the bed, unconscious. Charlet revived him and, deploying his often brutal humour, attempted to jolt him out of his depression. Though some have questioned this story, a suicide attempt does not seem far-fetched. On another occasion, when they were walking arm in arm along the banks of the River Thames, Charlet – sensing that Géricault had become clouded with dark thoughts – imagined that the painter wanted to pull him into the river so that they would both drown. On that occasion, to avoid calamity, Charlet swiftly urged his unstable friend away from the river's dangerous edge.[11]

Savigny's and Corréard's translated *Narrative* created considerable advance publicity for the London exhibition of Géricault's canvas, which now bore its original name, *The Raft of the Medusa*. Interest had been further stimulated by the opening, on May 29th, 1820, at London's Royal Coburg Theatre, of William Moncrieff's *Shipwreck of The Medusa, or, the Fatal Raft! – A Drama in Three Acts*. It was a spectacle that boasted the most extravagant and newfangled scenic effects: 'various Panoramic views of the Ocean & Red Deserts of Zaara' and a 'View of the Raft sailing amidst Novel & Extensive Moving Scenery'. The play was remarkable for the fact that *The Medusa* suddenly found herself with a British boatswain, Jack Gallant, whose primary function was to emphasize the honourable and fearless qualities of the British seaman. The introductory remarks to the printed text of the play strike that censorious note that the English so readily applied to the tragedy itself: 'Owing to a very relaxed state of discipline, and an ignorance of the common principles of navigation, that would have disgraced a private merchant ship, this frigate was suffered to run aground . . .'. Of the play itself, one can only hope that the language barrier would have protected Géricault from its chauvinistic froth.[12]

London was going *Medusa*-mad. Publicity for Bullock's exhibition of the painting began with announcements for the Private View on the front pages of *The Times* and the *Morning Chronicle* on Friday, June 9th, 1820:

> The Private Exhibition of Monsieur JERRICAULT'S GREAT PICTURE (from the Louvre), 24 feet by 18, representing the surviving Crew of *The Medusa* French Frigate, after remaining thirteen days on a raft without provision, at the moment they discover the vessel that saves them, will take place at the Egyptian Hall, Piccadilly, on Saturday, and will be opened to the public on Monday next.

From the press, we know that 'the Marquis of Stafford, the Bishops of Ely and Carlisle, and a number of the most eminent patrons of the Fine Arts together with several members of the Royal Academy' were present at the Private View. As for Géricault, perhaps his experience was much like that of Benjamin Robert Haydon, who only a few weeks earlier had, on the day of the Private View of *Christ's Entry into Jerusalem*, installed himself at Hatchett's Coffee Room, where he spent the time wondering whether anybody would turn up.

When the exhibition of *The Raft of the Medusa* opened to the public, visitors streamed into the outrageous building: through the doors sided by lotus columns and surrounded by hieroglyphs, down the passage to the main exhibition hall, through a 'Pasaltic cavern' resembling the Giant's Causeway, and through rooms that until the year before, when Bullock had auctioned off his own marvellous collection of objects and stuffed animals, had housed the most remarkable exhibits. Through these spaces of the newly established Bullock's Egyptian Sale-Room they moved, lured by the proprietor's promise of a large and dramatic picture, which portrayed such a recent and ghastly shipwreck and which had created 'universal interest . . . at the last exhibition of the Louvre'. Eager to spy on their recent enemy in his most abject hour, the public surged into the large Roman Gallery where *The Raft of the Medusa* was hanging, cunningly close to the ground, so that their approach would seem to continue on into the horrific scene. If Géricault had suffered from the first positioning of his work at the opening of the 1819 Salon, or from his compatriots' wish either to forget the tragedy it portrayed or to use his painting as a pretext for political wrangling, then in London, in the hands of a consummate showman, he certainly fared better. As with Haydon's exhibition, the 'rush was great and went on increasing'.[13]

For the most part, the reviews were intelligent and sympathetic. In *The Globe*, on June 12th, the reviewer noted that:

Monsieur Jerricault . . . has selected for his first great historical effort a subject of the utmost difficulty, and with a singular absence of the national vanity ascribed to his countrymen, one which it would be well for the naval character of France to have blotted from her maritime annals. The story of the shipwreck of *The Medusa* . . . records a narrative of the most criminal ignorance, pusillanimity, and individual suffering which has no parallel in modern history.[14]

The reviewer in *The Morning Post* on June 13th commented, 'This work far excels anything we have seen of the school to which it belongs . . . There is more of nature, of the grand simplicity of art, and of true expression than is usual with the highest of modern French painters . . .' This was a view that was elaborated in *The Times* of June 22nd: 'Though the painting bears marks of that cold pedantic school of which David may be considered the founder, yet the powerful talent of the artist has broken through the trammels of this system . . . the expression is energetic, true, and full of pathos.'[15] In contrast to the carping of many Parisian critics, two intelligent reviews appeared in *The London Literary Gazette: Journal of Belles Lettres*, noting, 'The Morgue seems to have been studied as far as it could without exciting horror' and 'the bold hand of the artist has laid bare the details of the horrid facts, with the severity of Michael Angelo and the gloom of Caravaggio . . . the whole of the colouring is so well suited to the subject.'[16]

The exhibition having opened with great success, Géricault returned to France. He arrived in Dieppe on June 19th and went on to Paris. Across Europe there were stirrings of liberal discontent. In Spain there was a successful revolt against the Bourbons. In July there were insurrections in Naples and Sicily, followed, in 1821, by stirrings of subversion in Portugal and Greece. There was liberal agitation in German univer-sities. Meanwhile in France, as one English visitor remarked, 'Since the assassination of the Duke de Berry, all has been distrust and suspicion.' Indeed, after that assassination on February 13th, 1820, which forced the resignation of Decazes, blamed for his tolerance of dissent, the govern-ment shifted markedly to the right. Henceforth there would be no question of reconciliation, only of two opposed factions. Louis XVIII's worst fears were realized as the country became bitterly divided. In March 1820, more laws enforcing press censorship and curtailing individual liberties were passed. In April, a control was imposed upon the publi-cation and distribution of engravings.

In May and June, medical and law students spearheaded the liberal reaction against the repressive measures and, in early June, they clashed with Royalists outside the Chamber

of Deputies, where a twenty-three-year-old law student
named Nicholas Lallemand was killed. The young man
became a liberal martyr and, after his funeral, student demon-
strators encited the workers of the faubourg St-Antoine to
riot, crying 'Long live the Charter!' and 'Down with the
Royalists!' A rebellious crowd formed and began to move
towards the Tuileries. Louis XVIII had not, as had been his
habit, removed his court to Saint-Cloud for the summer,
for he was acutely conscious of the danger and the threat
to his throne. The crowd swelled to cries of 'Down with
the King! and 'Long live Napoleon', until, to the relief of
the government, the mob was dispersed by a torrential
downpour. Over the following months, tension mounted
and there was, by late summer, a general anxiety that the
King and the benign institutions of his reign might be overthrown. The fact that the bourgeoisie felt as threatened by
such outbursts as the *ultras* consolidated the country's move
to the right; in the elections in early November 1820, the
left captured only eighty out of 430 seats, whereas the *ultras*
obtained 160, of which seventy-five had been held during
the ill-famed *chambre introuvable*.

Against this deteriorating political situation, Alexandre
Corréard was found guilty of publishing seditious material.[17]
He had already brushed with the law and had pamphlets
confiscated, but this time he was fined and imprisoned. As
the third edition of *The Shipwreck* was to be published by
Corréard in July of the following year, embellished by eight
engravings made by Géricault and others, it seems inevitable
that, during the artist's six-month stay in Paris, they would
have met to discuss the project and that Géricault would
have become further involved in the struggles of active
French liberals.

On December 30th, 1820, Bullock's exhibition of *The
Raft of the Medusa* closed. It had been a sensational success,
drawing up to 50,000 visitors. Géricault's share of the
London takings was between 17,000 and 20,000 francs, three

to four times as much as the sum that might be offered by the French establishment when purchasing canvases of this size and importance. Spurred on by success in London, where Bullock had exploited the similarities in size between Géricault's painting and the tremendously popular, contemporary entertainment of the panorama, the impresario took *The Raft of the Medusa* to Dublin, where the commercial success of the venture was ironically compromised by competition from an immense panorama shrewdly capitalizing on the current interest in the horrors of the raft. Shortly after Bullock's exhibition opened at the Rotunda, on February 5th, 1821, a notice appeared in a Dublin newsletter announcing that:

> Messrs Marshall respectfully beg leave again to solicit the kind patronage of the Nobility, Gentry and the public of Dublin, and its vicinity, for their lately finished, entirely novel *Marine Peristrephic Panorama of the Wreck of The Medusa French Frigate and the Fatal Raft*. Also the ceremony of crossing the line. Each view Accompanied by a full and appropriate band of music. The picture is painted on nearly 10,000 sq. feet of canvas, under the direction of one of the survivors, in a superior style of brilliancy and effect – the figures on the Raft and on the boat being the size of life.[18]

A month into the exhibition of Géricault's painting, Bullock's presentation was obviously struggling in the face of the loud, popular 'peristrephic' (or revolving) panorama. He was forced to reduce his entrance fee from one shilling and eight pence to a more competitive ten pence, 'In order that all ranks may have the opportunity of viewing this stupendous production of the pencil'.[19] Although Bullock was now offering Géricault at the same price as the cheapest ticket sold by the Marshalls for their panorama at the Pavilion, by the end of March the Géricault exhibition was forced to close, whereas the panorama continued to play in Dublin thrice-daily to packed houses until June 9th. Géricault's oblique, 430 square-foot (forty-square-metre) indictment of the leaders and organizers of the Senegal expedition – his grand metaphor for the fragility of the human condition – could not compete with an extravaganza that sensationally plunged the public into the event.

Eclipsed by pizzazz, Bullock's pride forced him to bluff his reasons for closure in Dublin by boasting of a booking in Edinburgh. Yet no evidence remains of *The Raft* having been exhibited there. In any case, as the Scottish public had already marvelled at the compelling effects of the Marshalls' panorama, the claim appears to have been humbug. Bullock had been commercially outmanoeuvred. The size of the panorama, the music, the sequence of scenes presented and the boast that each picture was painted 'under the direction of one of the survivors' caught the public's imagination. Unless the Marshalls had travelled to Paris to consult the loquacious Alexandre Corréard, it is likely that such authority derived from the *Narrative of the Voyage to Senegal*, information from which introduced each of the scenes that they presented.

Géricault had not been in London for the closure of his exhibition at the end of December 1820, but he returned to England shortly afterwards for a stay of about a year. During the winter of 1821, the painter lodged near fashionable Hyde Park, where he was able to ride.[20]

Although Géricault was participating in the equestrian pleasures of upper-class London, his continuing depression led him to seek out and explore the lower depths of the industrialized city. He observed those whose lives had been wrecked by the changing order, the castaways along the wharves and in the crippled byways of the city. Vestiges of Classicism which, in certain critics' eyes, had compromised the appalling horror of *The Raft*, could have no place here: Classicism was a style incapable of depicting the personal

misery and suffering that he encountered. Through his political awakening while working on *The Raft*, Géricault's
subject matter had become man's inhumanity to man, and
here, on the streets of London, was an appalling parade of
destitution and abuse. While *The Raft* was foundering in
Dublin, Géricault was hard at work. He collaborated with
the lithographer Charles Hullmandel on a series of twelve
images contrasting aspects of life in the capital: workhorses
and thoroughbreds, industrious blacksmiths and farriers were
treated, along with uncompromising images of the urban
poor.[21]

Although it has been observed that Géricault was working
in the tradition of Hogarth, in his attitude to the destitute
there is none of that artist's overt didacticism. Géricault's
view is objective, though not unsympathetic. In the muted
compassion of his lithographs, in their elucidation of a
shameful state of affairs, Géricault emerges as the first great
visual critic of the industrial revolution.

While devoting himself to an art 'that was a novelty in
London', Géricault wrote to Dedreux-Dorcy, on February
12th, reporting that he had been 'extremely sick'. He was
also far from happy. The circumstances surrounding the otherwise flattering attentions shown to him by a married 'woman
of great fortune who was not in her first flush of youth' can
only have acted as a painful echo of his complicated relations with Alexandrine and his uncle. This mysterious woman
fell head over heels in love with Géricault, calling him the
'God of Painting', but the affair – in a mocking reminder
of his uncle's early generosity – was made awkward by the
'thousand kindnesses' her husband extended to the young
man, even offering lodgings in his house so that Géricault
could work. Otherwise, the painter admitted to his friend
that 'I don't amuse myself at all. My life is that which I led
in Paris, working a lot in my room and then, to relax myself,
prowling the streets where there is always such movement
and variety that I'm sure that you wouldn't tire of it.'

Although, at the end of September, Géricault wrote that his health was better, during this time in London he suffered an attack of sciatica, provoked by a boat trip on the Thames. When the architect Charles Cockerell, whom Géricault had met in Rome, went with the artist to view some paintings on December 1st, he noted in his diary that Géricault looked 'ill and consumptive'. Bidding goodbye to him eleven days later, Cockerell summarized the painter's questionable style of life: 'lying torpid days and weeks, then rising to violent exertions. Riding, tearing, driving, exposing himself to heat, cold, violence of all sorts.' Cockerell concluded that he feared the artist was 'in a bad way'. Indeed, during his time in London, Géricault began to suffer from the first phases of what eventually developed into tuberculosis of the spine.[22]

On December 13th, the artist travelled to Dover and embarked for France the following day. He wrote of the crossing in a letter to a fellow French painter who had been living near him on the Edgware Road, perhaps gently mocking the current enthusiasm for nautical disaster:

I could easily give you a description of a marvellous storm, paint a picture of sails ripped, the masts swept by the furious waves, the captain up against it, abandoning the rudder and the sailors, petrified, fallen on their knees to invoke St Veronica. I would rather first put you at peace and tell you simply that there was no real disorder except in our stomachs, that all the basins were used; we arrived at Calais well purged and very pale . . .

Géricault found absolutely nothing changed in France 'except the ministers, but – they don't last long'.[23]

Indeed, on December 14th, the very day Géricault crossed the Channel to return home, a new *ultra* ministry came to power. Its use of the police would differ little from the previous, more moderate administration, but this new right-wing government proved more determined in its application of repressive measures. Louis XVIII was growing weaker and this new government had the support of the *ultra* Duc d'Artois, who was moving daily closer to the throne.

Two things, however, had changed in France while Géricault was away. Firstly, the death of Napoleon on May 5th, 1821 on the island of Saint Helena had brought the various factions opposing the monarchy closer together; there were no longer Bonapartists and liberals and Orléanists, but merely an anti-monarchical left, united in opposition. Secondly, the English abolitionist William Wilberforce had begun to make efforts to enlist French liberals in his cause.

Work on *The Raft of the Medusa*, his association with Alexandre Corréard and some disturbing news emerging from the colony in Senegal swept Géricault up into an issue that would preoccupy him for the rest of his short life. The residue of the *Medusa* fiasco was leading to the exposure of one of France's greatest scandals.

13

A Larger Struggle

'My second shipwreck'

IN the early 1780s, the father of Louis-Philippe d'Orléans, the last King of France, built an oblong, arcaded quadrangle enclosing a garden divided by gravelled paths. It was the Palais Royal. Having ruined himself gambling, this Duc d'Orléans turned the place into an immense 'temple of impurity – a den of Desperation' where 'you can see everything, hear everything, know everything' and within its precincts 'you may eat, drink, sleep, bathe . . . walk, read, make love, game and, should you be tired of life, you may buy powder and ball or opium to hasten your journey across the Styx'.[1]

Haunting its galleries were pickpockets, con-men, prostitutes, gamblers, procuresses, thieves and spies. During the Restoration there were visitors of every class and nation – one English tourist remembered that 'the military costume of every army in Europe, glared and rattled in the crowd'. The Palais Royal was to Paris of the Restoration what Piccadilly Circus and Times Square have been to London and New York: the hub of things. It was a focus for excitement and buzz, and tourists would make for its riot of 'unsanctioned dissipation' where, in its gambling dens, thousands would suffer 'shipwreck of fortune and character'. As night fell, within and behind its brilliantly lit arcades the Palais Royal became a 'laboratory of Venus', 'a world in itself . . . the temple of animal gratification', full of 'the most disgusting scenes of debauchery and vice'. There, as Balzac observed in his novel *La Peau de chagrin*, 'orgies began with wine and ended with suicides in the Seine'; he went on to remark that if 'Spain has its bullfights, if Rome had its gladiators, Paris is proud of its Palais Royal.'[2]

On three sides of the quadrangle, in the arcades under the stone galleries, were about 180 shops where tradesmen of every sort sold their goods and services at inflated prices. There were restaurants, florists, jewellers, print-sellers and an early incarnation of the Paris *Bourse*, where bankers and brokers met between four and five in the afternoon to buy and sell stocks. The fourth side of the structure terminated in a double row of wooden galleries that had been constructed as a temporary space and contained tall, windowed shops lit generously by natural light. These premises were largely occupied by milliners and booksellers. The sale of books and prints was an important aspect of trade in the Palais Royal, which, despite its proximity to the Tuilieries Palace and the Louvre, was a hotbed of anti-Bourbon protest. It had been in the Palais Royal that the first Revolutionary meetings had been held in 1789. The first *tricolore* had been hoisted in its garden, and it was there that the attack on the Bastille had been organized. More recently, during the *Cent-Jours*, its Café Montansier was a hub of Napoleonic fervour. Other cafés, such as the Corazza, were also meeting places for the politically active and, in the twenty-odd reading rooms scattered about the quadrangle, such people, 'for a very moderate monthly or weekly subscription', were able to keep up to date by consulting 'all the ephemeral productions of the press . . . the different public journals, magazines, reviews and pamphlets of every description'.[3]

In the temporary wooden galleries there were about 125

shops, the occupiers of which, since 1807, had been under notice to quit so that the passage could be rebuilt in stone. While shopkeepers in the other arcades were subject to high rents, premises were cheaper in this temporary section, which may well account for the fact that it was here that Alexandre Corréard, when he obtained his licence on September 9th, 1818, set up shop at no. 258 Galerie de Bois, an address that rapidly became an evening rendezvous for literary and political men hostile to the Crown.

If the Palais Royal, this 'Babylon in miniature', was not only a honeypot of licentiousness but also a nest of sedition, then 'swarms of spies and informers' were sure to be prowling. Relatively indulgent towards moral offences, the police nonetheless kept a keen eye on political agitators. This extensive spy network was a Napoleonic legacy, and these snoops, informers, letter-interceptors and plants were now, ironically, employed by the Restoration government to keep tabs on Bonapartists and liberals. Corréard, having set himself up in the centre of things, had also raised his cantankerous profile, rendering his subversive activities highly visible to the police.[4]

Corréard had bounced back. From penniless, uncompensated and semi-invalided shipwreck victim, he had, within three years, co-written a best-selling book and started up as a bookseller. Clearly, having lost everything on board *The Medusa*, he would have needed some kind of support or sponsorship.

One way in which the liberals scored public-relations victories against the authorities was to set up subscription funds for anyone who had been exiled or imprisoned for their political views, for military widows and for the victims of disasters caused by government incompetence. The fund created by the editors of the *Mercure de France*, Etienne Jay and Benjamin Constant, in favour of the victims of *The Medusa* had grown rapidly. When, because of governmental persecution, the *Mercure* cleverly rebaptized itself *La Minerve*

française in February 1818, it was able to announce a response
to the appeal totalling 18,278 francs. Not only was the sum
substantial, but the lists of donors published over the previous
months in the *Mercure* and *Minerve* provided a demographic
insight into liberal sympathy, with money pouring in from
the professional and merchant classes, as well as from the
disaffected military and working class. Indeed, the cause met
with such national support that no self-respecting celebrity-
seeker such as Clarisse Manzon, the star witness in the
Fualdès affair, could abstain from making a donation.[5]

During February 1818, a notice was placed in the
Minerve, summoning the shipwreck victims to the newspaper's offices on March 5th. With typical French bureau-
cratic caution, they were requested to bring proof that they
had been on the raft, along with a second document proving
that they were indeed the person they claimed to be. The
fund was to be divided among the survivors. One such,
Colonel Schmaltz's secretary, Griffon du Bellay, having apol-
ogized to Savigny for the document he had signed in Saint
Louis, now accused Corréard of pocketing a disproportion-
ately large part of the money. With several of the survivors
dead, others still in Senegal and one gone off to the West
Indies, there were only a few left in France to benefit from
the cash. Although that would provide a considerable
portion for each claimant, it took the further support of
the wealthy liberal banker and Deputy, Jacques Laffitte, one
of the administrators of the *Medusa* fund – as well of one
of its first and largest benefactors – to provide Corréard
with the extra finance necessary to establish himself as a
bookseller and publisher in the Palais Royal.[6] The shipwreck victim was thus able to become one of the most
vociferous private advocates for the liberal opposition.
Publishing was, as Corréard recalled, 'a profession that, in
giving me liberty, permitted me to serve the cause of that
same liberty'.[7]

Happily, the book trade was flourishing. In the first years

of the century, improvements in the production of paper had reduced costs and this contributed to the number of titles published annually in France nearly doubling between 1812 and 1825.[8] Despite the 300-odd booksellers in Paris, Corréard – already famous as a writer – chose a promising and lucrative line of business. Early on in his new career, however, he was forced to pursue three men who had pirated *The Shipwreck* by inserting twenty-nine pages of its text into a collection entitled *History of Shipwrecks*. Corréard lost the case, the judgement somewhat spuriously maintaining that because *The Shipwreck* was 400 pages long and the *History* 1,100, the twenty-nine pages copied represented only a trifling act of piracy. Furthermore, the judge ruled that Corréard's narrative was historic and belonged to everybody, and could only be recounted using the same words. Claiming, astoundingly, that the accused had no intention of piracy and even took the trouble to praise the original work, the judge suggested that there was no cause for protest. Although, as Corréard noted in summarizing the affair, the accused had actually confessed to having taken all the words from his text, the guilty parties were absolved by what seems a decidedly unjust ruling, and Corréard was ordered to pay costs.[9]

From early on in his new career, Corréard was harassed as a bookseller and publisher. In 1819, the author of one of the first works that he published, Claude-Henri de Saint-Simon, was called before the tribunal for offences against the royal family. The author was cleared by a judgement of the Assize Court, but the work was ordered to be destroyed and new proceedings were directed against him for his follow-up pamphlet, which Corréard also published. Between 1819 and 1822, Corréard went on to publish several inflammatory and contentious works by Saint-Simon. A typical proposition offered by the author was that if France kept its craftsmen, its thinkers or its artists, but lost all its rulers, it would hardly be affected. Corréard's publication of such material drew not only police attention, but menacing anonymous letters:

> Publisher Corréard, you are a madman and a scoundrel . . . I warn you that the authorities are watching you; make sure that they do not remain unsatisfied by just seizing the absurd inanities of the vile and contemptible Saint-Simon . . .[10]

Corréard was in obvious danger and set on a collision course with the new law of May 17th, 1819, which ruled for the suppression of books that were offensive to God, to the Crown, and to public and religious morality. In 1820, with the resurgence of the right after the assassination of the Duc de Berry, it was obvious that agitators such as Alexandre Corréard would be hounded. What is more, in the face of this deteriorating situation, Corréard was expanding his activity. In the spring of 1820, his list of projected publications ran to more than 150 brochures, priced at fifty centimes each, and among which could be found such provocative titles as 'Let's Defend Our Rights', 'The Wake-Up Call', 'Let's Speak – They'll Shut-Up', 'The Alliance of the Government with the *ultras*', 'What's Bred in the Bone Will Come Out in the Flesh', 'Does the Government Have a System?' and 'The Sleep-walking Minister – a tragedy in five acts'.

Corréard was also rashly distributing seditious texts in the Royalist south. A bookseller in Montauban, instead of selling works that he received from Corréard, took them straight to the police. The *Procureur Général* of Toulouse wrote to the Director of Criminal Affairs, insisting on Corréard's audacity in 'spreading the poison of false doctrines, disorder and rebellion everywhere'. The authorities, at last, decided to bring Corréard to trial.[11]

On June 14th, 1820, Corréard and the twenty-three-year-old Jacques Bousquet-Deschamps were tried as publisher and author of a pamphlet entitled *Questions of the Day*. On April 11th, the King's Prosecutor had seized ninety-three of the 1,000 copies of the work at Corréard's bookshop, as well as the manuscript at Dupont, the printers. Consistent with Articles 1, 3 and 6 of the law of May 17th, 1819, Bousquet-Deschamps was accused of provoking the destruction of the government, and Corréard was arraigned as an accomplice. With the challenging winged head of a snake-haired Medusa printed boldly on the title page above a garland reading '*Au Naufragé de la Méduse*', it certainly appeared as if Corréard was the publisher of the work. However, the printer testified that Corréard had told him he was only its vendor. Furthermore, the bookseller maintained that he had not even read the pamphlet. Given its mere sixteen pages, its subject matter and the fact that Corréard's establishment sought to attract and serve the liberal opposition, this claim seems far-fetched, if not downright mendacious.

'The moment that a government threatens liberty,' we read in the pamphlet, 'its relationship with society ceases to be legitimate.' Although the defence counsel sought to establish that such passages were merely philosophical considerations and not incitements to violence, and despite an impassioned plea for Corréard that played on his sufferings and his valour during the *Medusa* crisis, the author was sentenced to a year in prison and a fine of 3,000 francs for encouraging civil disobedience, and the alleged publisher to four months in prison and a fine of 1,000 francs.

The authorities, keen to destroy his irksome business, had Corréard back in court nine days later. His co-defendant was, once again, Bousquet-Deschamps, this time accused of having written a pamphlet called *Attention!*, which had been published a year to the day after the law censoring books had come into effect. Designating the *ultras* as 'the mortal enemies' of France, the work reflects upon the considerable human cost of the Revolution and asserts that, in France, 'there are today a million of our young men, children of the Revolution, who have sworn to defend to their dying breath, our constitutional liberties'.

Corréard, the publisher and vendor of the work, appeared in court without the young writer. Having already been arraigned before the Assize Courts twice, Bousquet-Deschamps had in fact already fled to England to escape his penalties. On this occasion, the authorities charged the author and publisher with provoking an attack on the King's person. The Assistant Public Prosecutor pointed out that, since the restitution of the laws of censorship governing newspaper and periodical publication, several writers or publishers had adopted the tactic of launching a series of pamphlets in quick succession. He insisted that the cheapness and frequency of such pamphlets enabled the author and publisher to disseminate articles that would be censored if written for the press. The long list of titles offered cheaply by Corréard suggests that this was exactly his tactic. The Assistant Public Prosecutor, anticipating Corréard's ruse of disclaiming knowledge of the pamphlet's contents, drew attention to the brevity of the document. It was unlikely, given Corréard's political sympathies, that he would have failed to enjoy the contentious passage, restricted as it was to just eleven lines on the final page. Corréard was found guilty, sentenced to four months in prison and fined 1,200 francs. Bousquet-Deschamps, in his absence, received the stiff default penalty of five years in prison and a 6,000-franc fine.

Five days later Corréard was back in the same court, accused (once again with Bousquet-Deschamps, author of *As Things Are*) of having outraged public and religious morality. This time the bookseller was awarded three months in prison and a fine of 400 francs, and the writer a year in prison and a fine of 500 francs. The court ordered the destruction of the brochure – as it had done with the previously condemned publications.

Just under a month later, on July 26th, Corréard was

charged, along with the booksellers Béchet and Mongie, with having distributed *History of the First Fortnight of June* by Bousquet-Deschamps. They were accused of producing a work that provoked rebellion and disobedience. The printer testified that the writer had instructed him to place the names of the three booksellers on the title page. Although the two other vendors were acquitted, Corréard – dubbed by the Assistant Public Prosecutor 'a great entrepreneur of sedition' – was condemned to four months in prison and a 500-franc fine, while the absent author collected another two years in prison and a 4,000-franc fine. Maintaining his innocence throughout, Corréard claimed that the work in question had never appeared in his catalogue. On the other hand, as a bookseller it was his job to sell books that were offered to him. In answer to observations about the unhealthy relationship between himself and the accused author, Corréard simply responded that, as a bookseller, he necessarily met men like Bousquet-Deschamps when they came to buy and sell.

The following day, July 27th, as a result of a complaint made at the end of May by the Ambassador of the King of Portugal and Brazil against a pamphlet entitled *Political Documents*, Corréard found himself once again in the Assize Court. The Assistant Public Prosecutor demonstrated that the pamphlet contained the libellous contention that the aforementioned Ambassador, the Marquis de Marialva, benefiting from the lack of a legitimate sovereign, was plotting to install a new family on the Portuguese throne. Taking Corréard to task as 'no ordinary editor', the Assistant Public Prosecutor seized on the scheme behind the announcement in the bookseller's brochure, promising 'a political pamphlet per day'. He again stressed that this was nothing other 'than a Daily in another format'. Corréard was really a newspaper publisher and was therefore responsible according to the laws governing journals. The result of the hearing was that Corréard was handed down another three-month prison sentence and a 400-franc fine.[12]

Within forty-three days the Public Prosecutor's Office had initiated five proceedings against Alexandre Corréard. Not only was he being targeted as a dangerous and key subversive, but he was also clearly extremely active. Lithograph portraits of Spanish revolutionary generals who had risen up against the Bourbons were displayed in his bookshop. He published documents in support of the parliamentary candidature of the abolitionist and supposed regicide, Abbé Grégoire. Seventeen works in all had been seized from his shop that year, and, hounded by the law, Corréard went to prison.[13]

In a back street on the Left Bank of the Seine, surrounded by thick, high walls, stood Saint-Pélagie, an ancient convent and refuge for prostitutes, which was now serving as a prison for debtors and political offenders. It was the third-largest prison in Paris with a population, in the year that Corréard was committed, of nearly 650 inmates. It was split into four divisions, including a section for young offenders between eight and sixteen years old, some of whom were serving prison terms of up to six years. To the left as you entered there was the debtors' prison; on the ground floor to the right was the *Détention*, which held 200 thieves and crooks 'with names like *Massacre* and *Quatre-Sous*'. When not silently 'familiarizing themselves with the Penal Code', so that when they got out they could 'specialize in crimes that carried low maximum penalties', they were loudly clattering about in their clogs, chorusing obscene songs. Above their cacophony was the *Corridor Rouge*, home to political prisoners, a 'paradise' compared with the other parts of Saint-Pélagie. In 1820, these inmates – men of letters, journalists, booksellers, printers and soldiers from the Imperial Army – were free to wander as far as the prison's inner grille and ceded the exercise yard to the debtors only in the hottest part of the day. They were not locked up in their cells at night and had the privilege to be visited at all hours. Indeed, the freedom enjoyed by these inmates meant that the political discussions of the Palais Royal could continue, their activities merely frustrated in the short term by their inability to turn words into actions. For a price, better food was available than elsewhere in Saint-Pélagie. Certain prisoners imported their own effects and furniture to make their stay more comfortable – Corréard among them, to judge from the Motte engraving of his cell printed in the later editions of *The Shipwreck*. During the period of Corréard's incarceration, numbers grew after the failure of the Bazar Conspiracy of August 1820, which had aimed to overthrow the Bourbons by capturing the Château de Vincennes and other strategic points around Paris before instituting a Provisional Government led by the Marquis de La Fayette. A delay resulted in the discovery of the plot, and many of the conspirators were subsequently committed to Saint-Pélagie.

Despite the privileges and relative comfort, Corréard's time in prison was not one of uninterrupted calm. At 6 a.m. on the morning of August 30th, Police Commissioner Valade burst into his cell and seized works that were considered to be seditious. Forty-eight hours later, Corréard spent the day before the magistrate answering an unrelated police accusation. Two weeks later, on September 14th, he was issued with an order advising him that he would be detained in prison until he had paid the fines imposed upon him.

Since the beginning of his detention, Corréard had been petitioning to be transferred to a nursing home. Supported by a letter from Dr Piron at Saint-Pélagie, Corréard claimed that scorbutic wounds from his thirteen days on the raft frequently reopened and that he was prone to rheumatism. These pleas were made in vain and he was left in Saint-Pélagie with his fines unpaid. He wrote to the Lord Chancellor, claiming that his shop had hardly been open before his enemies earmarked him as an opposition bookseller, just because he sold – as did many of his competitors – works from across the political spectrum. He noted that five works of which he had not been the publisher were seized in 1819. The seventeen works already seized in 1820 had not been, with one exception, confiscated from the shops of his competitors. He also appealed against an unjust fine of 3,700 francs, which it would, in any case, be impossible for him to pay.

Providentially, another subscription fund came to his rescue. The text accompanying the appeal's launch pointed out that 'since 1814, magistrates have not pursued booksellers' – that is, 'until the judgement against Corréard'. Persuasive in its appeal 'to French patriotism', the subscription fund provided Corréard with the wherewithal to terminate his imprisonment on November 28th. Summing up his incarceration for allegedly publishing seditious works, Corréard called it his 'second shipwreck'.[14]

Yet Corréard remained undaunted. In 1820, as the *ultras* once again became a force to reckon with, the liberals, anxious about the future, became increasingly militant in their behaviour. By the spring of 1821, a network of secret cells of resistance was set up, known as the *Charbonnerie* – the name taken from the Italian *Carbonari*, who had revolted in Naples in 1820. According to a police report, it was at 'Corréard's bookshop in the Palais Royal' that, every evening, 'a Jacobin circle met and shared news'. Corréard was marked by the police as an influential member of the *Charbonnerie*, as well as being a man who had links with other known subversives and agitators.[15]

By naming his bookshop 'At the Victim of the Shipwreck of the Medusa', Corréard had effectively created a trademark for sedition. *The Medusa*, and all that the name had come to signify, was now the flagship of the liberal opposition. Corréard was selling and publishing his own book in its third, fourth and fifth editions and was the champion of those writers and thinkers who sought to make France a republic.

Whatever he pleaded before the courts, so long as

Corréard kept his bookshop open, he sold and published material critical of the Bourbon regime. During this period he claimed that he was the victim of a 'permanent police initiative':

> I had works seized 130 times. I was accused 36 times and condemned 9 times to a total of 8 years in prison. Unjustified action never stops, and although the confiscation of belongings had been abolished, the authorities ordered the closure of my bookshop in the Palais Royal. I was hunted. My door was sealed and it was guarded for more than a month by the gendarmes. In 1823, I was again expelled from my premises, and pressured to sell all my merchandise for a base price.[16]

Though his skirmishes against a suspicious and threatened establishment undoubtedly furthered the liberal cause, during the militant years between the opening and closing of his shop Alexandre Corréard also involved himself with the greatest humanitarian crusade of the epoch. Born of his knowledge of what was really going on in Colonel Schmaltz's Senegal, Corréard became a force in the fight against slavery.

The condemned and the dying

In Géricault's *Raft of the Medusa*, the outstretched hand of Alexandre Corréard leads the spectator's eye towards the signalling arm of the black man standing on the barrel. Corréard is, in a sense, confirming the selection and positioning of the figure, as if he himself had something to do with the decision to show a black optimistically heralding a new dawn. There are certainly elements in his book *The Shipwreck of the Frigate, The Medusa* suggesting that such a reading of the gesture is justified. In the narrative, the would-be colonist shows himself eager to understand the cultures of various African peoples. He questions earlier writers such as Adanson, who noted that 'the Moors . . . either made captives, or killed, such Europeans, as had the misfortune to be ship-wrecked on their coast'. By contrast, Savigny's and Corréard's account of the interview that the naturalist Kummer had with the Moorish King Zaide revealed the ruler's civilization, his self-interested but intelligent curiosity about Napoleon and the *Cent-Jours* and his fair-mindedness. Furthermore, Corréard's choice of a portrait of King Zaide for the frontispiece of the second edition was surely a provocative act, suggesting that it was this comparatively enlightened ruler, rather than the barbarian Frenchmen Chaumareys or Schmaltz – or even Louis XVIII – who was the worthiest figure to preside over a book about events that occurred along the West African coast. The juxtaposition of Zaide's seemingly impeccable leadership with the maelstrom of French incompetence and cowardice that litters the pages of *The Shipwreck* acts as a strong reproach.[17]

Savigny's and Corréard's text, even in its earliest editions, made it clear that the eventual health and success of any colonial project depended on the abolition of slavery. When they published the information that the slave trade was thriving in Senegal, it was a provocative and, for many, surprising revelation. Although reports were beginning to circulate that French slave ships were active along the West African coast, slavery, at that time, was not widely discussed. Their narrative therefore makes a trail-blazing contribution to the burgeoning abolitionist critique of the French government's continued and devious complicity with the trade. The timely appearance of the third edition of *The Shipwreck*, just weeks after Benjamin Constant made a celebrated abolitionist speech to both Chambers, again demonstrates Corréard's ability to exploit opportunity. Abolitionism, with the growing awareness of the persistent flouting of France's anti-slave-trade laws, was newsworthy and the text would capitalize on the growing concern about what was actually going on in Senegal.[18]

A Larger Struggle

England had dominated the slave trade in the second half of the eighteenth century. But, under increasing pressure from humanitarian thinkers, coupled with a commercial desire to exploit the natural resources rather than the manpower of West Africa, the English abolished the slave trade in 1807. Although in France slavery and the slave trade had been ended by the *Convention* in January 1794, Napoleon had reversed the decree in May 1802. With the return of the Bourbons, England urged France, once again, to renounce the trade, but the artful Talleyrand, the principal architect of the Treaty of Paris, negotiated a five-year delay in implementing the ban, a period during which tax incentives were actually made available to stimulate the lucrative activity. As the French abolitionist Abbé Grégoire noted in a tract published in England:

> it is stipulated, that, for five years longer, the French shall be allowed to . . . steal or buy the natives of Africa, to tear them from their native country, from every object of their affections, to transport them to the West Indies, where, sold as beasts of burden, they shall moisten, with their labour, that soil, the fruits of which shall belong to others, and shall drag out a painful existence, with no other consolation at the close of each day, than that of having taken another step towards the grave.

When Napoleon returned for the *Cent-Jours*, seeking to appease England he declared the trade illegal and, on his second return to the throne, Louis XVIII, much indebted to the English, could hardly do anything but maintain abolition.[19] However, while his Ministry of Foreign Affairs was attempting to mollify the English, DuBouchage was besieged by ship-builders, ship owners and the Chambers of Commerce in ports such as Nantes and Bordeaux, who were anxious not to lose so abundant a source of income. About thirty of the naval officers who, at the outset of the

225

Restoration, had been forcibly retired on half-pay and thus denied their livelihood, had turned instead to the slave trade and, in 1816, at least thirty-six slaving ships plied their trade from French ports.[20]

Contemporary accounts of the appalling inhumanity and degradation of this commerce were appearing in English. The noted abolitionist Thomas Clarkson described the now-infamous conditions of the transatlantic crossing:

> In the best regulated ships, a full-grown man has no more space allowed him to lie upon than sixteen English inches in breadth, which gives him about as much room as a man has in his coffin, and about two feet eight inches in height. But there are very few vessels in which even this limited allowance is afforded . . . Besides this they are naked; and they have nothing to lie upon but the bare boards: on this account they suffer often very severely from the motion of the ship, which occasions different parts of their bodies to be bruised, and which causes their irons to excoriate their legs.
>
> But the situation is the most deplorable when it blows a heavy gale, and when the hatches or gratings are obliged to be fastened down. Their sufferings are, at this time, such as no language can describe. They are often heard, on such occasions, to cry out in their own language, 'We are dying, we are dying'.

Clarkson went on to describe that when they had 'fainted from heat, stench and corrupted air', they were brought up on deck where, affected by dysentery, they covered the planks 'with blood and mucus like a slaughterhouse'.[21]

In March 1820, an English squadron patrolling the West African coast boarded *La Jeune Estelle* and discovered two slaves crushed into casks in an attempt to conceal them. Another twelve had been flung overboard in the barrels that Commander Sir George Collier had noticed bobbing about

on the sea as they had approached the French ship, jettisoned by a captain hoping to escape the penalties of being
caught engaging in the forbidden trade. The French were
clearly continuing to participate in a traffic that they had,
once again, outlawed in 1818.

The Marquis of Lansdown stated in the House of Lords,
in July 1819, that the slave trade was 'carried on to a very
great extent under the flag of France'; and, three years later,
a distressed Thomas Babington wrote from Paris, 'No
member of the Ministry cares a fig for the abolition of the
Slave Carrying Trade, and many are really interested in its
continuance.' There were, however, voices beginning to be
raised against what Benjamin Constant called 'the unspeak-
able and sacrilegious commerce' that had, in the previous
quarter of a century, carried off more than 1.5 million
Africans.[22]

The sheer barbarity of the trade had been recorded in
Geoffrey de Villeneuve's *L'Afrique*, which had appeared in
Paris in 1814. He describes how the tribes from the north
side of the River Senegal would cross it on horseback in
bands of about twenty well-armed men. When they drew
close to a targeted village, they would watch and wait near
a spring until the women and children came for water.
Seizing them, they would carry their prize back to their
horses, fixing their victim's fingers between their teeth, ready
to bite if anyone cried out. Alternatively, they might attack
by night, yowling savagely as they set fire to an entire village
and capturing their prey as they fled the flames. Their prisoners were, at length, brought to the European trading posts
in single file, necks bolted into two-metre-long, forked
wooden yokes. The traders to whom the captives were sold
inspected the merchandise thoroughly; if a tooth was missing
or the eye dull, that would lower the price. They put the
captives through their paces, making them run, jump and
speak, and subjecting the women to a humiliating examination by a doctor. Breast size, held to be an indication of

fertility, partly determined their price, while the physique of the men, often acquired for studding, determined their value. Once purchased, they would arrive in Saint Louis or Gorée, where they were chained, branded and left, sometimes for months, in dark, dank, infected prisons in which dysentery was rife, awaiting transportation. While Europeans slowly became aware of the full horror of the trade and the degree to which their own countries were complicit, certain African peoples, obviously encouraged by local white slave traders, were reluctant to forgo the profitable commerce.[23]

When Julien Schmaltz eventually took possession of Senegal from the English on January 25th, 1817, he was instructed to rebuild forts, strengthen trading posts and re-establish relations with local chieftains. He was to improve hygiene, combat disease and spread Christianity. Slavery in the colony was to be terminated and blacks were to become hired labour, working to purchase their freedom. Schmaltz was, in short, supposed to transform what was little more than a military and commercial base into a tolerable settlement.

With severely depleted troops as a result of the shipwreck, and with disease devastating the camp on Cap Vert, Schmaltz set about reorganizing the remaining troops into two battalions, which, by mid-December, were strengthened by reinforcements arriving from France. He was then able to turn his attentions to costly – and often impractical – projects for establishing plantations, as well as to planning expeditions to explore and forge trading relations with the interior. But Schmaltz seemed to be curiously dilatory in carrying matters forward. It was not, for example, until the autumn of 1817 that an expedition – in which Brédif and Dechatelus were charged to assess the commercial interest of the natural resources around and about the River Senegal – was ready to depart. They made their way upriver, until, after two months, they were forced to turn back because of

Brédif's deteriorating health. Arriving in Saint Louis on December 29th, the man who had kept an eyewitness account of his first voyage, shipwreck and survival in the Sahara was dead in a matter of weeks.

Procrastination, bluff and a certain dissipation of his energies seem to have compromised Schmaltz's large plans and promises. A laxity was apparent in his sanctioning of the shameful plunder of *The Medusa* by the merchant ships of Saint Louis, and once Senegal came back into French hands he unhesitatingly revealed his appetite for less arduous and more rapid ways to enrich himself and his colony.[24]

A series of letters from English observers to the directors of the African Institution in London leave us in little doubt that when Schmaltz took repossession of Senegal, 'slave deals were waiting to be concluded as soon as the British quit the colony'. By June, a Mr Macauley writes that 'the coast is crowded with slave ships'. In July, the slave trade was seen to be 'raging dreadfully on the coast' and 'Gorée is become quite an emporium'. Writing from Saint Louis on November 8th, 1817, an Englishman gives a clear picture of how radically things had changed in the first nine months of Schmaltz's administration:

> To give you an idea of the extent to which this traffic has been carried on, I need only mention that four French vessels have been loaded here, the cargoes averaging, by the best information I can obtain, about 100 slaves each; and there are two schooners now in the river waiting for their cargoes which they have contracted for.

Lamenting that war had broken out between the peoples of the interior who had been unscrupulously armed by the slave traders, the correspondent continues:

> It must no doubt surprise you, as it does me, and the few English who remain in this settlement, that after the

solemn manner in which the French Government engaged to Abolish the Trade, that it should be carried on here so openly without any interruption from the authorities.

In March 1818, the trade is seen to be 'horribly increasing' and another correspondent notes that untold numbers of slaves are taken by Damiel, one of the most powerful kings in this part of Africa:

Damiel destroys his country, and for the purpose of selling for Rum and tobacco the last of his people, he has established a residence at Gandiol, nine miles down the river. What are the natives to think of the promise so repeatedly made by us, of the Slave Trade being abolished.

Arriving in London later that year, one of the correspondents reported that he had been spurned by Colonel Schmaltz. When he had confronted Schmaltz on the subject of slavery, the French governor snapped that it was none of his business and said 'that he would receive no information from him on the subject'. This eyewitness was convinced that the only time the administration interfered with the traders was when they were denied a rake-off from the profits.[25]

Coming under a good deal of pressure from the English during the winter and spring of 1818, the French pushed through an insufficient statute that punished a slave trader more leniently than a thief who had stolen a loaf of bread. The law, introduced by the Minister of the Navy, Comte Molé, provoked a thriving clandestine commerce; and Molé's successor, the Baron Portal, a Bordeaux merchant and Anglophobe, appeared indifferent to increases in the traffic. Such an attitude was hardly likely to placate abolitionists and liberals in France, particularly as appalled French residents and visitors to the colony wrote that Governor Julien

Schmaltz was encouraging and participating in the renewed trade.[26]

During the wreck of *The Medusa*, Schmaltz had exhibited scant regard for human life. It now seemed that rather than proceeding industriously to establish a genuine agricultural colony in Senegal, he appeared content to live off the ruin of the indigenous population. The Corsican priest Jean-Vincent Giudicelly, *préfet apostolique* to Senegal and Gorée, was well placed to observe the activities of the Governor. Giudicelly was unequivocal in his condemnation of both Schmaltz and his deputy. On the first page of an 1820 pamphlet he writes of 'the execrable commerce in human flesh . . . conducted in Senegal and Gorée under the administrations of Schmaltz and Fleuriau'. After his arrival in the colony in 1816, and during Schmaltz's 'calamitous administration', Giudicelly witnessed 'hundreds of unfortunate blacks embarked'.[27]

Schmaltz was temporarily recalled to Paris in late 1817, arriving with his depressed wife Reine, who had succumbed to a fifth attack of mania. In Paris, the Governor defended himself against accusations that emanated from the English press. Schmaltz reassured the Minister of his 'good faith', successfully whitewashing himself and deviously diverting blame onto Lieutenant-Colonel Gavot, the commander of Gorée. Schmaltz secured more troops for the colony and steamboats to navigate the River Senegal. He also discussed plans to replace undisciplined soldiers, who were poorly adapted to the climate, with natives – slaves bought from their owners and press-ganged for a period of ten to twelve years as sappers and workmen.[28]

During Schmaltz's absence from the colony, the interim governor, Aimé-Benjamin Fleuriau, selectively intercepted and seized certain ships suspected of slaving, while allowing the trade to continue elsewhere. *The Times* published a list of five French ships that were loaded in Senegal between November 9th, 1817 and March 19th, 1818 – ships from ports such as Nantes, Marseille and Bordeaux – noting that, as of mid-March, some were back, anchored in the River Senegal, waiting – along with two other ships – to be reloaded.[29]

By the end of June 1818 a French patrol route had been set up in an attempt to intercept and arrest slavers, but perversely the inconvenience of eluding capture made the trade more difficult – and therefore even more profitable – for those who escaped the authorities. What is more, interception did not lead to prevention, as some ships carried two captains on board and, when one captain was arrested, the other took over and the voyage continued.

When Schmaltz returned to Senegal, he pretended to make a stand against slavery by arraigning the owners and captain of *The Scholastique*, who were guilty of carrying a secret cargo of twenty blacks.[30] But this was mere public relations and the traffic, as Giudicelly recorded, was allowed to thrive:

> in the streets of the colony, as in the surrounding countryside, all unknown or unprotected blacks were arrested, sold, and embarked . . . What then is Monsieur Schmaltz doing, who claims there is no slave trade? He goes every morning to spend four hours in the *captiverie* of Potin, his accomplice, his consultant, his preferred . . . I heard publicly from several slave traders their complaints against Schmaltz who has given Potin an exclusive monopoly of the trade.

Corruption was evidently rife, and Giudicelly even coined a word for letters, ready for dispatch from the colony, being tampered with or censored: '*schmalisées*' or 'Schmaltzified'.[31]

There are reasons, perhaps, for questioning these reports about the extent and flagrancy of Schmaltz's and Fleuriau's involvement in the slave trade. Giudicelly was angry with both men over the question of arrears of pay, as well as the costs of his passage back to France. His anger may have led him to exaggerate the faults of men 'who can better manage their own interests than the affairs of the King'. Likewise, the British, who never doubted the desirability of Senegal, would not miss the opportunity to denounce or exaggerate a traffic which a good number of European governments had condemned as being 'repugnant to the principles of humanity and universal morality'.[32]

However, we also have the testimony of another witness – the agricultural botanist Joseph Morenas – who arrived in the colony in July 1818 as part of a team that would explore the River Senegal. Between his arrival and his departure in November 1819, Morenas confirmed many of Giudicelly's observations, stating that 'Saint Louis continues to be a market where these unfortunate Africans are sold publicly'. He noted that blacks were loaded for America from Potin's wharf, that the big traders such as the merchant Durécu went unpunished, and that Schmaltz and his aide-de-camp, Gouraud, were implicated in the trade. Morenas even claimed that a *captiverie*, or holding pen for slaves, was opened in the offices of the Navy by Colbrant, a member of Schmaltz's administrative team, and he provided a harrowing vision of the state of affairs in Senegal:

On 1st, December, 1817, a mother arrived in Saint Louis to free her ten-year-old son. His proprietor demanded eight-and-a-half ounces of gold. The unfortunate woman had only six and promised to go and fetch some more. Even before leaving, she was captured in the streets of Saint Louis. In her despair, she committed suicide by bashing her head against a wall. On 17th of the same month, the father, hoping to find justice under the flag of the King, came to Saint Louis to ask about his son, his wife and his gold. The reply he received was to be clapped in irons. When they offered him food, he drove a nail into his heart, screaming, 'God will avenge me in another world'.[33]

The government, needing to protect French commerce while, at the same time, wishing to appear receptive to persistent international pressure, was facing a dilemma. In 1819, the Baron Mackau was dispatched by the Minister of the Navy to refute the English accusation that slavery was thriving on the West African coast and to discredit the slanders heaped on the French governor of Senegal. Mackau's suppression of incriminating evidence, and his contention that accusations over slavery were 'odious calumnies', provoked Morenas to petition the government with an eyewitness account. He presented this *Petition Against the Slave Trade* before the Chamber of Deputies on June 14th, 1820.

The fact that this did not quite create the stir that his fellow abolitionists had hoped – the Minister skilfully dismissed it – did not deter men such as Giudicelly, Abbé Grégoire and La Fayette from making themselves heard. Morenas had, in fact, penned the first French abolitionist petition and the text was published by Alexandre Corréard. During the summer of 1820, Corréard's bookshop in the Palais Royal (its proprietor already condemned to prison) was used as the address at which readers could participate in the abolitionist debate.[34]

In the face of growing concern over legal abuses in the colony, supported by a swelling volume of evidence, Schmaltz was soon removed. He left Saint Louis on August 31st, 1820, his departure having been delayed by his wife succumbing to yet another attack of mania. Although the slave trade was far from finished, Corréard had helped to bring down the inhuman commander who had done him and thousands of others so much damage. The accounts written by Giudicelly in 1820, and by Morenas in 1820 and 1821, drew attention to the cause. Increased weight was added to the abolitionist movement by that important speech to the two Chambers by Benjamin Constant in June 1821 and by a lengthy address to the Chamber of Peers by the Duc de Broglie in March 1822. Several years later, Morenas produced his *Short History of the Slave Trade*, a text that benefited from his knowledge of the writings of the British abolitionists Thomas Clarkson and William Wilberforce. Nonetheless, 500-odd slave ships set sail from France or French colonial ports between 1818 and 1831, when a more rigorous law against the trade was passed. This was followed, seventeen years later, by a decree abolishing slavery in all French possessions.[35] During the years in which the transatlantic trade thrived, France transported fewer than half the number of slaves that England shipped, but it was in the last decades of that traffic that the pressure brought to bear by British abolitionists led to a rise in French consciousness. Slowly, a trade was suppressed that Morenas prophesied would 'shock future generations' — a trade that had ripped the heart and soul out of the peaceful residents of Senegal.[36]

Théodore Géricault's awareness of the international humanitarian liberal struggle had been stimulated by his close association with the circle of intellectuals, artists and soldiers who congregated in the studio of his neighbour, Horace Vernet, and through his friendship with Alexandre Corréard. His *Raft of the Medusa* had appeared before the public as the abolitionist movement in France was just beginning to coalesce. In June 1819, the influential La Fayette spoke out on the subject. In August of the same year, Benjamin Constant published a translation of *The Thirteenth Report of the Directors of the African Institution* in *La Minerve*, which revealed the true state of things in Senegal.[37]

As Géricault had distorted the facts of the raft by presenting bodies less emaciated than they were and by effacing the overt signs of cannibalism, so he modified the truth to make his plea for blacks. The account published by

Savigny and Corréard speaks of only one black survivor on the raft, whereas Géricault includes three, two of whom are very much alive. Writing about *The Raft of the Medusa* in 1845, the art critic Charles Blanc observed of the black man signalling against the sky that he is:

> . . . not in the bottom of the hold but the one who saves everybody. Isn't it admirable how great adversity has, all at once, re-established equality between the races? It's a poor slave who rescues these spurned and enslaved men and it takes place on the same coast where we go to take his brothers and put them in captivity.[38]

Spurred on by the growing momentum of French abolitionism, by his continuing friendship with Corréard, and by his now firmly established habit of responding to the topical issues of the day, Géricault embarked on the preparatory drawings for what would be a shocking image, intended to bring home to the public the inhumanity of a Senegalese slave market. Certainly the way slavers split up families – carrying off children, tearing them from their mothers and their fathers – resonated deeply in the painter's own psyche.[39]

Sadly, *The Slave Trade* never got beyond the planning stage: Géricault's deteriorating health and finances took care of that. He had returned from his long English visit in a precarious condition: his sciatica remained uncured and he was suffering from an overwhelming weariness caused by the early phase of tuberculosis of the spine. This physical weakness was soon compounded by two riding accidents. The exact circumstances of the first of these vary in early accounts: Géricault was out riding, either alone or with Vernet, when his particularly feisty horse threw him head over heels and he came down on his back onto either a stone or the knot of his belt. Whichever it was, the object pushed between two vertebrae, reactivating the infectious focus of the tuberculosis and provoking abscesses. Other accounts say that Géricault landed on his sciatic thigh, resulting in an abscess on his leg. Shortly afterwards, when the painter was travelling by carriage, a horse bolted, leaving him stranded. Determined to finish his journey on horseback, which in his condition would prove extremely painful, the artist suggested lancing an abscess in order to make the journey less awkward. Fortunately, he was prevented by those who were with him. As if bent on self-destruction, shortly afterwards he met with another accident that ended his days as a horseman. Galloping in the Champs-de-Mars, Géricault collided with another rider. The shock of the impact opened an abscess and confined him to his bed.[40] Accident and illness prevented him from preparing anything for the Salon of 1822, but he visited the exhibition and was struck particularly by Delacroix's debut, saying of the small, powerful *Barque of Dante* that it was a painting 'I would like to sign'.

An unsuccessful campaign to purchase *The Scene of a Shipwreck* for the King's own collection had been started shortly after the 1819 Salon by the sympathetic Comte Forbin, Director of Museums. In 1822, Forbin renewed his efforts to persuade the government to purchase Géricault's masterpiece for a sum of 6,000 francs. Forbin's plan was to place it in one of the large galleries at Versailles, arguing that it was a work highly esteemed both by French artists and by the general public in England. Perfectly aware that the subject matter would continue to prove a stumbling block for the government, Forbin unsuccessfully presented the canvas as revealing 'man struggling against a cruel death ... a homage to Providence which aided these unfortunate people', rather than 'a critique of the incompetence which abandoned them to danger'.[41]

By the beginning of 1823 Géricault's tuberculosis was firmly established. The disease, which had started with a bacterial infection in the lungs, had spread to other parts of his body, where it lay dormant until it slowly destroyed his spinal column. Géricault was visited by the King's eminent physician, Dupuytren, who diagnosed 'bone decay', and by another doctor, Laurent-Théodore Biett, who tended him regularly and, in token of gratitude, was presented with a sketch for the *Medusa*. Géricault was not, at this stage, completely bed-ridden, but he was depressed by the delays surrounding the Crown's purchase of his masterpiece.

The painter's melancholy and his delicate balance of health were not helped by the bankruptcy, in mid-August, of the stockbroker Félix Mussart, who fled Paris with about 78,000 francs of his clients' money, leaving enormous debts in his wake. Mussart had undertaken investments on the stock exchange for a circle of liberal friends, including Géricault. Much of the painter's considerable inheritance had been sacrificed to his expensive lifestyle, including the maintenance of several horses, as well as the purchase of the time in which to pursue his art. Left in dire straits after the added loss of the investment made by Mussart, Géricault, on the advice of his friends Colonel Bro and Dedreux-Dorcy, sold some work. The ailing painter was astonished that he raised 13,000 francs from the sale of small paintings, whereas the French government, when faced with a cost of 5,000–6,000 francs for *The Scene of a Shipwreck*, seemed unable to come to any conclusion about its purchase.[42]

During the last weeks of 1823, Géricault's disease became agonizing. He was wasting away. On November 30th, he made his will in favour of his father, Georges-Nicolas, who, two days later, made his own will in favour of Georges-Hippolyte, his unfortunate grandson, Géricault's illegitimate child. At the end of December, Delacroix described in his journal a visit he had paid to Géricault a few days earlier:

> He is dying; his emaciation is dreadful to see – thighs no thicker than my arms and a head like that of an ancient, dying man. I want him to live with all my heart but I dare not hope any longer . . . To die in the midst of all

this, which he has created in the full vigour and fire of his youth. And now, he cannot even turn in his bed without assistance![43]

In the early weeks of the new year, Géricault was close to the end. He had sufficient strength to make a drawing of his left hand, with its transparent skin revealing sinew and bone – some morbid curiosity seeming to motivate him, as it had done in his studies of the amputated limbs during his work on the *Medusa*. Indeed, he was so thin that he had taken on the haunting look of a raft survivor. He had reached the state, starved of life, in which he appears in a posthumous portrait painted by his friend Alexandre Corréard, the fiery '*Jacobin*' whom he had first met in a studio littered with death.

On January 17th–18th, 1824, Géricault suffered the excruciating pain of surgery. To no avail. He asked the lawyer Champion de Villeneuve to act as an adviser to his distant son, and, as he drew near death, he repeated over and over again the phrase 'Nothing replaces the love of a mother'. He may have been thinking of his own, supportive mother, who had died before he was old enough to show her how truly he merited her encouragement; but, most probably, he was dwelling on the predicament of his son, estranged from his mother, Géricault's own beloved, Alexandrine-Modeste Caruel.

In the early morning of Monday, January 26th, Théodore Géricault died, aged exactly thirty-two years and four months. Delacroix was painting the baby searching for the mother's breast in the *Massacre of Chios* when he heard the news the following morning: 'I cannot get used to the idea. Although everyone must have known that we would inevitably lose him before long, I almost felt that we could conjure death away by refusing to accept the idea. But death would not relinquish its prey, and tomorrow the earth will hide what little remains of him.'[44]

The funeral took place at the chapel of Saint-Jean-Porte-Latine on January 28th. The oration was delivered by the lawyer Mocquard, the man who had unsuccessfully defended Corréard in his trials of 1820. Mocquard spoke of the indefatigable dedication of those close friends who had attended the painter during his illness, most of whom had gathered on that bleak mid-winter day to mourn. One striking member of the congregation was the shipwrecked Turk, Mustapha, whom Géricault had found wandering the streets of Paris and had taken on as a domestic. The howling man stood a little apart and, according to the custom of his country, flung fistfuls of cinders at his head as a sign of grief. Among the other mourners were the Baron Jean-Baptiste Caruel de Saint-Martin and his wife, Alexandrine-Modeste. She had most probably not laid eyes on her handsome and beloved protégé since the early days of her pregnancy. Their son, Georges-Hippolyte, would now be left alone in the world, aged five and a half, prohibited by all the pressure of propriety from meeting his mother, denied by fate from ever knowing his father and not even carrying his name.

14

The Shipwreck and the Shipwrecked

WHILE Géricault had been wasting away, the King's health had also been deteriorating. By the summer of 1824, Louis XVIII was blind and could barely speak. Wet and dry gangrene attacked the base of his spine and his right foot, and on September 16th he died, leaving his younger brother, the *ultra*, Duc d'Artois, to become Charles X.[1] Corréard later summed up the ills of Louis's reign by stating that the Bourbons 'gave all the jobs to . . . their old and new accomplices who immediately and throughout our territory started to vex, plunder and massacre the citizens'. He might have added that Louis XVIII and his beloved Elie Decazes had skilfully used the *Medusa* catastrophe to their own political advantage, without doing anything for those people whose lives had been wrecked.[2]

A month after Corréard's licence was revoked, he obtained permission from the *Préfet de Police* to sell up his stock. There were more proceedings against him in 1823 and 1824, and after a number of serious judgements, Corréard at last took the advice that had been offered to him by Major Peddie when he had been hospitalized in Saint Louis – he fled to England, a decision that enabled him to escape the various sentences still pending.[3] The transportation of people by rail was only a few years away, and Corréard, who had fled to a 'country more of industry than of liberty', threw off the wearisome mantle of subversive publisher and busied himself with projects to construct railways. Not that this activity in any way stifled his spirits or made his passage through life any easier.

While he was building his new career as a railway engineer, the guilty architects of Corréard's misery fared less well. After being relieved of the governorship of Senegal in August 1820, Julien Schmaltz continued to work for the French administration, first in Mexico and then as Consul-General in Smyrna, where he died in 1827, apparently with little money to his name, a condition that suggests his profits from the illicit trade in Senegal had either been squandered or had not been spectacular.[4]

The man directly responsible for the shipwreck had a more pathetic fate. On release from prison, Hugues Duroy de Chaumareys retired to the small town of Haute-Vienne, where he lived with his family in disgrace and poverty amid the fading beauty of the Château de Lachenaud. He was consumed by remorse, and it was rumoured that he slept on vine shoots to atone for his failings. Although some sympathizers tried to obtain Géricault's painting of the raft in order to rip it up and efface the memory of the terrible event, the catastrophe pursued Chaumareys to the end. He was effectively forced to shut himself up in the garden of his château, because each time he walked abroad he was booed by peasants whose children pelted him with stones. His wife, Sophie, died in 1837, and his younger son, who had refused to marry because he did not wish to perpetuate the line, died the following year. The older son did, however, marry and produced four children. Three years after Chaumareys's death in 1841, this older son, crippled by debt, had his possessions seized and sold. He broke under the strain and committed suicide, his wife dying six months later, orphaning their four children, all of whom were under six years old.[5]

The other officers on the 1816 expedition to Senegal had varied fates. Joseph Reynaud, the man who was alleged to have cut the towropes, died in 1832, after contriving to remain largely port-bound. The energetic, brave and kindly Jean Espiaux was carried off by tetanus in Brazil in 1835 after an illustrious career. Pierre-Joseph Lapeyrère retired as a captain of a frigate in 1827, having been much troubled by a herpetic infection contracted during his march through the Sahara in the summer of 1816. Maudet died in 1845 with the rank of captain of a corvette, as did Chaudière in 1841, having contracted chronic dysentery during an expedition to Mexico. Sander Rang died of sunstroke in 1844 while he was governor of Nossi-Be in Madagascar. After a succession of commands, Gicquel des Touches, captain of *The Loire*, retired in 1845 to become Director of the Port of Brest. Captain Léon Parnajon of *The Argus*, the man who, because of a change in wind direction, had found the raft, rose to become captain of a frigate by the time he retired in 1837. Jean-Daniel Coudein, whose behaviour on the raft had been deemed 'courageous and zealous' by the Director of Navy Personnel, found himself involved in the shipwreck of *The Gloriole* in 1823. Surviving it, he went on to a long and successful career, reaching the rank of captain of a man-of-war in 1850 and retiring in 1853. Cornette de Vénancourt, despite the distinction of his seamanship, suffered after the July Revolution of 1830, never making the rank of admiral, which should have been the obvious conclusion to his long and distinguished career.[6]

After producing a self-vindicating thesis on calenture in 1818, Henri Savigny distanced himself from any of the controversies that raged around the wreck and its aftermath. He married the girl he had left behind him in 1816, and between 1821 and 1829 served as Mayor of Soubise, a village near Rochefort. In 1831 he received the *Légion d'honneur* from King Louis-Philippe, as did the other survivors of the raft. Until his death in 1843, frequently ill and haunted by horrific scenes, Savigny remained embittered, melancholic and racked by grief. When his wife died, the keepsake she had given to the surgeon as a 'Godspeed' before he set out on the doomed expedition, discoloured by sea water and stained with blood, was placed in her coffin.[7]

Alexandre Corréard's technique for survival was relentless action and agitation. Having returned to France by 1831, he found himself back in his old role of protesting to the government on behalf of the victims of Restoration injustice. Throughout the 1830s and 1840s, however, he passed a chequered time developing projects for railways. In 1838 he found his competence questioned for grossly underestimating the cost of the Paris–Versailles route. In 1842 he found himself embroiled in a quarrel over who first carried out the surveys for the Paris–Bordeaux line. And in the mid-1840s, seeking compensation for ten years' work and the considerable costs he had sustained, he learned that the government had refused to grant him the concession on this project. Seemingly wearied by such endless struggles, he retired, with his wife Hortense, to the Château des Basses-Loges, a property of twelve hectares of gardens and orchards situated in the middle of a forest at Avon, near Fontainebleau. It would seem that Corréard had, at last, discovered a haven from the battles of the world. But not so. Finding cause to involve himself in lawsuits with his neighbours, he also, in 1848, proposed himself as a candidate for the Chamber of Deputies, advertising himself as 'the engineer of *The Medusa*'. Taking the historic opportunity offered in 1848 to shrug off the Bourbon yoke, Corréard predictably proposed a grand reform of the Constitution, tax and budget cuts, and supported Louis Napoleon. His disposition remained embittered and his endless offensive zeal was one way of never allowing himself to become too preoccupied with some of the unanswered questions surrounding the wreck and the raft.[8]

Among the officers, crew and passengers on board *The*

Medusa, there had been a number of people who, for a variety of reasons – personal and political – recorded their adventures. These notes or narratives are often contradictory. The various writers had seen things differently. What is more, their trudge through the desert or drifting in the raft had resulted in a delirium in which actions and motives, like the hours and days, kaleidoscoped into one another. Charles-Marie Brédif is alone in having made on-the-spot notes. Otherwise, the only surviving record kept during the voyage was Captain Vénancourt's log. On board *The Echo*, Vénancourt could cast only a wary eye over the dubious manoeuvres made by Captain Chaumareys.

Others who provided accounts of the voyage did so after the event. Charlotte Picard, who married Dard, the schoolmaster in Saint Louis and published under her married name, alleges that among her reasons for chronicling her adventure was the opportunity it offered of correcting 'what is wanting in exactitude' in the famous narrative by Savigny and Corréard. Her corrections mainly concern her slog through the desert and she quite reasonably asks, 'how could they know from their raft, what took place . . . in the Sahara?' To be fair to the authors, they did have access to the survivors of both desert marches, as well as the benefit of Brédif's notes, with which, as early as the second edition, they augmented their own story. In any case, Charlotte Picard's emendations are slight and one of the principal aims of her narrative is consistent with that of Savigny and Corréard: she berates Governor Schmaltz, who favoured the rights of the large commercial enterprises of Saint Louis over those of colonists seeking to establish plantations. Above all, she seeks to vindicate her father, who had received no help from the leaders whom he had criticized so frankly during the events of July 1816, and who died in the colony in August 1819.[9]

The narrative by the Royalist and Protestant Midshipman Sander Rang is not always to be trusted. He praises the efficacy of Colonel Schmaltz and, on the subject of the evacuation of *The Medusa*, writes that Chaumareys's barge had taken as many people as it could carry – sheer self-exculpation, as he had been among the twenty-eight people on board a boat that could easily have accommodated fifty. Rang suggests that the cry of '*Vive le roi*' resounding from the various lifeboats was a 'cry of love, a sound that rallies all good Frenchmen' and that it 'gave us strength and increased our desire to save everybody'. This is either a naive evaluation of the scene or empty bombast.

Like Rang, Anglas de Praviel and Schmaltz's secretary, Griffon du Bellay, are, in their respective accounts, very much at odds with Savigny and Corréard. An annotated copy of the second edition of *The Shipwreck of the Frigate, The Medusa*, in which page after page reveals Griffon du Bellay's refutation or contradiction of its authors, does not, however, deny the principal circumstances of the events chronicled.[10]

Savigny and Corréard saw themselves, first and foremost, as victims of incompetent leadership, which, in turn – and particularly in Corréard's estimation – revealed the insufficiencies of the new regime. Yet they also had some bizarre events and dubious actions to explain away, and to that end, throughout their narrative, it was necessary for them to create impeccable characters for themselves. Of their choosing to go on the raft they write, 'Monsieur Savigny . . . might have stayed on board a boat, but an invincible attachment to his duty made him forget the danger'. Corréard, who 'among others, was to go in one of the boats', finding that his workmen were being forced aboard the raft, 'thought that in his capacity as commander of engineers, it was his duty not to separate from the majority of those who were in his care'. Their noble blend of duty, compassion and loyalty is pitched to contrast with the selfish character of the leaders of the expedition. Nonetheless, as if to pre-empt any charges that might be levelled against them for their actions on the raft, they grant a degree of sympathy to those who abandoned them, while leaving us in no doubt as to their guilt: 'in forsaking the raft, the minds of those who did so were greatly agitated, and the desire of withdrawing themselves from danger made them forget that a hundred and fifty unfortunate men were going to be abandoned to the most cruel sufferings'. Such unexpected empathy for their oppressors surely serves no other purpose than to encourage readers to be lenient in their judgement of the two authors for whatever atrocities took place on board the raft. By way of pleading their cause, Savigny and Corréard frequently crave the reader's indulgence.[11]

Savigny's explanation of calenture is deployed as an irrefutable defence. He claims that delirium seized the minds of those on board the raft as early as the second night. The 'hallucinations', the 'burning fever', the 'insanity', the sensation of inhabiting a 'horrendous dream' indemnified them for the horrors of the following days: the slaughter, the cannibalism, the murder. As 'darkness brought with it a renewal of the disorder in our weakened intellects', any aberration could be attributed to the debilitating affliction. The publication of his thesis on calenture provided further medical justification for the 'insanity', 'egotism . . . brutality' and 'barbarous indifference' of those who were in command of the raft.[12]

When it comes to the fraught question of cannibalism, the authors preface their account with a guilt-drenched appeal to the reader, worthy of the narrator of a Gothic novel:

We tremble with horror at being obliged to mention that which we made use of! We feel our pen drop from our hand; a deathlike chill pervades all our limbs; our hair stands erect on our heads! Reader, we beseech you, do not feel indignation towards men who are already too unfortunate; but have compassion on them, and shed some tears of pity on their unhappy fate.

Despite their remorse, Savigny and Corréard cannot conceal their powerful will and strong survival instinct. Inconsistencies between their narrative and other accounts are explained partly by their desire to whitewash their questionable roles on the raft and partly by their need to blacken the perceived villains of the piece in order to further their political aim.[13]

In their description of the soldiers from the Africa Battalion boarding the raft, they write that, although these men were forbidden to bring their muskets and cartridges on board, some managed to retain their carbines and sabres. Lieutenant Anglas de Praviel, who supervised this embarkation, incisively described the same scene:

> I watched with sorrow as these brave soldiers were forced to abandon their arms, and, despite what Monsieur Savigny says, I can confirm that none of them was carrying a sabre or a rifle. This measure, which had such dire results, was undertaken through prudence; we were worried about overloading the raft.

In discussing the so-called 'mutinies', it served the interests of Savigny, whom some accused of having orchestrated the slaughter of the lower ranks on board the raft, that some soldiers should be seen to have been armed and therefore capable of initiating the violence against their leaders.[14]

Anglas de Praviel is immortalized by Corréard and Savigny as the officer whom the frenzied members of the Africa Battalion were seeking to kill on the raft. These soldiers mistakenly believed that he was on board and wished to destroy him because of his allegedly abusive behaviour in the barracks on the Île de Ré before departure. Thus maligned and even implicated as a pretext for the riot on the second night, it is hardly surprising that de Praviel, in a text that was published after Savigny's and Corréard's, should set out to discredit them. He questions Savigny's and

Corréard's self-aggrandizing claims about their sense of duty, compassion and loyalty, asking caustically 'what became of the twelve workmen for whom Corréard made such a generous sacrifice?'

An important discrepancy between their accounts is that de Praviel took Schmaltz for a 'man of honour', who was 'ceaseless' in his rallying of the boats, despite the general perception that the Governor's Barge, along with the Captain's Barge and the Pinnace, remained at some distance from the frigate. But in stark contradiction, it is de Praviel whom Savigny and Corréard describe as taking aim at the Governor's Barge as it fled from the stricken frigate.

Surely, the rather pompous oath that de Praviel secured from the fifty-seven victims washed up on the shore at Cap Mirick is placed in his text as a blatant denunciation of what Savigny and Corréard guiltily confessed had taken place on board the raft. The oath urged them to do nothing that would allow people to say that the French 'have drunk the blood of their brothers, stuffed themselves with their flesh' – in short, to say 'the French were cannibals'. To that end, de Praviel dwells on the Gothic horror of the platform when it was discovered – the survivors with their hands and mouths still dripping with blood, 'their pockets stuffed with hunks of flesh on which they had fed'.[15]

After returning home to France for health reasons, de Praviel found that the celebrity of Savigny and Corréard had penetrated even to the depths of the country. When he eventually obtained their text, he exclaims:

Imagine my surprise when this report was contrary to the facts of which I was witness, to the observations that I made, to the details that I collected. Alteration of the most essential circumstances, impardonable omissions, people blamed who, up to now, I had valued . . . I seriously asked myself if my shipwreck had not been a dream, an illusion, or if my memory had not been weakened,

deranged in the burning sands of the Sahara . . .
Recovering from this momentary uncertainty, I was
unable to resist the desire to employ the leisure imposed
by a long convalescence and write down the awful facts
as I saw them.

In his own narrative, Sander Rang records an observation of Honoré Thomas, the helmsman, which is at odds
with Savigny and Corréard. He claims that the leaders had
deliberately placed a barrel in the middle of the raft and
broached it, leaving the soldiers free to drink their fill.
Tempted by such largesse, they soon got drunk, which
resulted in the inevitable disorder and subsequent massacre.[16]
This version of events is supported by Brédif. When he
visited his old school friend, Valéry Touche-Lavillette, who
was lying in the hospital in Saint Louis, the latter suggested
that Dr Savigny and two or three leaders behaved like brigands and committed murder when it was by no means necessary. He put it to Brédif that they had organized a sinister
plan to nettle these ill-fated, frenzied people into destroying
one another.

Lavillette, as a member of the *Société philanthropique*, seems
to have had no overt motive for questioning Savigny, and
he would also have been one of the souls whom Corréard
felt it his duty to accompany onto the raft. In any case,
doubt is cast on Lavillette's own position by Honoré Thomas,
who claims that Lavillette was a keen euthanasiast, helping
those who were slowly drowning to die by thrusting them
through with his sabre, perhaps in collusion with the leaders
on board.[17]

The health and judgement of these men were severely
affected, not only during their ordeal, but also in its aftermath. We can legitimately question statements, observations
and accusations made in the hospital in Senegal. Lavillette
was, after all, one of the signatories of the Schmaltzified
declarations brought to the sickbeds of the recuperating

survivors in Saint Louis. This declaration indeed names Savigny, 'who, by his counsel and his discourse . . . was the principal provoker and executor' of the outrages on the raft.[18] But these letters were later refuted, as the signatories claimed that they had been pressured to sign them and had not been altogether lucid when they had done so. Lavillette subsequently went to Géricault's studio and made the painter a model of the raft. At whose invitation? Most probably through the Corréard connection – which suggests, perhaps, that any acrimonious differences were subsequently patched up.

Certainly, Savigny has been accused of ruthless brutality on the raft. But whose version of events can stand as truth? Savigny left Senegal in considerable haste and wasted no time in getting his version of events down on paper, in a report that was unexpectedly published in the press. The surgeon went on to collaborate with Corréard on a full-length book. As this was the longest account of the tragedy to appear, it gave authority to Savigny's viewpoint. Midshipman Coudein, as senior naval officer on board the raft and therefore responsible for everything that happened, understandably followed Savigny and Corréard in his report to his minister. He suggested that the leaders had acted in legitimate defence and that Savigny's composure had been 'very helpful in maintaining order' in that small, packed and precarious space in which violence was certain to erupt.[19]

A tiny band of bourgeoisie, floating aimlessly on an impossible platform in the tropical heat with insufficient rations and dangerously outnumbered by cut-throats and brigands, would naturally be anxious. According to the mores of the period, the leaders on the raft felt themselves superior to these 'scum of all countries, the refuse of the prisons' with whom they shared the makeshift space. The struggle on the raft, whoever initiated it, was inevitably a class battle in which the leaders believed that they had a greater claim to life – much as Schmaltz and Chaumareys had done.[20]

The least pardonable aspect of survival on the raft remains the self-confessed elimination of the weakest. It is of the same immoral order as the decision to cut the towrope, and Savigny and Corréard, sensing this, make an attempt to deflect their guilt by, once again, appealing to their public: 'Readers . . . recollect, at least, that it was other men, fellow countrymen and comrades, who had placed us in this abominable situation.' Nonetheless, the tactical cull continues to haunt the story of the shipwreck of *The Medusa*, casting a macabre light across the all-too-human instinct for self-preservation.

Our inability to discover the truth behind the terrible events that have been variously recounted, according to the particular – and sometimes conflicting – interests of their authors, remains problematic. What comes down to us is, inevitably, a distortion of the truth: a mosaic of probabilities. Confusingly, in Savigny's and Corréard's narration of the first days, the raft is one minute so crammed that no one can move, but the next, the mutineers are seen advancing against the leaders. If Savigny and Corréard were candid about eliminating those who were least likely to survive during their last days on the raft, why would they not be frank about the inescapable need to reduce numbers early on? Furthermore, we have to question whether it is not more likely that a murderous rout would have been started by a rabble of combustible professional killers than by a lone doctor, albeit a plucky and frightened one. And though it is true that Savigny rapidly distanced himself from the *Medusa* controversy, haunted by nightmarish memories, Corréard was less eager to let sleeping dogs lie. The polemicist and would-be politician had to live with an episode in his past that was inevitably blurred, and he most probably came to accept the version of the truth as given in *The Shipwreck*, not least because it served a larger political end.

The main elements of the catastrophe are universally agreed upon. It is a story in which the villains are obvious, the heroes few, and the chroniclers are not altogether to be trusted. At a time when tales of shipwrecks were commonplace, a particularly distressing example was presented to an appalled public in France and was manipulated by various parties – including, ironically, the King and his chief adviser – to drive one more nail into the coffin of the French monarchy. The burial process may have been slow, but the *Medusa* scandal played its part in disparaging the procedures of the *ancien régime* and toppling, albeit briefly, the *ultra* faction. The event was also used, through Géricault's painting, to present a new, Romantic evaluation of the human predicament.

Much of the hard evidence surrounding the *Medusa* tragedy has perished in the sea, or on the desert sands, and what is left has been swirled and sifted by partial, prejudiced and imperfect narratives. Ultimately, what is of interest to perpetuity is not the exact truth of the contestable details, but rather to what end the various versions of these errors and follies have been used.

In 1828, the writer and newspaper editor Arnold Scheffer called Géricault the 'head of a new school', by which he meant the Romantic movement in art. This was born in opposition and crisis, and disturbed the models provided by religion and rigid hierarchy. Romantics often troubled readers or spectators by plunging them into the eerie or the ugly, and denied redemption by placing them in an agony of endless longing. Themes of abandonment and false hope in Géricault's painting touch the wider Romantic agony provoked by the loss of faith in religion.[21] Géricault's painting presents man grasping for salvation from a stinking, sinking, makeshift raft. His painting inhabits the same world as Caspar David Friedrich's *Wreck of Hope*[22] and Coleridge's 'Ancient Mariner'. Like the eponymous hero of Mary Shelley's *Frankenstein*, published in 1818 at the time Géricault began working on *The Raft*, the painter spent 'days . . . in charnel-houses'[23] studying decay, pushing himself to the very edge in his preparations for his painting. But in its realization, transcending the Gothic horrors of the bloodied raft, Géricault aimed to be grandly Romantic in his seizure of the large metaphor.

Famously, the historian Jules Michelet saw that the real subject of Géricault's painting was 'France herself, our whole society . . . loaded on *The Medusa*'; Géricault, he believed, 'paints the shipwreck of France'. His viewpoint gains support from the fact that when *The Medusa* set sail from Rochefort, she carried on board a dangerous brew of jarring political approaches – a Restoration France in miniature.

Géricault lived most of his short adult life through a time that is often dismissed as something that almost did not happen – the Restoration, the sad coda to the Eroica of Revolution and Empire. Yet, in a sense, the period was so tempestuous that it might just as easily be viewed as a chapter in the ongoing French Revolution. Certainly, down through the nineteenth century, as the country continued to wrangle with the question of her political identity, *The Raft of the Medusa* remained a symbol of France riven. Even as the spectator stands before the painting, the composition seems to pull apart, flying off towards the corners, because the centre cannot hold.[24]

In November 1824, there was a sale of works and effects from Géricault's studio, which achieved modest returns. Lot 66, including sketches and figure studies for *The Raft*, went for sixty francs. The Duc d'Orléans, for a total of just over 5,000 francs, bought lots 93 and 94, the magnificent *Officer of the Chasseurs* and *The Wounded Cuirassier*. Happily, at long last, the Comte Forbin, who had been a persistent champion of Géricault's work, was able to purchase *The Raft of the Medusa* for the Louvre. The sum agreed (6,005 francs) did not appear derisory when compared with the going rate for similarly sized works.[25]

On October 24th, 1848, the year that saw the end of the Bourbon monarchy, a mason's ladder punctured *The Raft of the Medusa*, damaging some of the sky and the side of the hand of the sailor waving for rescue. The severely bubbling rectangular repair is visible today. In the late 1850s two painters, Guillemet and Ronjat, pointed out to the Director of Museums the extent to which Géricault's masterpiece had deteriorated. The bituminous paint was cracking and darkening, and Guillemet and Ronjat set about making a full-size copy using more stable paint. This now hangs in the *Musée de Picardie* in Amiens, where it provides a far better indication of how Géricault's masterpiece would have appeared to visitors at the 1819 Salon than the original, which hangs in the Louvre.[26]

Its collection swollen as a result of Napoleonic plundering, the Louvre had been, in the first days of the Restoration, a favoured destination for visitors to the French capital. No other city boasted such a magnificent museum, and Géricault was heartbroken to learn that much of the pillage was to be restored to its rightful owners. One hundred and twenty years later, the fragile, supposedly unmovable *Raft of the Medusa* had to be carried off to spend six years hidden in the Château de Sarthe to avoid its falling into the hands of the plundering Nazis. But, after the Second World War, the masterpiece was back in the Louvre, where it remains to this day, one of that great museum's major attractions.[27]

As for *The Medusa* herself, beached on the Arguin sand bank with 90,000 francs in three strong boxes deep in the gunner's storeroom, she too has been the focus of considerable interest. Rear-Admiral de Rosily, anxious to improve the faulty maps that had contributed to the shipwreck, ensured that a mission was swiftly undertaken to chart the dangerous West African coast. The 1817–18 hydrographic expedition under Commandant Roussin, contending with fogs, sandstorms and mirages, established that Cap Blanc, which had proved so elusive to Captain Chaumareys, was actually four nautical miles farther south than it appeared on the existing map. The officers, attempting to protect

themselves by duping their captain, had been sailing closer
to the mark than they could have known.

On April 4th, 1817, the hydrographic expedition spotted
the carcass of *The Medusa* lying on its port side, with its
starboard hull still intact, withstanding the repeated battering
of the ocean's waves. After that, the frigate broke up and
disappeared beneath the shallow waters of the Arguin sand
bank, lost until interest in its whereabouts was rekindled and
determined efforts were made to find the wreck.

In 1960, the French ambassador to Mauritania, Pierre
Anthonioz, searched for *The Medusa* with navy divers. The
following year, during a bathymetric survey of the sand
bank, a team pinpointed the wreck at 19° 53' 4" west
and 19° 18' 8" north. Under the direction of Professor
Monod of the Research Group for the Identification and
Exploration of the Wreck of *The Medusa*, a boat set sail
from Rochefort in October 1980 to study whatever
remained of the frigate. In early December, Jean-Yves Blot
and his team found the wreck. Their search profited from
the generous loan of sophisticated equipment. The fame
of Géricault's painting persuaded companies that such
support would, with industry's love of sponsoring established art, prove a fabulous public-relations opportunity.
Assisted by satellite positioning equipment and computers,
they located the remains of the frigate. They also found
an inexplicable mystery. There was no sign of the untraced
90,000 francs. Over the years there had been theories about
how Schmaltz or Chaumareys had managed to appropriate
the fortune – perhaps even before *The Medusa* had set sail
– but, if that were so, it seems strange that Schmaltz should
die in reduced circumstances in Smyrna and that
Chaumareys would die in debt, after decades of genteel
poverty. Perhaps one of the enterprising commercial giants
of Saint Louis, such as Valentin, Potin or Durécu, unsatisfied by their fortunes made from the slave trade, managed
to wrest the treasure from the frigate. Or perhaps it lies

there still, broken up, scattered and swallowed in the shifting sands of the Arguin Bank.[28]

Several survivors associated with the events and achievements surrounding the wreck of *The Medusa* lived on for decades. Corréard's determined agitation contributed to the eventual success of the abolitionist movement in France and to the eventual demise of the monarchy. To those ends, he lived for most of his life under the perpetual burden of somebody in opposition. The failure of his attempt for public office can only have added to his unhappiness at the end of his life. Still in pain from the numerous wounds he had sustained on the raft, he was grief-stricken by the death of his wife. Indeed, such was his distress at her passing that he kept a dressmaker's mannequin sitting in the window of his house at Basses-Loges in Avon. Every day he would change her clothes, dressing the life-sized doll in his dead wife's garments – a lonely, sorrowful fetishist, longing for things lost.

When Corréard died on February 16th, 1857, he took the truth of what happened on the raft to his grave.[29] His struggle to keep the *Medusa* story before the public at a time when the establishment thought it best forgotten had been much aided by Théodore Géricault's decision to make a painting. Géricault had, of course, been drawn to the subject as a result of the dark mood that had displaced his youthful happiness. Painted by him at about the same time, a shipwreck scene entitled *The Storm* revealed a mother and her infant thrown up on a desolate shore. The painting hints at the dashed hopes of Alexandrine and her third son, Georges-Hippolyte, the child she was never allowed to know.[30]

Having negotiated the scandal of the illegitimate birth, Alexandrine continued to live as the wife of Baron Caruel de Saint-Martin in the relative isolation of the Château du Grand-Chesnay. In 1847 her husband died, aged ninety.

Despite her impropriety, Caruel was generous to Alexandrine in his will, increasing her private annual income by 20 per cent, as well as giving her 40,000 francs in gold, along with the silverware from his Paris mansion and all the books he owned – useful companions in her secluded life.[31]

Alexandrine-Modeste Caruel lived on, never able to meet her lost child, and reached the same ripe age as her husband by the time of her death in August 1875. Towards the end of her life she watched, perhaps with misgivings, when her younger son Paul (as his father had before him) finally married at the age of fifty. As Paul's unstable older brother, Louis-Sylvestre, had been placed under legal guardianship in 1845 and spent the last thirty-two years of his life in a mental institution at Ivry-sur-Seine, Paul inherited the Château du Grand-Chesnay. As he produced only female children, the year after Paul's death in 1889 the château – the place where the romance between aunt and nephew had flourished – was sold.[32]

Mental disturbance in the maternal line of Géricault's family claimed many victims. Not only had Jean-Baptiste Caruel's older son, Louis-Sylvestre, succumbed, but his nephew, Théodore Géricault, suffered a breakdown and severe depression after months of tortured emotional distress, followed by the failure of his masterpiece at the Salon. While there is no evidence of treatable mental illness, it seems that Géricault's illegitimate son, Georges-Hippolyte, was over-wrought and unable to forge a satisfactory life.[33]

There were resources to ensure that Géricault's child was brought up in comfortable circumstances, but from the outset things did not go well. Paul Clouard, Géricault's cousin, tricked the painter's father into changing the will that he had made in favour of his grandson, effectively cheating Georges-Hippolyte of most of his inheritance, but nonetheless leaving him two farms in Normandy. Furthermore, Auguste Brunet, whom the dying Géricault had asked to act as a guardian to his son, met with an unexpectedly early death in February 1827, and so it fell to the families of other old friends to step into the breach.[34]

The wasted life of Géricault's son, a man vainly in search of the harbour of parental affection, played out its course over several sad decades. In September 1839, recently turned twenty-one, he successfully petitioned the *Garde des Sceaux* for the right to bear the name Géricault. Shy, small and dressed in a nondescript manner, Georges-Hippolyte spent the last twenty years of his life living in austere lodgings just beneath the attic in the modest *Hôtel du Lion d'Or* in Bayeux. He had settled there in order to be near the source of his income, the farms at Saint-Martin. How piercing the sound of that name must have seemed, reminding him daily of his overwhelming desire to meet and get to know his mother, the Baroness de Saint-Martin. At last, after years of silence, he managed through an intermediary to secure word from her. The message was brief. His mother insisted that they should not make contact. Her son must forget her – society would not permit otherwise.

His life dragged emptily, unhealthily on; his lodging seemed to a friendly visitor like a cell in which he waited for death to claim him. When he eventually died with the year, on December 31st, 1882, his property fell to the state because he had no legal heirs. Georges-Hippolyte had outlived the mother whom he had never known by just seven years; their enforced separation was the only thing they had shared.[35]

It had been well over half a century since two scarred men met in an eerie studio in Saint-Phillipe du Roule, two men whose lives had been shattered – one in a senseless shipwreck with a particularly cruel and ghoulish aftermath, the other whose wreck had been emotional. Both had grown up amid the turbulence of revolutionary France and their respective fates had swept them up and set them on a course of political engagement that would involve them with the largest humanitarian issue of their time. Their meeting had

259

proved fruitful: Corréard had become midwife to one of the great masterpieces of Western art, helping Géricault to crown his short but magnificent career.

For Corréard, the wreck had been a rite of passage into the arena of political challenge. After his long and combative life, he was laid to rest in the cemetery at Avon, on the banks of the Seine, just a stone's throw from Féricy, where Géricault had gone to recuperate after completing *The Raft of the Medusa*. A little way downriver, in the celebrated Parisian cemetery of Père Lachaise, stands a memorial tomb to the Romantic master. A bronze bas-relief of Géricault's most famous composition emblazons the front of the monument, reminding the visitor that the young man interred below had been someone of artistic genius, who had kept the terrible story of the wreck of *The Medusa* alive. Around the base of the structure is a railing only twenty centimetres high. In his will, Georges-Hippolyte had left money to embellish the tomb of his father, and the wrought-iron railing remains as a son's acknowledgement of the parents he never knew. It is a message from the unfortunate who occupies an almost anonymous grave nearby. The railing's repeating motif is a 'G' embracing a heart transpierced by two arrows. It is a son's silent testimony to the brief love between Théodore Géricault and Alexandrine-Modeste Caruel, a secret witness to the shipwreck of lives caught up in an unrelenting passion.

Notes

1: A Severed Head

1   Benjamin Robert Haydon, *Life of Benjamin Robert Haydon,
     historical painter, from his Autobiography and his Journals*, ed.
     and completed by Tom Taylor (London: Longman, Brown,
     Green and Longman, 1853), Vol. I, 238.
2   William Dorset Fellowes, *Paris During the Interesting Month
     of July, 1815, a Series of Letters* (London: Gale and Fenner,
     1815), 22.
3   Alain Monestier & Jacques Cheyronnaud, *Le Fait divers*.
     (Paris: Éditions de la Réunion des musées nationaux,
     1982), 50.

2: Voyages Out

1   Philip Mansel, *Louis XVIII* (Stroud: Sutton Publishing,
     1999), 119, 170, 186–7.
2   Alexandre Corréard, *Élections des Représentants du peuple à
     l'Assemblée législative – Alexandre Corréard, Ingénieur (du
     Radeau de 'La Méduse') aux électeurs du département de Seine-
     et-Marne* (Batignolles: n.d. [1848]); Jean-Paul Besse,
     Compiègne dans l'histoire: une ville impériale et royale (Paris:
     Éd. D.U.C., 1992), 2.
3   Guillaume de Bertier de Sauvigny, *La Restauration* (Paris:

Flammarion, 1955, pbk 1999), 11; Philip Mansel, *Paris Between Empires 1814–1852* (London: Phoenix Press, 2003), 4.

4   Haydon, *Life*, 232, 237.

5   Mansel, *Paris Between Empires*, 16.

6   Bertier de Sauvigny, *La Restauration*, 63–4.

7   Louis XVIII, quoted in Jeanne Gilmore, *La République clandestine 1818–48* (Paris: Aubier, 1997), 9.

8   Corréard, *Élections des Représentants du peuple à l'Assemblée législative*, 2.

9   Edmond Hugues, *Alexandre Corréard de Serres, naufragé de la 'Méduse'* (Gap, 1920), 5.

10   Charles-Pierre de Nazarieux, *Mémoire pour la Société coloniale philanthropique, présenté à son excellence Mgr. le Ministre Secrétaire d'Etat de la Marine et des colonies par MM. les membres composant la Commission administrative de la Société coloniale* (Paris, November 25th, 1816), 30; Alexandre Corréard et Henri Savigny, *Naufrage de la frégate la Méduse faisant partie de l'expédition du Sénégal en 1816*, 5th edn (Paris: Chez Corréard, Libraire, 1821), 64–5; Roger Mercier, 'Le Naufrage de "La Méduse" – 'Réalité et imagination romanesque', in *Revue des Sciences Humaines*, Fasc. 125 (Lille: Université de Lille, January–March 1967), 55.

11   Eugène Titeux, *Histoire de la Maison militaire du Roi de 1814 à 1830* (Paris: Baudry, 1890), 29; Mansel, *Louis XVIII*, 221.

12   *Le Moniteur universel*, March 20th, 1815, quoted in Mansel, *Louis XVIII*, 227.

13   Mansel, *Paris Between Empires*, 80–1.

14   E. Chevalier, *Histoire de la Marine Française de 1815–1870* (Paris: Hachette, 1900), 8–9; Henri Legohérel, *Histoire de la Marine française* (Presses universitaires de France, 1999), 59–66.

15   Legohérel, 68–77.

16   Present-day Java.

17   Georges Bordonove, *Le Naufrage de 'la Méduse'* (Paris: R. Laffont, 1973), 18–21, 23–9.

18 Nazarieux, 8–9, 30.

19 Germain Bazin, *Théodore Géricault, étude critique, documents et catalogue raisonné*, Vol.1 (Paris: Wildenstein Institute, La bibliothèque des arts, 1987), 21, doc. 1; Jean Sagne, *Géricault* (Paris: Fayard, 1991), 15; Denise Aimé-Azam, *Mazeppa, Géricault et son temps* (Paris: Plon, 1956), 11–12; Gilles Buisson, *Géricault – de Mortain à Paris* (Coutances, OCEP, 1976), 22; Charles Clément in his biography, *Géricault – Etude biographique et critique* (Paris: Didier & Co., 1868), 15–16; Bruno Chenique, 'Géricault, une vie', *Géricault* (Paris: Éditions de la Réunion des musées nationaux, 1991), 263.

20 Louis Batissier, 'Géricault', reprint from *Revue du dix-neuvième Siècle* (Rouen, n.d. [1842 is a mistake in many citations] 1824), 4; Michel Le Pesant, 'Documents inédits sur Géricault', *Revue de l'Art*, No.31 (Paris: Flammarion, 1976), 74–5, 78; Clément, 16.

21 Charles Blanc, *Histoire des peintres français au XIX siècle* (Paris, 1845), 408–9; Clément 43.

22 See Blanc, 408–9.

23 The posthumous inventory of Géricault's possessions included two copies of works by Ruysdaël and Wynants – artists included in Alexandrine-Modeste's dowry. See Philippe Grunchec, 'L'inventaire posthume de Théodore Géricault', *Bulletin de la Société de l'histoire de l'art français* (Paris, 1976), 395–420; Bazin, I, 178–94.

24 Bazin, I, 32; Lorenz Eitner, *Géricault – Sa vie, son oeuvre* (Paris: Gallimard, 1991), 98; Stefan Germer, '"Je commence une femme, et ça devient un lion": On the Origin of Géricault's Fantasy of Origins', *Géricault, Conférences et colloques du Louvre* (Paris: La documentation française, 1996), Vol.1, 439.

25 Batissier, 6–7; Bazin, I, 32–6.

26 Mansel, *Louis XVIII*, 204–5; Bertier de Sauvigny, *La Restauration*, 80.

27 Titeux, 33; Frederick Antal, 'Reflections on Classicism

and Romanticism – III' in *The Burlington Magazine* (London, September 1940), 73.

28 See Mansel, *Paris Between Empires*, 27; Bertier de Sauvigny, *La Restauration*, 70–5; Irene Collins, ed. *Government and Society in France, 1814–1848* (London: Edward Arnold, 1970), 12; Mansel, *Louis XVIII*, 184.

29 Bertier de Sauvigny, *La Restauration*, 118.

30 ibid., 124, 273; Mansel, *Louis XVIII*, 266–7; Alfred M. Nettement, *Souvenirs de la Restauration* (Paris: Jacques Lecoffre et Cie, 1858), 272–3, 275, 277; Edgar Leon Newman, *Historical Dictionary of France from the 1815 Restoration to the Second Empire*, 2 vols (Westport, Conn.: Greenwood Press, 1987), Vol.I, 300; Mansel, *Paris Between Empires*, 123.

31 Bertier de Sauvigny, *La Restauration*, 132–3; Collins, *Government and Society in France*, 19; Newman, Vol.I, 275; Bertier de Sauvigny, *La Restauration*, 132–3; Pierre Darmon, *La Rumeur de Rodez* (Paris: Albin Michel, 1991), 14–15.

32 John Scott of Gala, *Paris Revisited in 1815, by way of Brussels* (London: Longman, Hurst Rees & Brown, 1816), 400, 401; Daniel P. Resnick, *The White Terror and the Political Reaction after Waterloo* (Cambridge, Mass.: Harvard University Press, 1966), 117–18; Gilmore, 11–12; Bertier de Sauvigny, *La Restauration*, 136; Newman, Vol.II, 1125.

33 Bertier de Sauvigny, *La Restauration*, 79.

34 Terence Grocott, *Shipwrecks of the Revolutionary and Napoleonic Eras* (London: Caxton Editions, 2002), xv; Chevalier, 1–3; E.H. Jenkins, *Histoire de la marine française* (Paris: Albin Michel, 1977), 334; Gicquel des Touches, 'Souvenirs d'un marin de la République', *Revue des Deux-Mondes*, Parts I & II, Vol.28 (Paris, 1905), 434.

35 Bordonove, 30–3; Phillippe Masson, *L'Affaire de la Méduse* (Paris: Tallandier, 1989), 155–6.

36 J. Breillout, 'La vie dramatique de M. de Chaumereix', in *Bulletin de la Société des lettres, sciences et arts de la Corrèze*

(Tulle, 1933), 242–4; Bordonove, 34–6, 39–40; Masson, 155–63.

37 Hugues Duroy de Chaumereys, *Relation de M. de Chaumereix, officier de la marine, échappé aux massacres d'Aurai et de Vannes, suivie de quelques observations sur l'esprit public en Bretagne* (London: J. de Bouffe, 1795), 3.

38 ibid., 43.

39 Bordonove, 43.

40 Touches, 'Souvenirs d'un marin de la République', 181, 434.

41 M. de Brisson, *Histoire du naufrage et de la captivité de M. De Brisson* (Genève & Paris, 1789), 14–25; René-Claude Geoffrey de Villeneuve, *L'Afrique ou Histoire, moeurs, usages et coutumes des Africains. Le Sénégal*, 4 vols (Paris: Nepveu, 1814), Vol.I, 9, 22–57.

42 Touches, 434.

43 Grocott, x–xi.

44 Bordonove, 75–6, 224; Vénancourt's log quoted in Bordonove, 80.

45 Geoffrey de Villeneuve, Vol.I, 133.

46 Under her married name of Dard, Charlotte Picard has left a detailed account of her voyage to West Africa: Mme Dard (née Charlotte-Adelaide Picard), *La chaumière Africaine, ou Histoire d'une famille française jetée sur la côte de l'Afrique, à la suite du naufrage de la Frégate la Méduse* (Dijon: Noellat, 1824), 14–15.

47 ibid., 6–12; Serge Daget, 'France, Suppression of the Illegal Trade, and England 1817–50', *Abolition of the Atlantic Slave Trade*, ed. Eltis and Walvin (Madison: The University of Wisconsin Press, 1981), 195.

48 Charles-Marie Brédif, 'Le naufrage de la Méduse, mon voyage au Sénégal', *Revue de Paris*, No.11 (Paris, 1907), 636–7.

49 ibid., 639–41; Dard, 18–19. There is a dating discrepancy between Brédif and Dard's narrative; Mme Dard, writing eight years after the event, seems more likely to have mistaken the date, whereas Brédif, given to

taking measurements and recording events as he goes along, is more trustworthy.

50 Brédif, 641; Jean-Yves Blot, *La Méduse – Chronique d'un naufrage ordinaire.* (Paris: Arthaud, 1982), 90–1; Aimé-Azam, *Mazeppa, Géricault et son temps*, 225.

51 Brédif, 643; Serge Daget, 'France, Suppression of the Illegal Trade', 194; Service historique de la Défense –Vincennes: BB 3 432 – letter of March 17th, 1816 from the Director of Construction at Rochefort; Corréard & Savigny, 5th edn (Paris, 1821), 396.

52 Geoffrey de Villeneuve, Vol.I, iii & Vol.II, 156–7; Bordonove, 46; Parson, *Premier rapport de M. Parson, chef de la délégation envoyée au Cap-Verd par la Société coloniale philanthropique à l'effet de reconnoître les lieux les plus propres à la fondation des colonies agricoles* – 2e édition avec des Notes par M. Sevigny (Paris: Au bureau de la Société coloniale philanthropique, 1817), 19; Darcy Grimaldo Grigsby, *Extremities* (New Haven and London: Yale University Press, 2002), 171.

53 Service historique de la Défense – Vincennes: Dossier marine, François-Marie Cornette de Vénancourt (b. 1778); Bordonove, 66–7; Daget, 'France, Suppression of the Illegal Trade', 195.

54 Touches, 184–6, 417, 425–6, 428.

55 Service historique de la Défense – Vincennes: Dossier marine, Léon Henry de Parnajon; Bordonove, 67.

56 Jenkins, 334; Service Historique de la Défense –Vincennes: Dossier marine, Joseph Pierre André Reynaud (b. 1786); Bordonove, 54, 56. Service historique de la Défense – Vincennes: Dossier marine: Jean Espiaux (b. 1783, Carcassonne), including the evaluation of his commander aboard *The Medusa* in 1814; Bordonove 44–5, 49, 51.

57 Corréard & Savigny, 5th edn (Paris, 1821), 23; Gaspar Mollien, *Découverte des sources du Sénégal et de la Gambie en 1818* (Paris: C. Delagrave, 1889), 20.

58 Parson, iii–iv; Henri Savigny & Alexandre Corréard,

Notes

Narrative of a Voyage to Senegal in 1816 (London: Henry Colburn, 1818), 4–5.

59 Brédif, 644; Dard, 20–2.

60 Savigny & Corréard (London, 1818), 12; Mollien, *Découverte*, 20–1; Brédif, 783–4.

61 Bordonove, 84.

62 Brédif, 785; Service historique de la Défense – Vincennes: BB 4 3 93; Bordonove, 85.

63 Corréard and Savigny get this date wrong, claiming it to be June 27th, which (if you follow their text through) would make the arrival in Tenerife the 30th and not the 29th – which was indeed the case, as June 29th is St Peter's Day and the island bells were tolling for the festival. Viz. Brédif, 785–91; Bordonove, 87.

64 Corréard & Savigny, 5th edn (Paris, 1821), 28–9.

65 Brédif, 786–7; Corréard & Savigny, 5th edn (Paris 1821), 13–16; Bordonove, 87.

66 Savigny & Corréard (London, 1818), 16; Paulin d'Anglas de Praviel, *Relation nouvelle et impartiale du naufrage de la frégate la Méduse* (Nîmes: Paulin d'Anglas de Praviel, 1858), included in *Relation complète du naufrage de la frégate la Méduse* (Paris: J. de Bonnot, 1968), 275; M. Adanson, *A Voyage to Senegal, the Isle of Gorée and the River Gambia* (Dublin: Ewing, James & Bradley, 1759), 22; Sander Rang (Alexandre Rang des Adrets, *dit* Sander Rang), *Voyage au Sénégal, Naufrage de la Méduse* (Paris: Editions E.P.I., 1946), 13; According to Brédif, it was at 8 a.m. that the boat was lowered (788). Though Rang was on the boat, Brédif was keeping a diary. It was at 10 a.m. according to Charlotte Picard: Dard, 24; Brédif, 788.

67 Bordonove, 91.

68 Brédif, 787; Dard, 24–7.

69 Based on an account given in a popular anonymous fictional account, *Le Naufrage de la Méduse* (Paris: Delarue, 1842), 2–8; Brédif, 789–90.

70 Brédif, 790.

71   Charles Cochelet, *Narrative of the Shipwreck of the Sophia on the 30th May, 1819, on the Western Coast of Africa* (London: Sir Richard Phillips and Co., 1822), introduction; Geoffrey de Villeneuve, Vol.1, 9; James Riley, *Loss of American Brig 'Commerce' wrecked on Western Coast of Africa in the month of August 1815* (London: J. Murray, 1817), 55, 72.

72   Savigny & Corréard (London, 1818), 24; Corréard and Savigny, 5th edn (Paris, 1821), 38, 40–1; Dard, 28; Mollien, *Découverte*, 21.

73   Corréard & Savigny, 5th edn (Paris, 1821), 44–6; Bordonove, 93, 99–102.

74   Corréard & Savigny 5th edn (Paris, 1821), 41–3; Savigny & Corréard (London, 1818), 30; Dard, 30–1; Praviel, 276; Bordonove, 96, 176–7.

75   Savigny & Corréard (London, 1818), 31; Rang, 20; Brédif, 791; Dard, 32, 34–5; Praviel, 278; Mollien, *Découverte*, 22; Bordonove, 102.

76   Mansel, *Louis XVIII*, 330, 340, 411; Mansel, *Paris Between Empires*, 110; Berthier & Savigny, *La Restauration*, 128, 138; Bazin, Vol.V, 50.

77   Blanc, 415.

78   Benjamin Constant, speaking in 1822, and quoted by Alan B. Spitzer, *The French Generation of 1820* (Princeton, New Jersey: Princeton University Press, 1987), 4.

79   Blanc, 415.

80   Chenique, 'Géricault: une vie', in *Géricault*, 275.

81   Théodore Lebrun to Batissier, April 6th, 1836, quoted in Clément, 79–81; Bazin Vol.I, doc. 1, 22.

82   Clément, 77–8. Chenique, 'Géricault, une vie', in *Géricault*, 276.

3: The Wreck

1   Rang, 25; Praviel, 278; Brédif, 792–3; Corréard & Savigny, 5th edn (Paris, 1821), 50; Savigny & Corréard (London,

1818), 35–6; Mollien, *Découverte*, 22–3; Bordonove, 111–12.

2 Savigny & Corréard (London, 1818), 36–7.

3 Auguste Bailly, *Le Radeau de la Méduse* (Paris, 1929), 27–8.

4 Royou in his *La Biographie pittoresque et contemporaine des hommes de mer et d'eau douce* (1811), quoted in Corréard & Savigny, 5th edn (Paris, 1821), 278ff.

5 L. Jore, 'La vie diverse et volontaire du Colonel Julien Désiré Schmaltz . . . Consul Général de France à Smyrne (Turquie) 1771–1827', *Revue d'histoire des colonies*, Vol.XL, 2nd trimestre 1953, 265–312 (Paris, 1953), 269–70; Bordonove, 60.

6 Etienne Esquirol, *Des maladies mentales considérées sous les rapports médical, hygiénique et médico-légal* (Paris, 1838), Vol.II, 172–3.

7 Jore, 272–6; Esquirol, Vol.II, 172.

8 Jore, 278–83; Masson, 21–2.

9 Esquirol, Vol.II, 173; Erwin H. Ackerknecht, *Medicine at the Paris Hospital 1784–1848* (Baltimore: Johns Hopkins Press, 1967), 48, 168–70; Corréard & Savigny, 5th edn (Paris, 1821), 50.

10 Grocott, ix–x; Dard, 35–7; Corréard & Savigny, 5th edn (Paris, 1821), 56; Savigny & Corréard (London, 1818), 35–8; Mollien, *Découverte*, 24–5.

11 Savigny & Corréard (London, 1818), 39–41; Corréard & Savigny, 5th edn (Paris, 1821), 56–7.

12 Service historique de la Défense – Vincennes: Dossier marine, Jean Espiaux; Rang, 79–80; Dard, 36; Savigny & Corréard (London, 1818), 56–9.

13 Dard, 41–3; Praviel, 279.

14 Marie-Antoine Rabaroust, 'Récit inédit du naufrage de La Méduse', in *L'Intermédiaire des chercheurs* (Paris, January 10th, 1902), column 45; Dard, 42; Brédif, 793; Savigny & Corréard (London, 1818), 43–4.

15 Dard, 46–50; Brédif, 793–4; Praviel, 280.

16 Dard, 49–51; Rang, 81; Praviel, 281–2; Rabaroust,

column 46; Savigny & Corréard (London, 1818), 50–1, 71–2.

17   Brédif, 793–4; Corréard & Savigny, 5th edn (Paris, 1821), 69–70.

18   Dard, 51; Brédif, 793; Corréard & Savigny, 5th edn (Paris, 1821), 71.

19   Dard, 53–6.

20   Rabaroust, column 46; Rang, 37–9; Praviel, 280–2; Savigny & Corréard (London, 1818), 52, 60–7, 71; Corréard & Savigny, 5th edn (Paris, 1821), 87–94; Dard, 59–63; Rabaroust, column 46; Mollien, *Découverte*, 27–8.

21   Dard, 61–4.

22   Brédif, 795.

4: On a Scorching Shore

1   Praviel, 284–5; Mollien, *Découverte*, 28; Brédif, 795. They give conflicting numbers for those who stayed on board. Praviel gives the figure as forty-three, but Brédif, who was on board and writing at the time, has twenty-seven.

2   Brédif, 796–9; Rang, 66; Mollien, *Découverte*, 28–31.

3   Dard, 68, 77–95; Mollien, *Découverte*, 31; MacDonald Critchley, *Shipwreck – Survivors, a Medical Study* (London: J. & A. Churchill, 1943), 30.

4   Dard, 95–104; Brédif, 799; Rang, 69–70.

5   See Cochelet's impression: Cochelet, 5.

6   Jean Baptiste-Léonard Durand, *Voyage au Sénégal* (Paris: Chez Henri Agasse, 1802), 2.

7   Frank Lestringant, *Cannibal: The Discovery and Representation of the Cannibal from Columbus to Jules Verne* (Cambridge: Polity Press, 1997), 80–6.

8   G.H. von Langsdorff, *Voyages and Travels in Various Parts of the World during the Years 1803, 1804, 1805, 1806, and 1807* (London: Henry Colburn, 1813), 141.

9   Cochelet, 4.

10   Louis-Marie-Joseph Ohier, Comte de Grandpré, *Voyage à*

la côte occidentale d'Afrique fait dans les années 1786 et 1787,
2 vols (Paris: Dentu, an IX [1801]) vi–xi; Grigsby, 185–6.

11 Geoffrey de Villeneuve, Vol. II, 18–20.

12 Brédif, 799–800; Mollien, *Découverte*, 32; G. Mollien, *Travels in the Interior of Africa to the Sources of the Senegal and Gambia Performed by Command of the French government in the year 1818* (London: Colburn & Co., 1820), 3–4; Adanson, 79; Critchley, 31; Andrew Boorde, *Dyetary*, ed. F.J. Furnivall, Early English Text Society, e.s. 10 (London, 1870).

13 Dard, 100–19; Brédif, 799–800; Rang, 70; Savigny & Corréard (London, 1818), 163–4; Mollien, *Découverte*, 33–5; Adanson, 46.

14 Dard, 119–29; Brédif, 800–2; Mollien, *Découverte*, 39.

15 Brédif, 803; Dard, 129–32; Mollien, *Découverte*, 39.

16 Mollien, *Travels*, 3–4; Brédif, 802–3.

17 Brédif, 803.

18 Dard, 133–6; Brédif, 803–4.

19 Dard, 137–58; Brédif, 804.

20 Jacques-Joseph Le Maire, *Les Voyages du Sieur Le Maire aux Isles Canaries, Cap-Verd, Sénégal et Gambie* (Paris, 1695), 51; Mollien, *Travels*, 3–4; Praviel, 287–8.

21 Praviel, 289–91; Critchley, 28–30.

22 Praviel, 292–3; Geoffrey de Villeneuve, Vol. I, 6, 40; Mollien, *Découverte*, 47–9; Critchley, 33–4.

23 Praviel, 293–5; Geoffrey de Villeneuve, Vol. II, 43–4.

24 Praviel, 296–8; Mollien, *Découverte*, 47–50; Adanson, 46.

5: The Raft

1 Savigny & Corréard (London, 1818), 60–1, 68, 72–77, 100–11; Corréard & Savigny, 5th edn (Paris, 1821), 99–102; Rang, 82; Critchley, 24, 42; Denis Escudier, *L'affreuse vérité de M. Savigny: second chirurgien de la frégate la 'Méduse', naufragé du radeau, miraculeusement sauvé par l'Argus le 17 juillet 1816* (Saint-Jean-D'Angely: Bordessoules, 1991), 16,

62; Henri Savigny, 'Relation Manuscript', reproduced in Escudier, 67; Jean Griffon du Bellay, *Les Griffon pendant cinq cent ans* (Garnes: privately printed, 1979), 26ff.

2 Savigny & Corréard (London, 1818), 78–80; Corréard & Savigny, 5th edn (Paris, 1821), 103–5.

3 Savigny & Corréard (London, 1818), 80–104; Corréard & Savigny, 5th edn (Paris, 1821), 105–29; Jean-Baptiste Savigny, '*Observations sur les effets de la faim et de la soif eprouvées après le naufrage de la frégate du roi la Méduse en 1816*' (Paris, May 26th, 1818), reproduced in Escudier, 101–16; Griffon du Bellay, letter to his uncle from Senegal, reprinted in Jean Griffon du Bellay, 26–7.

4 Fournier de Pescay, 'Notice sur la Calenture, maladie particulière aux gens de mer', *Annales des faits et des sciences militaires: faisant suite aux 'Victoires et conquêtes des Français de 1792–1815'*, ed. Jean Denis Barbié du Bocage, 4 vols (March 1818).

5 Corréard & Savigny, 5th edn (Paris, 1821), 125–33; Savigny & Corréard (London, 1818), 104–11; Langsdorff, 142–3; *The Book of Deuteronomy*, XXVIII, v.53; Brian A.W. Simpson, *Cannibalism and the Common Law: The Story of the Tragic Last Voyage of the Mignonette and the Strange Legal Proceedings to Which it Gave Rise* (Harmondsworth: Penguin, 1986), 114–16, 123–5; Critchley, 44; John Graham Dalyell, *Shipwrecks and Disasters at Sea* (London: George Routledge and Sons, 1866 edn), 198–202; Grigsby, 186; Savigny, 'Observations', reproduced in Escudier, 101–2.

6 Critchley, 26, 49; Eric Martini, 'Treatment for Scurvy not Discovered by Lind', *The Lancet*, Vol.364 (London, December 18th/25th, 2004), 2180; Savigny & Corréard (London, 1818), 111–15, 129; Corréard & Savigny, 5th edn (Paris, 1821), 133–8, 149.

7 Savigny & Corréard (London, 1818), 116–20; Corréard & Savigny, 5th edn (Paris, 1821), 139–42.

8 Savigny, 'Observations', in Escudier, 103–4; Corréard &

Savigny, 5th edn (Paris, 1821), 142, 147–8; Savigny, & Corréard (London, 1818), 121–3, 127–8; Critchley, 25.

9 Savigny, 'Observations', in Escudier, 104; Savigny, 'Relation' ms., reprinted in Escudier, 30; Savigny & Corréard (London, 1818), 123–9.

10 Service historique de la Défense – Vincennes: BB 4 393 – Parnajon to Schmaltz, July 19th, 1816; Savigny, 'Observations', in Escudier, 104–5; Critchley, 31, 44–5, 47; Savigny & Corréard (London, 1818), 126–45; Corréard & Savigny, 5th edn (Paris, 1821), 142–5, 147–66; Bordonove, 170–1, 265; Escudier, 132.

6: Tea and Pastries in Senegal

1 Rang, 42–52, 53–7.

2 A.W. Lawrence, *Trade Castles and Forts of West Africa* (London: Jonathan Cape, 1963), 30, 41, 78; Bordonove, 47; Durand, vi–xx.

3 Major John Peddie, letter of August 3rd, 1816, in the National Archives, CO 2/5.

4 Governor Brereton to Governor-designate Schmaltz, July 9th, 1816, in Service historique de la Défense –Vincennes: BB 4 393.

5 Dard, 154–5, 174–5; Geoffrey de Villeneuve, Vol.1, 63–6; map of Saint Louis, National Archives, M.P.G. 220.

6 Dard, 65–6, 156–7, 162–3, 165–7; Rang, 63.

7 Brédif, 138; Dard, 162–3; Savigny & Corréard (London, 1818), 203–4.

8 Service historique de la Défense – Vincennes: BB 4 394 – Vénancourt's report on Cap Vert; Le Maire, 57–8; Geoffrey de Villeneuve,Vol.I, 114; Brédif, 148; Bordonove, 173–5; Praviel, 301; Mollien, *Découverte*, 43, 50–1.

9 Geoffrey de Villeneuve, Vol.I, 103; Savigny & Corréard (London, 1818), 232.

10 Rang, 79; Brédif, 141–3; Savigny & Corréard (London, 1818), 147.

11   Grigsby, 190–1; Rang, 78.

12   Brédif, 143.

13   Savigny & Corréard (London, 1818), 163–92; Corréard & Savigny, 5th edn (Paris, 1821), 215–43; Brédif, 142; Rang, 97–8.

14   Brédif, 143; Praviel, 300.

15   Savigny & Corréard (London, 1818), 200, 213–26; Corréard & Savigny, 5th edn (Paris, 1821), 268–9.

16   Savigny & Corréard (London, 1818), 202–7; Corréard & Savigny, 5th edn (Paris, 1821), 244–61; Dard, 58–9; Escudier, 27.

17   Savigny & Corréard (London, 1818), 210–13; Corréard & Savigny, 5th edn (Paris, 1821), 255–60; Claude Faure, '*La Garnison européenne du Sénégal et le recrutement des premières troupes noires (1779–1858)*', in *Revue de l'histoire des colonies françaises*, No.8, 3e trimestre (Paris: Société de l'histoire des colonies françaises, 1920), 17.

18   Service historique de la Défense: Dossier marine, Cornette de Vénancourt, Report of September 17th, 1816; Parson, *Premier rapport*, vii; Savigny & Corréard (London, 1818), 232–4, 251.

19   This manuscript may well be the one in the *Bibliothèque Municipale de Saintes* (donation of Baron Eschasseriaux) – a notebook of forty pages, which bears a resemblance to the article eventually published in *Le Journal des débats* – see Escudier, 20, 29, 34.

20   *Archive Nationale*, Paris – Marine BB4 393 f° 122; Blot, 153–4; Bordonove, 186–7, 190–2.

7: Sex and the Street

1   Clément, 77–8.

2   Christopher Sells, 'New Light on Géricault, his Travels and his Friends, 1816–23', *Apollo*, Vol.CXXIII, No.292 (London: June 1986), 391; Géricault, letter of October

18th to Dedreux-Dorcy, quoted in full in Chenique, 'Lettres et documents', in *Géricault*, 318; Géricault, letter of November 27th to Dedreux-Dorcy, quoted in Clément, 84–5.

3   Pierre Courthion, *Géricault raconté par lui-même et par ses amis* (Vésenaz-Genève: P. Cailler, 1947), 89–90; Wheelock Whitney, *Gericault in Italy* (New Haven and London: Yale, 1997), 19.

4   Whitney, 158, 161; René-Paul Huet, *Paul Huet d'après ses notes, sa correspondance, ses contemporains* (Paris: H. Laurens, 1911), 224; Lorenz Eitner, 'Erotic Drawings by Gericault', *Master Drawings*, Vol.XXXIV, No.4 (New York, Winter 1996), 375–7.

5   Whitney, 158, 170–1, 181.

6   Montfort, quoted in Bazin, Vol.I, 201; Mme Meuricoffre, quoted in Whitney, 11; Régis Michel, 'Le Mythe de l'oeuvre', in *Géricault* (1991), 66.

7   Courthion, 93; Clément, 111; Batissier, 8.

8   Stendhal, *Racine et Shakespeare* (Paris, 1823), Chapter III; Isaiah Berlin, *The Roots of Romanticism*, ed. Henry Hardy (London: Chatto & Windus, 1999), 14.

8: Breaking News and Stifling Scandal

1   Decazes, quoted in Roger Langeron, *Decazes, ministre du roi* (Paris: Hachette, 1960), 76; Ernest Daudet, *Louis XVIII et le duc Decazes 1815–1820* (Paris: Plon, Nourrit et Cie, 1899), 142–3.

2   Bertier de Sauvigny, *La Restauration*, 150; C.L. Lesur, *Annuaire historique universel Pour 1818* (Paris: Thoisnier-Deplaces, 1825), 36; Irene Collins, 'Liberalism and the Newspaper Press during the French Restoration 1814–1830', *History*, Vol.XLVI (London: RKP, 1961), 26; Langeron, 97, 117–18; Louis Girard, *Les Libéraux français, 1814–1875* (Paris: Aubier, 1985), 61.

3   Decazes, quoted in Daudet, *Louis XVIII*, 142.

4   Daudet, *Louis XVIII*, 132–3, 135.

5   Decazes, in notes to be used for his memoirs, quoted in Langeron, 71.

6   Decazes, quoted in Daudet, *Louis XVIII*, 146–7; Ephraim Harpaz, *L'école libérale sous la Restauration, le Mercure et la Minerve, 1817–1820* (Geneva: Droz, 1968), 68.

7   Service historique de la Défense – Vincennes: BB 4 393.

8   ibid.; Masson, 111–14; Bordonove, 187–9.

9   Service historique de la Défense – Vincennes: BB 4 393; Louis XVIII, Ordinance Dissolving the Chamber signed on September 5th, Palais de Tuileries, and printed in *Journal des débats*, September 8th, 1816; *La Quotidienne*, Friday September 6th, 1816; *Le Moniteur universel*, September 8th, 1816.

10   Daudet, *Louis XVIII*, 148–9; Mansel, *Louis XVIII*, 344; Bertier de Sauvigny, *La Restauration*, 138–40; *La Quotidienne*, September 13th, 1816; François-René de Chateaubriand, *Mémoires d'outre-tombe*, ed. Levaillant (Paris: Le Club français du livre, 1969), Vol.III, 8.

11   *La Quotidienne*, Wednesday, September 11th, 1816.

12   Corréard & Savigny, 5th edn (Paris, 1821), 305–8.

13   Collins, 'Liberalism and the Newspaper', 21–2.

14   *Journal des débats*, September 13th, 1816.

15   Corréard & Savigny, 5th edn (Paris, 1821), 307–9.

16   Vicomte DuBouchage in *La Quotidienne*, September 15th, 1816.

17   Savigny, letter to *le Moniteur universel*, September 13th, 1816, reprinted in *La Quotidienne*, Monday September 16th, 1816; Corréard & Savigny, 5th edn (Paris, 1821), 306.

18   *La Quotidienne*, September 22nd, 1816; *Le Constitutionel & Journal des débats*, September 23rd, 1816; Collins, *The Government and the Newspaper*, 14–16; Collins, 'Liberalism and the Newspaper', 22.

19   Bordonove, 196, 197–8, 210–13.

20   Service historique de la Défense – Vincennes; BB 2 152;

Bertier de Sauvigny, *La Restauration*, 150; *The Times*, London, September 16th & 17th, 1816; Anon, *The History of The Times: The Thunderer in the Making 1785–1841* (London: *The Times*, 1935), 212–20, 467.

21   Service historique de la Défense – Vincennes; BB 4 393; Savigny & Corréard (London, 1818) 255–63; Corréard & Savigny, 5th edn (Paris, 1821), 309–17.

22   National Archives Ex 11/11; Parson, *Premier rapport*, v; Dard, 170.

23   Savigny & Corréard (London, 1818), 238–45; Corréard & Savigny, 5th edn (Paris, 1821), 288–93.

24   Service historique de la Défense – Vincennes: BB 4 393; Touches, 435; Savigny & Corréard, (London, 1818), 247–9; Corréard & Savigny, 5th edn (Paris, 1821), 298–304; Bordonove, 206.

25   Savigny & Corréard (London, 1818), 249–50, 261–2; Corréard & Savigny, 5th edn (Paris, 1821), 314–17.

26   Savigny & Corréard (London, 1818), 263–8; Corréard & Savigny, 5th edn (Paris, 1821), 317–22.

27   Chaumareys, *Relation*, 31–2; Bordonove, 176–7, 188–9, 214–48; Masson, 131–43.

28   'Jugement de M. Hugues Duroys de Chaumareys', in Corréard & Savigny, 5th edn (Paris, 1821), 373–82; Masson, 145–54, 189–92; Bordonove, 248.

29   Bertier de Sauvigny, *La Restauration*, 141–2.

30   Savigny & Corréard (London, 1818), 270–7; Corréard & Savigny, 5th edn (Paris, 1821), 323–9; Alexandre Corréard, letter to Decazes, June 27th, 1818, in the *Archives Nationales*, F/18/1749.

31   Mansel, *Louis XVIII*, 356; Bertier de Sauvigny, *La Restauration*, 147; Chevalier, 3–4; Newman, I, 341; Bordonove, 302–3; *Journal des débats*, October 22nd, 1817.

32   Savigny & Corréard (London, 1818), 200–1; Corréard & Savigny, 5th edn (Paris, 1821), 247.

33   C.L. Lesur, *Annuaire historique 1818*, 19–22.

34   A. Imbert, *Biographie des imprimeurs et des libraires* (Paris,

1826), 43, 48, 57; Jean de La Tynna, *Almanach du commerce de Paris, des départements de la France et des principales villes du monde* (Paris: Bureau de L'Almanach du Commerce, 1818 & 1822), 78, 98, 135; *Bibliographie de la France*, 1817, 602, entry no.3404.

35   *Le Mercure de France*, November 1817, 340–55; *Journal des débats*, November 4th, 1817.

36   *Le Journal du commerce*, November 29th, 1817; Harpaz, 156; Corréard & Savigny, 5th edn (Paris, 1821), 448–58.

9: The Fualdès Affair and the Love Affair

1   Darmon, 21; Peter Shankland and The Rt. Hon. Sir Michael Havers, Q.C., *Murder with a Double Tongue* (London: Souvenir Press, 1990), 73; Lesur (1818), 523.

2   Robert Simon, 'Géricault and l'affaire Fualdès', *Géricault, Conférences et colloques du Louvre*, Vol.1, 169–70; Darmon, 14–15, 36, 137, 158–9, 206–7; Bazin, V, 50–1; Shankland and Havers, 26–8, 71, 89, 143–6; Mansel, *Louis XVIII*, 161.

3   Manzon, quoted in Darmon, 69.

4   *La Quotidienne*, September 18th, 1817 quoted by Shankland and Havers, 137.

5   Darmon, 142–3; Shankland and Havers, 158, 255.

6   Perrot, quoted by Simon, 'Géricault and the fait divers', *Géricault, Conférences et colloques du Louvre*, Vol.1, 258; see also 257 and the rest of this excellent essay; E. Auger, quoted in M. Angenot, *Le Roman populaire; Recherches en paralittérature* (Montréal: Presses de l'Université du Québec, 1975), 16–18; Roland Barthes, 'La structure du fait divers', *Essais critiques* (Paris: Éditions Seuil, 1964), 188.

7   Linda Nochlin, 'Géricault or the Absence of Women', *Géricault, Conférences et colloques du Louvre*, Vol.I, 415.

8   Chantal Gleyses, *La Femme coupable* (Paris: Éditions Imago, 1994), 85; Patricia Mainardi, *Husbands, Wives, and*

Lovers (New Haven and London: Yale University Press, 2003), 1–3, 7, 13, 16–19; Patricia Mainardi, 'Husbands, Wives and Lovers. Mazeppa or Marriage and its Discontents in Nineteenth Century France', *Géricault, Conférences et colloques du Louvre*, Vol.1, 277–9, 280, 282–3; Patricia Mainardi, 'Mazeppa', *Word & Image*, Vol.16, No.4 (London, October 2000), 340; Bertier de Sauvigny, *La Restauration*, 236, 244.

10: Trips to the Morgue

1   Batissier, 8; Aimé-Azam, *Mazzeppa*, 159.
2   Bazin, Vol.VI, 90, Vol.I, 41–2; Donald A. Rosenthal, 'Géricault's Expenses for the Raft of the Medusa', in *Art Bulletin*, Vol.LXII (New York: College Art Association of America, December 1980), 639.
3   Buisson, 40; Edward Planta, *A New Picture of Paris or The Stranger's Guide to the French Metropolis* (London: Samuel Leigh, July 1814), 49; Mainardi, *Husbands and Wives*, 25, 193; Bertier de Sauvigny, *La Restauration*, 243; Chenique, 'Géricault, une vie', in *Gericault* (1991), 281; Le Pesant 76–8.
4   Jean-Baptiste Savigny, *Observations sur les effets de la faim*; Fournier de Pescay, 'Notice sur la Calenture, maladie particulière aux gens de mer', *Annales des faits et des sciences militaires*; Albert, Alhadeff, *The Raft of the Medusa* (Munich: Prestel, 2002), 54–5.
5   Clément, 129; Henri Houssaye, 'Un Maître de l'école française – Théodore Géricault', *Revue des deux-mondes* (Paris, November 15th, 1879), 384.
6   The present-day 80 rue du Faubourg-St-Honoré. Clément, 137; Pierre Vallery-Radot, 'L'anatomie et la psychiatrie dans la vie et l'oeuvre de Géricault', in *La presse médicale*, 66, no.27 (Paris: Masson, April 5th, 1958), 614; Eitner, *Raft*, 23–4.
7   Charles Fournel, *L'hôpital Beaujon. Histoire depuis son origine*

Medusa

jusqu'à nos jours (Paris: Dentu, 1884), 48–50, 82–7; Martial Guédron, *La plaie et le couteau: La sensibilité anatomique de Théodore Géricault 1791–1824* (Paris: Kimé, 1997), 90; Bazin, Vol.VI, 29.

8 Vallery-Radot, 'L'anatomie et la psychiatrie', 614; Hector Berlioz, *La vie de Berlioz racontée par Berlioz* (Paris: R. Juliard, 1954), 36, quoted in Inken D. Knoch, 'Une peinture sans sujet? Étude sur les fragments anatomiques', *Géricault, Conférences et colloques du Louvre*, Vol.I, 148.

9 Mansel, *Paris Between Empires*, 7, 49–50; Bertier de Sauvigny, *La Restauration*, 258–9.

10 Anon., *The Picture of the Palais Royal* (London: William Hone, 1819), 141–2; Pierre Vayre, *Les Larrey. Dominique, Hippolyte . . . et les autres* (Paris: Editions Glyphe, collection 'Société, histoire et médecine, 2005) Disarticulation is different from amputation – the bones are simply separated at a joint, rather than being sawn through, which is swifter and less dangerous on the battle-field than amputation.

11 C. Leymarie, 'Michelet et Géricault', *L'Artiste* (1897), quoted in Courthion, 191–2; Guédron, 90–2; Guillaume de Bertier de Sauvigny, *Nouvelle histoire de Paris: La Restauration* (Paris, 1977), 190; Haydon, 240.

12 Eugène Delacroix, quoted in Eitner, *Géricault's Raft*, 36.

13 Clément, 131–2; Vallery-Radot, 614; Jean-François Debord, *À propos de quelques dessins anatomiques de Géricault*', in *Géricault – Dessins et estampes des collections de l'École des Beaux-Arts* (Paris: École nationale supérieure des Beaux-Arts, 1997), 65, n.82.

14 Nina Athanassoglou-Kallmyer, 'Géricault's Severed Heads and Limbs: The Politics and Aesthetics of the Scaffold', *The Art Bulletin*, Vol.LXXXIV, No.4 (New York, December 1992), 614.

280

Notes

11: *The Raft of the Medusa*

1 Marie-Claude Chaudonneret, *L'Etat et les artistes de la Restauration à la monarchie de Juillet (1815–1833)* (Paris: Flammarion, 1999), 55–7, 72–5.

2 Grigsby, 232.

3 Montfort, quoted by Clément, 138–40.

4 Letter from Théodore Lebrun to Louis Batissier, April 8th, 1836, quoted in Bazin, Vol.I, 22.

5 Delacroix, quoted in Eitner, *The Raft*, 34.

6 Clément, 143–5.

7 Corréard & Savigny, 5th edn (Paris, 1821), 383–96.

8 Alhadeff, 137, 163, 166–7.

9 Christopher Sells, 'New Light on Géricault, his Travels and his Friends', 391–2; Clément, 137.

10 Théodore Géricault, quoted in Bazin, Vol.I, 73; Eitner, *Raft*, 32.

11 See Bazin, Vol.VI, 16; Savigny & Corréard (London, 1818), 79 (inadvertently printed between 96 & 98).

12 Clément, 144–5; Eitner, *Raft*, 38.

13 Vicomte DuBouchage, report to Louis XVIII of September 1816, in Service historique de la Défense – Vincennes BB 4 393.

14 Chaudonneret, 60, 80; Eitner, *Raft*, 2, 5–6.

15 Chaudonneret, 76, 97.

16 Clément, 147–8; Eitner, *Raft*, 2, 5, 40.

17 Jean Sagne, 'Géricault et l'opinion libérale', *Géricault, Conférences et colloques du Louvre*, Vol.II, 597–8; Bertier de Sauvigny, *La Restauration*, 152; Chaudonneret, 125; Bazin, Vol.1, 44, where the remark seems to have come to Jean Gigoux via the painter Gros, its authenticity questioned.

18 *La Quotidienne*, August 30th, 1819, 4; Pierre Angrand, *Le Comte Forbin et le Louvre en 1819* (Lausanne-Paris/Bibliothèque des Arts, 1972), 172.

19 Aimé-Azam, *Mazeppa*, 169.

20 *La Minerve française*, September 10th, 1819; *Le Moniteur universel*, October 12th, 1819; Eitner, *Raft*, 40–1.

21 *Gazette de France*, August 31st, 1819; Gustave Jal, *L'Ombre de Diderot et le bossu du Marais; Dialogue critique sur le Salon de 1819* (Paris: Corréard, 1819), 128.

22 *L'Indépendant*, August 29th, 1819, 3.

23 Alphonse Rabbe, 'Nécrologie, Géricault peintre d'histoire', *La Pandore, Journal des spectacles, des lettres, des arts, des moeurs et des modes*, No.198 (Paris, January 29th, 1824).

24 Géricault, letter to M. Musigny, quoted in Batissier, 14; *Le drapeau blanc*, August 26th, 1819, 3.

25 Eitner, *Raft*, 52–4, 60.

26 Le Pesant, 77; Eitner, *Raft*, 61; Bazin, Vol.1, 129; Sells, 'New Light on Géricault, his Travels and his Friends', 395; Christopher Sells, 'Two Letters from Gericault to Madame Horace Vernet', *The Burlington Magazine*, Vol.CXXXI, No.1032 (London: March 1989), 217.

12: *The Medusa* Sails On

1 Paul Joannides, '*The Raft of the Medusa*' (a review of Eitner's monograph), *The Burlington Magazine*, Vol.CXVII, No.864 (London: March 1975), 171–2.

2 John McLeod, *Voyage of His Majesty's late ship 'Alceste' along the coast of Corea to the island of Lewchew, with an account of her subsequent shipwreck in the straits of Gaspar*, compiled from the papers of John McLeod (London: John Murray, 1818), 3, 207–15, 220–1, 248, 253, appendix; John McLeod, *The Shipwreck of the Alceste, an English frigate in the straits of Gaspar; also the Shipwreck of the Medusa*, compiled from the papers of John McLeod and the narrative by Savigny and Corréard (Dublin: E.Tute, 1822), 157.

3 Houssaye, 387.

4 Mansel, *Paris Between Empires*, 41, 44, 149–50; Mansel, *Louis XVIII*, 214.

5 Suzanne Lodge, 'Géricault in England', *Burlington*

Notes

Magazine, Vol.CVII, No.753 (London, December 1965), 617–18; Thomas Jessop, *Journal d'un voyage à Paris en septembre–octobre 1820,* ed. F.C.W. Hiley (Paris: 1928), 18–19; Bertier de Sauvigny, *La Restauration,* 331; Eric J. Evans, *Britain Before the Reform Act: Politics and Society 1815–1832* (London and New York: Longman, 1989), 1–5, 15, 19, 22–4, 50; John Belchem, *Popular Radicalism in Nineteenth Century Britain* (London: Macmillan, 1996), 47–8; Mansel, *Paris Between Empires,* 142–4.

6   Sells, 'New Light on Géricault', 390; Théodore Géricault, letter to Dedreux-Dorcy, April 23rd, 1820, quoted in Courthion, 96; Lodge, 'Géricault in England', 617; Clément, 189–90.

7   Christine Riding, '*The Raft of the Medusa* in Britain – Audience and Context', *Crossing the Channel, British and French Painting in the Age of Romanticism,* ed. by Patrick Noon (London: Tate Publishing, 2003), 71; Hugh Honour, 'Curiosities of the Egyptian Hall', *Country Life,* Vol.CXV, No.2973 (London January 7th, 1954), 38–9; Richard Altick, *The Shows of London* (Cambridge, Mass., and London: The Belknap Press, 1978), 235, 236–8.

8   Haydon, *Life,* 367, 378; *The Literary Gazette: Journal of Belles Letters,* July 1st, 1820, 427, quoted in Riding, 'The Raft of the Medusa in Britain – Audience and Context', 72.

9   Sells, 'New Light on Géricault', 392; Boime, 'Géricault's African Slave Trade and the Physiognomy of the Oppressed', 574–5; Nina Athanassoglou, 'Géricault and La Liberté des Peuples', text submitted for publication in *Art History,* n.d., 21 (copy in The Sackler Library, University of Oxford); *Le Conservateur littéraire* (Paris, 1820), 208.

10   Belchem, 49; Evans, *Britain Before the Reform Act,* 18, 26–7; E.P. Thompson, *The Making of the English Working Class* (New York: Vintage Books, 1963), 702–5.

11   Although he was with Géricault at the time, Charlet's account of this incident has been strongly contested, as has Silvestre's story concerning the aftermath of a drunken

283

dinner. On the advice of Dedreux-Dorcy, Clément discredited these stories and rather suggests that, although Géricault had his dark moments, 'he was relatively happy and tranquil while he was living in England'. Clément points out that a letter of April 23rd to Dedreux-Dorcy shows no signs of despair; Chenique, 'Géricault: une vie', *Géricault*, 290–1; Clément, 187–8; Houssaye, 388: Sells, 'New Light on Géricault', 392.

12   W.T. Moncrieff, *Shipwreck of The Medusa, or, the Fatal Raft! – A Drama in Three Acts* (London, 1830), introduction & 17.

13   *The Morning Post*, June 13th, 1820; William Bullock, *Sale Catalogue of the Bullock Museum – 1819* (facs. – London: Johnson and Hewett, 1979); W.H. Mullens, 'William Bullock's London Museum', in *Museums Journal*, No.17 (London: October 1917), 54; Honour, 38; Haydon, *Life*, 371–3; Johnson, '*The Raft of the Medusa* in Great Britain', *The Burlington Magazine,* Vol.XCVI, No.617 (London, August 1954), 250.

14   *The Globe*, June 12th, 1820, quoted in Eitner, *Raft*, 64.

15   *The Morning Post*, June 13th, 1820 and *The Times*, June 22nd, 1820 – both quoted in Johnson, '*The Raft of the Medusa* in Great Britain', 250.

16   *The London Literary Gazette: Journal of Belles Lettres*, June 10th and July 1st, 1820, 427, quoted in Johnson, '*The Raft of the Medusa* in Great Britain', 250–1.

17   Jessop, *Journal*, 65; Anon., *Souscription en faveur du libraire Corréard, condamné pour avoir vendu des brochures politiques, dont les auteurs et les éditeurs étaient connus* (Paris: 1820), 2; Alan B. Spitzer, *Old Hatred and Young Hopes – The French Carbonari against the Bourbon Restoration* (Cambridge, Mass.: Harvard University Press, 1971), 62–3; Mansel, *Louis XVIII*, 375; Mansel, *Paris Between Empires*, 172, 177–8; Bertier de Sauvigny, *La Restauration*, 163–6, 168, 172.

18   Johnson, '*The Raft of the Medusa* in Great Britain', 251–2 and quoting *Saunder's News-Letter*, 17th February, 1821.

19   *Saunder's News-Letter,* March 5th, 1821, quoted in Johnson, '*The Raft of the Medusa* in Great Britain', 251.

20   Sells, 'New Light on Géricault', 392; Bazin, Vol.VII, 20.

21   Sells, 'New Light on Géricault', 390; Michael Twyman, *Lithography 1800–1850* (London: Oxford University Press, 1970), 183, 185; Bruno Chenique, '*Théodore Géricault, lithographe d'avant garde', Géricault — Dessins et estampes des collections de l'École des Beaux-Arts* (Paris: École nationale supérieure des Beaux-Arts, 1998), 118.

22   Théodore Géricault, letter to Dedreaux-Dorcy of February 12th, 1821, quoted in Courthion, 98; Chenique, 'Géricault: une vie', 295, 257; Cockerell's diaries, quoted in Lee Johnson, 'Géricault and Delacroix seen by Cockerell', in *The Burlington Magazine*, Vol.CXIII, No.822 (London, September 1971), 547–51; Bazin, Vol.VII, 10.

23   Théodore Géricault, letter to Jules Auguste of December 27th, 1821, quoted in Bazin, Vol.1, 65.

13: A Larger Struggle

1   Jessop, 70–1; Mansel, *Paris Between Empires*, 41–2; Major W.E. Frye, *After Waterloo — Reminiscences of European Travel 1815–19* (London, 1908), 59–60; H. Déterville, *Le Palais Royal ou les filles en bonne fortune* (Paris: 1815), ix, 15.

2   Lewis Tronchet, *Picture of Paris, being a complete guide to all the public buildings, places of amusement, and curiosities in that metropolis* (London: Sherwood, Neely and Jones, 1814), 160; Déterville, 15–17; Planta, 54; Anon., *The Picture of the Palais Royal*, 25, 40, 151; Honoré de Balzac, *La Peau de chagrin* (1831) (Paris: Gallimard, 1974), 23–4.

3   Anon., *The Picture of the Palais Royal*, 14–17, 27, 29, 52, 60, 144–5; John Scott of Gala, 281–2; Bertier de Sauvigny, *Nouvelle Histoire de Paris: La Restauration*, 381.

4   Anon., *The Picture of the Palais Royal*, 21, 29–31, 83–4;

Hugues, 21; Jessop, 73; Frye, 61; Jeanne Gilmore, *La République clandestine*, 30; *Archives nationales*, F/18/1749.

5 *Le Mercure de France,* December 1817, 603; Harpaz, 155–6; Shankland & Havers, 156.

6 Griffon du Bellay, 28; *La Minerve française*, February 1818, 104.

7 Alexandre Corréard, *Élections des Représentants du Peuple*, 2.

8 Mansel, *Paris Between Empires*, 307; Bertier de Sauvigny, *La Restauration*, 340.

9 Corréard & Savigny, 5th edn (Paris, 1821), 398–405; Arnold Charles Scheffer, *De l'Etat de la liberté en France* (Brussels, 1818), preface.

10 Bruno Chenique, 'On the Far Left of Géricault', in Serge Guilbaut, Maureen Ryan and Scott Watson, eds, *Théodore Géricault – The Alien Body: Tradition in Chaos* (Vancouver: Morris and Helen Belkin Art Gallery, 1997), 73–5.

11 The copy of Jacques Bousquet-Deschamps, *Questions à l'ordre du jour* (Paris: Chez Corréard, April 8th, 1820), in the *Archives nationales*, BB/18/999, and other items like the letter from the *Procureur Général* of Toulouse, dated April 1820; Jean Sagne, 'Géricault et l'opinion libérale', *Géricault, Conférences et colloques du Louvre,* Vol.2, 605.

12 J.-Lucien Bousquet-Deschamps, *Attention!* (Paris: Corréard, May 17th, 1820), 15–16; Corréard & Savigny, 5th edn (Paris, 1821), 406–43.

13 Werdet, *De la librairie française: son passé, son présent et son avenir* (Paris, 1860), 178; Nina Athanassoglou, 'Géricault and La Liberté des Peuples', 10–11; Hugues, 21; *Archives nationales*, F/18/1749.

14 Léonard Gallois, *Promenade à Saint-Pélagie* (Paris, Leroux, 1823), 6, 11–12, 14, 21–22, 31, 32–9; Newman, 80–1, 939; Sauvigny, *Nouvelle Histoire de Paris*, 47, 463; Collins, *Government and Society in France*, 27–8; Néret, 119; Corréard & Savigny, 5th edn (Paris, 1821), 443–7; Anon, *Souscription en faveur du libraire Corréard*, 1–3; *Je sais tout,*

Notes

July 15th, 1916, in the Corréard deposit in the Archives Départmentales, Gap; *Archives nationales*, BB/18/999.

15 Spitzer, *Old Hatred and Young Hopes*, 2–3, 6–7, 58, 105–16; Bertier de Sauvigny, *La Restauration*, 180–1; Bordonove, 288–9.

16 Alexandre Corréard, *Élections des Représentants du peuple à l'Assemblée Législative*, 2.

17 Alhadeff, 123–5; Savigny & Corréard (London, 1818), 179–84; Adanson, *A Voyage to Senegal*, vii, 48–9.

18 Guilbaut, Ryan and Watson, eds, *Théodore Géricault – The Alien Body*; 'Liberal Ironies, Colonial Narratives and the Rhetoric of Art: Reconsidering Géricault's *Radeau de la Méduse*', 30–1.

19 Henri Grégoire, *On the slave-trade and on the slavery of the blacks and of the whites, by a friend of men of all colours* (London: Josiah Conder, 1815), 2; Boime, 'Géricault's African Slave Trade and the Physiognomy of the Oppressed', in *Géricault, Conférences et colloques du Louvre*, 567.

20 Chevalier, *Histoire de la Marine Française*, 7–8; Hugh Thomas, *The Slave Trade* (London: Papermac, 1998), 587; Savigny & Corréard (London, 1818), 311–17.

21 Thomas Clarkson, *The Cries of Africa to the inhabitants of Europe; or, a Survey of that Bloody Commerce called the Slave-Trade* (London, 1822), 26–7.

22 James Walvin, *England, Slaves and Freedom 1776–1838* (London: Macmillan, 1986), 126–7; *The Times*, July 10th, 1819; 'De la traite des Nègres au Sénégal', a translation of the *13th Report of the Directors of the African Institution, London of March 24th, 1819*, presented by Benjamin Constant in *La Minerve française*, 113, 116; J. Morenas, *Pétition contre la Traite des Noirs qui se fait au Sénégal, présentée à la Chambre des Députés le 14 juin, 1820* (Paris: Corréard, 1820), 10.

23 Geoffrey de Villeneuve, Vol.IV, 40–1, 44, 49.

24 Paul Marty, *Études Sénégalaise* (Paris: Société de l'Histoire

des Colonies Françaises et Librairie Larose, 1925), 95, 101, 105, 157; Faure, 'La garnison européenne', 17–18; Gabriel Debien, 'J.E. Morenas à Saint Louis en 1818–19', in *Bulletin de l'Institut français d'Afrique noire*, series B, XXX, 2 (April 1968), 692.

25 Letters from English observers in Sierra Leone and Senegal, variously dated March 6th, 18th, 19th, June 28th, July 21st and November 8th, 1817 in the National Archives FO/95/9/2.

26 Serge Daget, 'L'Abolition de la traite des noirs en France de 1814 à 1831', *Cahiers d'études africaines II* (1971), 28–9; Bertier de Sauvigny, *La Restauration*, 157; Thomas, 620.

27 Jean-Vincent Giudicelly, *Observations sur la traite des Noirs en réponse au rapport de M. Courvoisier sur la pétition de M. Morenas* (Paris: Chez les Marchands de Nouveautés, 1820), 1, 12.

28 Marty, 195–6; Faure, 19, 29, 30–1; Daget, 'L'Abolition . . .', 27.

29 *The Times*, June 13th, 1818; Serge Daget, *Répertoire des expéditions négrières françaises à la traite illégale (1814–1850)* (Nantes, 1988), 32–3, 36, 52, 53, 55, 65, 87.

30 Daget, 'L'Abolition . . .', 30, 193; Serge Daget, *La répression de la traite des Noirs au XIX siècle* (Paris: Éditions Karthala, 1997), 69; Esquirol, Vol.II, 172–3.

31 Giudicelly, *Observations sur la traite des Noirs*, 22, 23.

32 Jean-Vincent Giudicelly, *Réponse de M. l'abbé Giudicelly, ex-préfet apostolique du Sénégal et de Gorée, à une lettre de S. Exc. le Bon Portal, ministre de la marine, 30 Avril, 1821* (Paris: Impr. de Mme Jeunehomme-Crémière, 1821), 10, 15; Gueye, 'L'Afrique et l'esclavage . . .', 202–3; Daget, 'L'Abolition . . .', 31; Thomas, 584; *The Times*, July 20th, 1818; Morenas, *Pétition contre la Traite des Noirs*, 5–6.

33 Morenas, *Pétition contre la Traite des Noirs*, 4–7, 12; J. Morenas, *Seconde Pétition contre La Traite des Noirs présentée*

à la Chambre des Députées le 19 Mars, 1821 (Paris, 1821), 55; Debien, 694.

34   Daget, 'L'Abolition . . .', 34; Debien, 693; Gueye, *L'Afrique et l'esclavage* (Paris: Éditions Martinsart, 1983), 204.

35   Daget, 'L'abolition . . .', 36; M'Baye Gueye, 'La Fin de l'esclavage à Saint Louis et à Gorée en 1848', in *Notes d'Histoire Coloniale*, No.102 – extract from *Bulletin de l'I.F.A.N.*, Vol.28, Series B, No.3–4 (Dakar, 1996), 641; Alhadeff, 155, 157.

36   Morenas, *Pétition* (1820), 12; Thomas, 805; Joseph Elzéar Morenas, *Précis historique de la traite des Noirs et de l'esclavage colonial contenant l'origine de la traite, ses progrès, son état actual et un exposé des horreurs produites par le despotisme des colons; ouvrage dans lequel on prouve qu'on a exporté d'Afrique, depuis 1814 jusqu'à présent, plus de 700 000 esclaves, dans un grande nombre sous pavillon français* (Paris, 1828), 176.

37   Jacques de Caso, 'Géricault, David d'Angers, le Monument à l'émancipation et autres objects ou figures du racisme romantique', *Géricault, Conférences et colloques du Louvre*, Vol.2, 538; *La Minerve française*, August 9th, 1819, 113–14.

38   Charles Blanc, 421.

39   Boime, *The Art of Exclusion*, 62–3.

40   Bro de Comères, 162; Clément, 227–30; Chenique, 'Géricault, une vie', in *Géricault*, 298–9, for extracts from all the early accounts of these accidents.

41   Chaudonneret, 40; Comte Forbin, quoted in Chaudonneret, 40.

42   Bazin, Vol.1, 74, 83–5 & Vol.VI, 20; letter of Count de Forbin, quoted in Chenique, 'Géricault, une vie', *Géricault*, 303.

43   Eugène Delacroix, *The Journal of Eugène Delacroix* (London: Phaidon, 1951, pbk 1995), 19.

44   ibid., 24.

14: The Shipwreck and the Shipwrecked

1   Mansel, *Louis XVIII*, 399–404.

2   Alexandre Corréard, *Pétition des membres de la commission des condamnés pour causes politiques, adressée aux deux chambres* (Paris: 1832), 7–8.

3   Alexandre Corréard, *Résumé pour le sieur Corréard*, 2, 6; Werdet, 178; Alexandre Corréard, *Mémoire sur le projet d'un chemin de fer de Paris à Bordeaux* (Paris: Librairie Scientifique et Industrielle, 1838), 5; Alexandre Corréard, *Mémoire sur les différents moyens qui peuvent être employés par l'État pour intervenir dans l'exécution des chemins de fer en France, contenant des renseignements sur l'affaire du chemin de fer de Paris à Tours* (Paris: L. Mathias, 1837), 66.

4   Jore, *La vie diverse*, 306; Bordonove, 320–1; Corréard, *Mémoire sur le projet d'un chemin de fer*, 5.

5   Breillout, 248–50; Masson, 233–4.

6   Service historique de la Défense – Vincennes: Dossiers, Vincent Marie Martin Chaudière, Francis Cornette de Vénancourt, Jean Daniel Coudein, Jean Espiaux, Pierre Joseph Lapeyrère, Joseph Michel Maudet, Léon Henry de Parnajon, Alexandre Léonard Rang des Adrets, Joseph Pierre André Reynaud, Jean Baptiste Henri Savigny.

7   Louis Robert, 'Une odyssée atroce: le Radeau de la Méduse. La tragique Origine d'une thèse de médecine', in *La Presse médicale*, 61, No.51 (Paris: Masson, August 8th, 1953), 1084; Michel Savigny, in *L'Intermédiaire des Chercheurs*, No.934 (Paris: May 30th, 1901), column 1010.

8   Alexandre Corréard, *Chemin de fer de Paris à Versailles, rive gauche. Causes de la ruine de l'entreprise et réponses critiques aux attaques de la Compagnie* (Paris: L. Mathias, 1839), 3; Alexandre Corréard, *Chemin de fer de Paris à Bordeaux, par Chartres. Pétition sur l'usurpation par les Ponts et chaussées du projet de chemin de fer de Paris à Bordeaux, pour la partie comprise entre Tours et Bordeaux, présentée à la Chambre des*

Pairs par Alexandre Corréard (Paris, 1842), 2–8; Alexandre Corréard, *Élections des Représentants du peuple à l'Assemblée Législative*; Alexandre Corréard, *Projet d'un barrage éclusé et mobile* (Paris, 1856), 16–17; Hughes, 20.

9   Dard, iii, 141, 226, 287; Mercier, 59–60; *La Minerve française* (1819), 122; Debien, 692; Corréard & Savigny, 5th edn (Paris, 1821), 14–15: Brédif, 79.

10   Rang, 39; Griffon du Bellay, 27.

11   Savigny & Corréard (London, 1818), 46, 56, 69–70, 88, 100.

12   Corréard & Savigny, 5th edn (Paris, 1821), 121–4; Savigny & Corréard (London, 1818), 104; Savigny, 'Observations de la faim et de la soif', Escudier, 112, 116; Bordonove, 161, 285.

13   Savigny & Corréard (London, 1818), 107–8, 119–20; Corréard & Savigny, 5th edn (Paris, 1821), 131.

14   Savigny & Corréard, 5th edn (Paris, 1821), 61–2; Anglas de Praviel, *Relation*, 281.

15   Savigny & Corréard (London, 1818), 98; Anglas de Praviel, *Relation*, 280, 283, 287–8, 8, 309.

16   Rang, 88; Bordonove, 155–6.

17   Brédif, 143; Bordonove, 156–7.

18   Quoted by Griffon du Bellay in *Les Griffons*, 27.

19   Service historique de la Défense – Vincennes: Dossier marine, Jean Baptiste Henri Savigny.

20   Savigny & Corréard (London, 1818), 94–5, 120; Grigsby, 173, 176.

21   Arnold Sheffer, 'Salon de 1827', in the *Revue Française*, t. 1, 197, quoted in Chaudonneret, 82; Berlin, *The Roots of Romanticism*, 15.

22   This is the traditional title of a painting now known as *The Polar Sea* in the Kunsthalle, Hamburg.

23   Mary Shelley, *Frankenstein* (1819) (London: Wordsworth Editions, 1993), 41.

24   Jules Michelet, 'L'Enfant du siècle', 5ème leçon, quoted in Courthion, 112, 114.

25 Chaudonneret, 40; Clément, 252–3, n.1; Philippe Grunchec, 'L'inventaire posthume de Théodore Géricault', 406; Lorenz Eitner, 'The Sale of Géricault's Studio in 1824', *Gazette des Beaux-Arts*, Vol.LIII (Paris and New York: Presses universitaires de France), 122; Bazin, Vol.I, 92.

26 Bazin, Vol.I, 107, 110.

27 Mansell, *Paris Between Empires*, 49.

28 Bordonove, 263, 265–6; Jean-Yves Blot, 'Sur les traces de la Méduse', in François Bellec, *L'affaire de la Méduse* – Musée de la marine, Palais de Chaillot, 14 mai–21 juin 1981 (Paris: Musée de la marine, 1981).

29 *Archives départmentales*, Gap; Hughes, 23; Bazin, Vol.VI, 84–5.

30 Sagne, *Géricault*, 272; Bazin, Vol.VI, 65.

31 Bazin, Vol.I, 106.

32 ibid., 116, 150.

33 Louise Becq de Fouqières to Georges-Hippolyte Géricault, July 19th, 1863, quoted in Bazin, Vol.I, 126; Bazin, Vol.I, 129, 138, 186; Le Pesant, 73, 77; Mainardi, 'Husbands, Wives and Lovers', 285.

34 Le Pesant, 77; Chenique, 'Le Tombeau de Géricault', *Géricault, Conférences et colloques du Louvre*, Vol.II, 725–6.

35 Bazin, Vol.I, 122, 124, 126, 157–8, 160, 163.

Bibliography

Abrahams, Aleck, 'The Egyptian Hall, Piccadilly', *The Antiquary*, 42. London, 1906.

Ackerknecht, Erwin H., *Medicine at the Paris Hospital 1784–1848*. Baltimore: Johns Hopkins Press, 1967.

Adanson, M., *A Voyage to Senegal, the Isle of Gorée and the River Gambia*. Dublin: Ewing, James & Bradley, 1759.

Aimé-Azam, Denise, *Mazeppa, Géricault et son temps*. Paris: Plon, 1956.

Aimé-Azam, Denise, *La Passion de Géricault*. Paris: Fayard, 1970.

Alhadeff, Albert, *The Raft of the Medusa*. Munich: Prestel, 2002.

Altick, Richard, *The Shows of London*. Cambridge, Mass., and London: The Belknap Press, 1978.

Angenot, Marc, *Le Roman populaire; recherches en paralittérature*. Montreal: Presses de l'Université du Québec, 1975.

Anglas de Praviel, Paulin d', '*Relation nouvelle et impartiale du naufrage de la frégate la Méduse* (Nîmes: Paulin d'Anglas de Praviel, 1858), in *Relation complète du naufrage de la frégate la Méduse*. Paris: J. de Bonnot, 1968.

Angrand, Pierre, *Le Comte de Forbin et le Louvre en 1819*. Lausanne-Paris: Bibliothèque des Arts, 1972.

Année, Antoine, *Le livre noir de Messieurs Delavau et Franchet, ou Répertoire alphabétique de la police politique sous le ministère déplorable; ouvrage imprimé d'après les registres de l'Administration*. Paris: Moutardier, 1829.

Anon., *Le Naufrage de la Méduse*. Paris: Delarue, 1842.

Anon., *Le Naufrage de la Méduse – Légendes populaires.* Paris: P. Martinon, 1863.

Anon., *Souscription en faveur du libraire Corréard, condamné pour avoir vendu des brochures politiques, dont les auteurs et les éditeurs étaient connu.* Paris, 1820.

Anon., *The History of The Times 'The Thunderer' in the Making 1785–1841.* London: The Times, 1935.

Anon., *The Picture of the Palais Royal.* London: William Hone, 1819.

Anon., *The Shipwreck of the Alceste . . . The Shipwreck of the Medusa.* Dublin: E. Tute, 1822.

Antal, Frederick, 'Reflections on Classicism and Romanticism', Parts III, IV and V, *The Burlington Magazine.* London, September 1940, December 1940 and January 1941.

Athanassoglou, Nina, 'Géricault and La Liberté des Peuples'. Text submitted for publication in *Art History*, n.d., copy in the Sackler Library, University of Oxford.

Athanassoglou-Kallmyer, Nina, Géricault: politique et esthétique de la mort', in *Géricault, Conférences et colloques du Louvre*, Vol.1. Paris: La documentation française, 1996.

Athanassoglou-Kallmyer, Nina, 'Géricault's Severed Heads and Limbs: The Politics and Aesthetics of the Scaffold', *The Art Bulletin*, Vol.LXXIV, No.4, 599–619. New York, December 1992.

Athanassoglou-Kallmyer, Nina, '*Imago Belli*: Vernet's *L'Atelier* as an Image of Radical Militarism under the Restoration', *The Art Bulletin*, Vol.LXVII, No.2, 268–80. New York, June 1986.

Athanassoglou-Kallmyer, Nina, 'Liberals of the World Unite: Géricault, his Friends and *La Liberté des Peuples*', *Gazette des Beaux-Arts*, Vol.CXVI, 227–42. Paris, December 1990.

Bailly, Auguste, *Le Radeau de la Méduse.* Paris: la Renaissance du Livre, 1929.

Balzac, Honoré de, *La Peau de chagrin.* Paris: Gallimard, 1974.

Baron, Auguste, *Naufrage de la Méduse.* Limoges: E. Ardant, 1879.

Barthes, Roland, '*La structure du fait divers*', in *Essais critique.* Paris: Éditions Seuil, 1964.

Batissier, Louis, 'Géricault', reprint from *Revue du dix-neuvième Siècle* (Rouen, n.d., [1842 is a mistake in many citations] 1824).

Bibliography

Bazin, Germain, *Théodore Géricault, étude critique, documents et catalogue raisonné*, Vols I–VII. Paris: Wildenstein Institute: la Bibliothèque des arts, 1988–97.

Belchem, John, *Popular Radicalism in Nineteenth Century Britain*. London: Macmillan, 1996.

Bellanger, Claude, et al., *Histoire générale de la presse française, Vol.II 1815–1871*. Paris: Presses universitaires de France, 1969.

Bellec, François, *L'affaire de la Méduse* – Musée national de la marine, Palais de Chaillot, 14 mai-21 juin 1981. Paris: Musée national de la marine, 1981.

Berger, Klaus, *Géricault's Drawings and Watercolors*. New York: H. Bittner, 1946.

Bergot, François, *Géricault* – *tout l'oeuvre gravé*. Rouen: Musée des beaux-arts de Rouen, 1981.

Berlin, Isaiah, *The Roots of Romanticism*, edited by Henry Hardy. London: Chatto & Windus, 1999.

Berlioz, Hector, *La vie de Berlioz racontée par Berlioz*. Paris: R. Juliard, 1954.

Bertier de Sauvigny, Guillaume de, *La Restauration*. Paris: Flammarion, 1955, pbk 1999.

Bertier de Sauvigny, Guillaume de, *Nouvelle Histoire de Paris: La Restauration*. Paris: Hachette, 1977.

Besse, Jean-Paul, *Compiègne dans l'histoire: une ville impériale et royale*. Paris: Éd. D.U.C., 1992.

Bjelajac, David, *American Art – A Cultural History*. London: Laurence King, 2000.

Blanc, Charles, *Histoire des peintres français au XIX siècle*. Paris: Cauville frères, 1845.

Blot, Jean-Yves, *'La Méduse' – chronique d'un naufrage ordinaire*. Paris: Arthaud, 1982.

Blot, Jean-Yves, *'Sur les traces de la Méduse'*, in Bellec, *L'affaire de la Méduse* – Musée national de la marine, Palais de Chaillot, 14 mai-21 juin 1981. Paris: Musée national de la marine, 1981.

Boime, Albert, 'Géricault's African Slave Trade and the Physiognomy of the Oppressed, in *Géricault, Conférences et colloques du Louvre*, Vol.II. Paris: La documentation française, 1996.

Boime, Albert, *The Art of Exclusion: Representing Blacks in the Nineteenth Century*. Washington, D.C.: Smithsonian Institution Press, 1990.

Boorde, Andrew, *Dyetary*, edited by F.J. Furnivall. Early English Text Society, e.s. 10. London, 1870.

Bordonove, Georges, *Le Naufrage de 'la Méduse'*. Paris: R. Laffont, 1973.

Bousquet-Deschamps, Jacques-Lucien, *Attention!* Paris: Corréard, May 17th, 1820.

Bousquet-Deschamps, Jacques-Lucien, *Pièces politiques*. Paris: Corréard, 1820.

Bousquet-Deschamps, Jacques-Lucien, *Questions à l'ordre du jour*. Paris: Corréard, April 8th, 1820.

Brédif, Charles-Marie, 'Le naufrage de la "Méduse", mon voyage au Sénégal', *La Revue de Paris*, Nos 11, 12 & 13. Paris: 1907.

Breillout, J., 'La vie dramatique de M. de Chaumereix', *Bulletin de la Société des lettres, sciences et arts de la Corrèze*, 238–51. Tulle, 1933.

Brisson, M. de, *Histoire du Naufrage et de la captivité de M. De Brisson*. Geneva & Paris, 1789.

Bro, Louis, *Mémoires du général Bro (1796–1844)*, edited by Bro de Comères, Le Baron Henry. Paris: Plon-Nourrit et Cie, 1914.

Broglie, Achille-Charles-Léonce-Victor, Duc de, *Discours prononcé par M. le duc de Broglie, à la Chambre des Pairs, le 28 mars 1822 sur la traite des nègres*. Paris, 1822.

Brookner, Anita, *Romanticism and its Discontents*. New York: Viking, 2000.

Brown, David Blayney, 'Literature and History: Shakespeare, Scott, Byron and Genre Historique', in *Crossing the Channel, British and French Painting in the Age of Romanticism*, edited by Patrick Noon. London: Tate Publishing, 2003.

Brown, David Blayney, *Romanticism*. London & New York: Phaidon, 2001.

Brunet, Auguste, *De l'Aristocratie et de la démocratie, de l'importance du travail, et de la richesse mobilière*. Paris: Corréard, 1819.

Buisson, Gilles, *Géricault: de Mortain à Paris*. Coutances: OCEP, 1976.

Bibliography

Bullock, William, *Sale Catalogue of the Bullock Museum – 1819*. London: Johnson and Hewett, 1979.

Byron, George Gordon, Lord, *Byron, A Self Portrait, Letters and Diaries 1798 to 1824*, Vol.II, edited by Peter Quennell. New York: Charles Scribner's & Sons, 1950.

Carey, David, *Life in Paris*. London: John Fairburn, 1822.

Caron, François, *Histoire des chemins de fer en France*, Vol.I. Paris: Fayard, 1997.

Caso, Jacques de, 'Géricault, David d'Angers, le Monument à l'émancipation et autres objets ou figures du racisme romantique', in *Géricault, Conférences et colloques du Louvre*, Vol.II. Paris: La documentation française, 1996.

Castel, René-Richard, *Lettres de René-Richard-Louis Castel . . . au comte Louis de Chevigné*. Rheims: Delaunois, 1883.

Chateaubriand, François-René de, *Mémoires d'outre-tombe*, Vol.III, edited by Levaillant. Paris: Le Club français du livre, 1969.

Chaudonneret, Marie-Claude, *L'Etat et les artistes de la Restauration à la monarchie de Juillet – 1815–1833*. Paris: Flammarion, 1999.

Chaumareys, Hugues Duroy de, *Relation de M. de Chaumereix, officier de la marine, échappé aux massacres d'Aurai et de Vannes, suivie de quelques observations sur l'esprit public en Bretagne*. London: J. de Boffe, 1795.

Chenique, Bruno, 'Géricault posthume', in *Géricault, Conférences et colloques du Louvre*, Vol.II. Paris: La documentation française, 1996.

Chenique, Bruno, 'Géricault: une vie' & 'Lettres et documents', in *Géricault*, edited by Régis Michel. Paris: Éditions de la Réunion des musées nationaux, 1991.

Chenique, Bruno, 'Le tombeau de Géricault', in *Géricault, Conférences et colloques du Louvre*, Vol.II. Paris: La documentation française, 1996.

Chenique, Bruno, 'On the Far Left of Géricault', in *Théodore Géricault – The Alien Body: Tradition in Chaos*, edited by Serge Guilbaut, Maureen Ryan and Scott Watson. Vancouver: Morris and Helen Belkin Art Gallery, 1997.

Chenique, Bruno, 'Pour une étude de milieu: le cercle amical de Géricault', in *Géricault, Conférences et colloques du Louvre*, Vol.1. Paris: La documentation française, 1996.

Chenique, Bruno, 'Théodore Géricault, lithographe d'avant garde', in *Géricault – dessins et estampes des collections de l'École des beaux-arts*. Paris: École nationale supérieure des beaux-arts, 1997.

Chevalier, E., *Histoire de la Marine Française de 1815–1870*. Paris: Hachette, 1900.

Clarkson, Thomas, *The Cries of Africa to the Inhabitants of Europe; or, a Survey of that Bloody Commerce called the Slave-Trade*. London: Harvey and Darton and W. Phillipps, 1822.

Clément, Charles, *Géricault – étude biographique et critique*. Paris: Didier & Co., 1868.

Clinch, Dermot, 'Hans Werner Henze – Profile', *New Statesman*. London: June 21st, 1996.

Cochelet, Charles, *Narrative of the Shipwreck of the Sophia on the 30th May, 1819, on the Western Coast of Africa*. London: Sir Richard Phillips and Co., 1822.

Cohen, William B., *The French Encounter with Africans: White Response to Blacks 1530–1880*. Bloomington: Indiana University Press, 1980.

Collier, Peter, 'Newspaper and myth: migrations of the Romantic image', in *Artistic Relations: Literature and the Visual Arts in Nineteenth-Century France*, edited by Collier & Lethbridge. New Haven and London: Yale University Press, 1994.

Collins, Irene, ed., *Government and Society in France, 1814–1848*. London: Edward Arnold, 1970.

Collins, Irene, 'Liberalism and the Newspaper Press during the French Restoration 1814–1830', in *History*, Vol.XLVI, 17–32. London: RKP, 1961.

Collins, Irene, *The Government and the Newspaper Press in France 1814–1881*. London: Oxford University Press, 1959.

Conservateur littéraire, Le, Vol.II. Paris, 1820.

Constant, Benjamin, introducing '*De la traite des Nègres au Sénégal*'. A translation of 'The 13th Report of the Directors of the

Bibliography

African Institution, London of March 24th, 1819', *La Minerve française*, 113–24. Paris, 1819.

Constitutionnel, Le. Paris, 1815–17.

Corréard, Alexandre, *Bases d'un projet de loi à intervenir dans l'intérêt des condamnés pour délits politiques sous les deux derniers règnes*. Paris, n.d. [1831].

Corréard, Alexandre, *Chemin de fer de Paris à Bordeaux, par Chartres. Pétition sur l'usurpation par les Ponts et chaussées du project de chemin de fer de Paris à Bordeaux, pour la partie comprise entre Tours et Bordeaux, présentée à la Chambre des Pairs par Alexandre Corréard*. Paris, 1842.

Corréard, Alexandre, *Chemin de fer de Paris à Versailles, rive gauche. Causes de la ruine de l'entreprise et réponses critiques aux attaques de la Compagnie*. Paris: L. Mathias, 1839.

Corréard, Alexandre, *Élections des Représentants du peuple à l'Assemblée législative. Alexandre Corréard, Ingénieur (du Radeau de 'La Méduse') aux électeurs du département Seine-et-Marne*. Batignolles, n.d.

Corréard, Alexandre, *Mémoire sur le project d'un chemin de fer de Paris à Bordeaux*. Paris: Librairie Scientifique et Industrielle, 1838.

Corréard, Alexandre, *Mémoire sur les différents moyens qui peuvent être employés par l'État pour intervenir dans l'exécution des chemins de fer en France, contenant des renseignements sur l'affaire du chemin de Paris à Tours*. Paris: L. Mathias, 1837.

Corréard, Alexandre, *Pétition des membres de la commission des condamnés pour causes politiques, adressée aux deux chambres*. Paris, n.d. [1832].

Corréard, Alexandre, *Project d'un barrage éclusé et mobile*. Paris, 1856.

Corréard, Alexandre, *Résumé pour le sieur Corréard*. Paris: n.d.

Corréard, Alexandre and Savigny, Henri, *Naufrage de la frégate la Méduse faisant partie de l'expédition du Sénégal en 1816*, 5th edn. Paris: Chez Corréard, Libraire, 1821.

Corréard, Alexandre et al., *A MM. les députés des départements. Réclamations des anciens condamnés politiques*. Paris, July 25th, 1831.

Courthion, Pierre, *Géricault raconté par lui-même et par ses amis.* Vésenaz-Généve: P. Cailler, 1947.

Critchley, MacDonald, *Shipwreck-Survivors, a Medical Study.* London: J. & A. Churchill, 1943.

Daget, Serge, 'France, Suppression of the Illegal Trade, and England 1817–50', in *The Abolition of the Atlantic Slave Trade*, ed. Eltis and Walvin. Madison: The University of Wisconsin Press, 1981.

Daget, Serge, 'L'Abolition de la traite des noirs en France de 1814 à 1831', *Cahiers d'Études Africaines*, Vol. XI, No. 41. Paris: École Pratique des Hautes Études, 1971.

Daget, Serge, *La répression de la traite des Noirs au XIX siècle.* Paris: Éditions Karthala, 1997.

Daget, Serge, *Répertoire des expéditions négrières françaises à la traite illégale (1814–1850).* Nantes: Centre de recherche sur l'histoire du monde atlantique: Comité nantais d'études en sciences humaines, 1988.

Dalyell, John Graham, *Shipwrecks and Disasters at Sea* (Edinburgh, 1812). London: George Routledge and Sons, 1866.

Dard, Mme, née Charlotte-Adelaïde Picard, *La chaumière Africaine, ou Histoire d'une famille française jetée sur la côte de l'Afrique, à la suite du naufrage de la Frégate la Méduse.* Dijon: Noellat, 1824.

Darmon, Pierre, *La Rumeur de Rodez.* Paris: Albin Michel, 1991.

Daudet, Ernest, *La police politique: chroniques des temps de la Restauration 1815–1820.* Paris: Plon-Nourrit, 1912.

Daudet, Ernest, *Louis XVIII et le duc Decazes 1815–1820.* Paris: E. Plon, Nourrit et Cie, 1899.

Debien, Gabriel, 'J.E. Morenas à Saint Louis en 1818–19', *Bulletin de l'Institut Français d'Afrique noire*, series B, XXX, 2. Paris, April 1968.

Debord, Jean-François, 'À propos de quelques dessins anatomiques de Géricault', in *Géricault – dessins et estampes des collections de l'École des beaux-arts.* Paris: École nationale supérieure des beaux-arts, 1997.

Delacroix, Eugène, *The Journal of Eugène Delacroix.* London: Phaidon, 1951, pbk 1995.

Deslys, Charles, *Le naufrage de la Méduse.* Paris: G. Havard, 1859.

Bibliography

Déterville, H., *Le Palais-Royal ou les Filles en bonne fortune.* Paris: L'Écrivain, 1815.

Drujon, Fernand, *Catalogue des ouvrages, écrits, et dessins poursuivis, supprimés ou condamnés depuis le 21 octobre 1814 jusqu'au 31 juillet 1877.* Paris: Edward Rouveyre, 1879.

Dubaut, Pierre and Aubry, Claude, *Géricault dans les collections privées françaises.* Paris: Galerie Claude Aubry, 1964.

Dukay, Pierre, *Le Naufrage de 'la Méduse'.* Paris: Éditions Jules Tallandier, 1932.

Durand, Jean-Baptiste-Léonard, *Voyage au Sénégal.* Paris: Chez Henri Agasse, 1802.

Eitner, Lorenz, 'Erotic Drawings by Gericault', *Master Drawings,* Vol.XXXIV, No.4, 375–89. New York, 1996.

Eitner, Lorenz, *Géricault – His Life and Work.* London: Orbis Press, 1983.

Eitner, Lorenz, *Géricault – Sa vie, son oeuvre.* Paris: Gallimard, 1991.

Eitner, Lorenz, *Géricault's 'Raft of the Medusa'.* London: Phaidon, 1972.

Eitner, Lorenz, 'The sale of Géricault's Studio in 1824', *Gazette des Beaux-Arts,* Vol.LIII, 115–26. Paris and New York: Presses universitaires de France, February 1959.

Escudier, Denis, *L'affreuse vérité de M. Savigny: second chirurgien de la frégate la 'Méduse', naufragé du radeau, miraculeusement sauvé par l'Argus, le 17 juillet 1816.* Saint-Jean D'Angely: Bordessoules, 1991.

Esquirol, Etienne, *Des maladies mentales considérées sous les rapports médical, hygiénique et médico-légal.* Paris: 1838.

Evans, Eric J., *Britain Before the Reform Act: Politics and Society 1815–1832.* London and New York: Longman, 1989.

Falconbridge, Alexander, *An Account of the slave trade on the coast of Africa.* London: J. Phillips, 1788.

Faure, Claude, 'La garnison européenne du Sénégal et la recruitement des premières troupes noires (1779–1858)', *Revue de l'histoire des colonies françaises,* No.8, 3ᵉ trimestre. Paris: Société de l'histoire des colonies françaises, 1920.

Fellowes, William Dorset, *Paris During the Interesting Month of July, 1815, a Series of Letters.* London: Gale and Fenner, 1815.

Fournel, Charles, *L'hôpital Beaujon. Histoire depuis son origine jusqu'à nos jours*. Paris: Dentu, 1884.

Frye, Major W.E., *After Waterloo — Reminiscences of European Travel 1815–19*. London: Heinemann, 1908.

Gallois, Léonard, *Promenade à Saint Pélagie*. Paris: Leroux, 1823.

Geoffrey de Villeneuve, René-Claude, *L'Afrique ou Histoire, moeurs, usages et coutumes des Africains. Le Sénégal*, 4 vols. Paris: Nepveu, 1814.

Germer, Stefan, '"Je commence une femme, et ça devient un lion": On the Origin of Géricault's Fantasy of Origins', in *Géricault, Conférences et colloques du Louvre*, Vol.1. Paris: La documentation française, 1996.

Gilmore, Jeanne, *La République clandestine 1818–48*. Paris: Aubier, 1997.

Girard, Louis, *Les Libéraux français, 1814–1875*. Paris: Aubier, 1985.

Giudicelly, Jean-Vincent, *Observations sur la traite des Noirs en réponse au rapport de M. Courvoisier sur la pétition de M. Morenas*. Paris: Chez les Marchands de Nouveautés, 1820.

Giudicelly, Jean-Vincent, *Réponse de M. l'abbé Giudicelly, ex-préfet apostolique du Sénégal et de Gorée, à une lettre de S. Exc. le Bon Portal, ministre de la marine, 30 Avril, 1821*. Paris: Impr. de Mme Jeunehomme-Crémière, 1821.

Gleyses, Chantal, *La femme coupable*. Paris: Éditions Imago, 1994.

Grandpré, Louis-Marie-Joseph Ohier, Comte de, *Voyage à la côte occidentale d'Afrique fait dans les années 1786 et 1787*, 2 vols. Paris: Dentu, an IX [1801].

Grate, Pontus, 'La critique d'art et la bataille romantique', *Gazette des Beaux-Arts*, Vol.54, 129–44. Paris and New York: Presses universitaires de France, September 1959.

Grégoire, Henri, *On the Slave-Trade and on the Slavery of the Blacks and of the Whites, by a Friend of Men of all Colours*. London: Josiah Conder, 1815.

Griffon du Bellay, Jean, *Les Griffons pendant cinq cent ans*. Garnes: privately printed, 1979.

Grigsby, Darcy Grimaldo, *Extremities*. New Haven and London: Yale University Press, 2002.

Bibliography

Grocott, Terence, *Shipwrecks of the Revolutionary and Napoleonic Eras*. London: Caxton Editions, 2002.

Grunchec, Philippe, 'L'inventaire posthume de Théodore Géricault', *Bulletin de la Société de l'histoire de l'art français*, 395–420. Paris, 1976.

Guédron, Martial, *La plaie et le couteau: La sensibilité anatomique de Théodore Géricault 1791–1824*. Paris: Kimé, 1997.

Gueye, M'Baye, 'La fin de l'esclavage à Saint Louis et à Gorée en 1848', *Notes d'histoire coloniale*, No.102 – extract from *Bulletin de l'I.F.A.N.*, Vol.28, series B, Nos 3–4. Dakar, 1966.

Gueye, M'Baye, *L'Afrique et l'esclavage: une étude sur la traite négrière*. Romorantin: Éditions Martinsart, 1983.

Guilbaut, Serge, 'Théodore Géricault: The Hoarse Voice of History', in *Théodore Géricault – The Alien Body: Tradition in Chaos*, edited by Serge Guilbaut, Maureen Ryan and Scott Watson. Vancouver: Morris and Helen Belkin Art Gallery, 1997.

Hardcastle, Ephraim, *Wine and Walnuts or After Dinner Chit-Chat*. London: Longman, Hurst, Rees, Orme and Brown, 1823.

Harpaz, Ephraim, *L'Ecole libérale sous la Restauration, le Mercure et la Minerve, 1817–1820*. Geneva: Droz, 1968.

Haydon, Benjamin Robert, *Life of Benjamin Robert Haydon, historical painter, from his Autobiography and his Journals*, edited and completed by Tom Taylor. London: Longman, Brown, Green and Longman, 1853.

Henze, Hans-Werner and Schnabel, Ernst, *Das Floss der Medusa: oratorio volgare e militare in due parte*. Berlin: Deutsche Grammophon Gesellschaft, 1968.

Honour, Hugh, 'Curiosities of the Egyptian Hall', *Country Life*, Vol.CXV, No.2973, 38–9. London, January 7th, 1954.

Houssaye, Henri, 'Un Maître de L'École française – Théodore Géricault', *Revue des Deux-Mondes*, 374–91. Paris, November 15th, 1879.

Huet, René-Paul, *Paul Huet d'après ses notes, sa correspondance, ses contemporains*. Paris: H. Laurens, 1911.

Hugues, Edmond, *Alexandre Corréard de Serres, naufragé de la 'Méduse'*. Gap, France, 1920.

Imbert, Auguste, *Biographie des imprimeurs et des librairies*. Paris, 1826.

Imbert, Auguste and Bellet, B.L., *Biographie des condamnés pour délits politiques*. Brussels, 1827.

Jal, Auguste, *L'Ombre de Diderot et le bossu du Marais; Dialogue critique sur le Salon de 1819*. Paris: Corréard, 1819.

Jenkins, E.H., *Histoire de la marine française*. Paris: Albin Michel, 1977.

Jennings, L.C., 'The Abolition of French Slavery', in *De la traite à l'esclavage. Actes du colloque international sur la traite des Noirs*, edited by Serge Daget. Nantes, 1985; Paris and Nantes, 1988.

Jessop, Thomas, *Journal d'un voyage à Paris en septembre–octobre 1820*, edited by F.C.W. Hiley. Paris: 1928.

Joannet, Henri, *Le Radeau de la Méduse ou Comment un Serrois montre du doigt l'espérance au reste du monde*. Serres: Groupement d'action pour le développement de la vallée du Buèch: 'Notre Pays', 1999.

Joannides, Paul, 'The Raft of the Medusa', review of *Géricault's 'Raft of the Medusa'*, by Lorenz Eitner, *The Burlington Magazine*, Vol.CXVII, No.864. London: March 1975.

Johnson, Lee, 'Géricault and Delacroix seen by Cockerell', *The Burlington Magazine*, Vol.CXIII, No.822, 547–51. London, September 1971.

Johnson, Lee, '"La grosse Suzanne" uncovered', *The Burlington Magazine*, Vol.CXXIII, No.937. London, April 1981.

Johnson, Lee, '*The Raft of The Medusa* in Great Britain', *The Burlington Magazine*, Vol.XCVI, No.617, 249–54. London, August 1954.

Jore, L., 'La vie diverse et volontaire du Colonel Julien Désiré Schmaltz . . . Consul Général de France à Smyrne (Turquie) 1771–1827', *Revue d'histoire des colonies*, Vol.XL, 2nd trimestre 1953, 265–312. Paris, 1953.

Journal des débats et des décrets. Paris, 1814–24.

Knoch, Inken D., 'Une peinture sans sujet? Étude sur les *Fragments anatomiques*', in *Géricault, Conférences et colloques du Louvre*, Vol.1. Paris: La documentation française, 1996.

Bibliography

La Tynna, Jean de, *Almanach du commerce de Paris, des départements de la France et des principales villes du monde*. Paris: au bureau de l'Almanach du commerce, 1818 and 1822.

La Tynna, Jean de, *Dictionnaire topographique, historique et étymologique des rues de Paris*. Paris, 1816.

Landow, George, 'Iconography and Point of View in painting and literature; the example of the shipwreck', *Studies in Iconography*, III, 89–104. Highland Heights, Kentucky: Northern Kentucky University, 1977.

Langeron, Roger, *Decazes, ministre du roi*. Paris: Hachette, 1960.

Langsdorff, Georg Heinrich Freiherr von, *Voyages and Travels in Various Parts of the World during the Years 1803, 1804, 1805, 1806, and 1807*. London: Henry Colburn, 1813.

Lawrence, A.W., *Trade Castles and Forts of West Africa*. London: Jonathan Cape, 1963.

Le Maire, Jacques-Joseph, *Les Voyages du Sieur Le Maire aux Isles Canaries, Cap-Verd, Sénégal et Gambie*. Paris, 1695.

Le Pesant, Michel, 'Documents inédits sur Géricault', *Revue de l'Art*, No.31, 73–81. Paris: Flammarion, 1976.

Ledré, Charles, *La Presse à l'assaut de la monarchie 1815–1848*. Paris: Armand Colin, 1960.

Legohérel, Henri, *Histoire de la Marine française*. Paris: Presses universitaires de France, 1999.

Lestringant, Frank, *Cannibals: The Discovery and Representation of the Cannibal from Columbus to Jules Verne*. Cambridge: Polity Press, 1997.

Lesur, C.L., *Annuaire historique universel Pour 1818*. Paris: Thoisnier-Deplaces, 1825.

Lodge, Suzanne, 'Géricault in England', *The Burlington Magazine*, Vol.CVII, No.753, 616–27. London, December 1965.

McLeod, John, *The Shipwreck of the Alceste, an English frigate in the straits of Gaspar; also the Shipwreck of the Medusa*, compiled from the papers of John McLeod and the narrative by Savigny and Corréard. Dublin: E. Tute, 1822.

McLeod, John, *Voyage of His Majesty's late ship 'Alceste' along the coast of Corea to the island of Lewchew, with an account of her subsequent shipwreck in the straits of Gaspar*, compiled from the papers of John McLeod. London: John Murray, 1818.

Mainardi, Patricia, 'Husbands, Wives and Lovers. *Mazeppa* or Marriage and its Discontents in Nineteenth Century France', in *Géricault, Conférences et colloques du Louvre*, Vol.1. Paris: La documentation française, 1996.

Mainardi, Patricia, *Husbands, Wives, and Lovers*. New Haven and London: Yale University Press, 2003.

Mainardi, Patricia, 'Mazeppa', *Word & Image*, Vol.16, No.4. London: Taylor & Francis, October 2000.

Mansel, Philip, *Louis XVIII*. Stroud: Sutton Publishing, rev. edition 1999.

Mansel, Philip, *Paris Between Empires 1814–1852*. London: John Murray, 2001, pbk 2003.

Manson, Marie and Latouche, Henri de, *Mémoires de Madame Manson*, 7th edition. Paris: Pillet, 1818.

Martini, Eric, 'Treatment for scurvy not discovered by Lind', *The Lancet*, Vol.364, 2180. London, December 18–25th, 2004.

Martini, Michel, *La tuberculose ostéo-articulaire*. Berlin-Heidelberg: Springer-Verlag, 1988.

Marty, Paul, *Études Sénégalaise*. Paris: Société de l'Histoire des Colonies Françaises et Librairie Larose, 1925.

Masson, Philippe, *L'Affaire de la Méduse*. Paris: Tallandier, 1989.

Matteson, Lynn R., 'Géricault and "English Street Cries"', *Apollo*, October 1977, 304–6. London, 1977.

Mellon, Stanley, *The Political Uses of History*. Stanford: Stanford University Press, 1958.

Mercier, Roger, 'Le Naufrage de "La Méduse" – Réalité et imagination romanesque', *Revue des Sciences Humaines*, Facs. 125, 53–66. Lille: Université de Lille, January–March 1967.

Michel, Régis, ed., *Géricault, Conférences et colloques du Louvre*, 2 vols. Paris: La documentation française, 1996.

Michel, Régis, Chenique, Bruno et. al., *Géricault*. Paris: Éditions de la Réunion des musées nationaux, 1991.

Mishory, Alec, 'Theodore Gericault's *A Paraleytic (sic) Woman*',

*Gazette des Beaux-Arts,*Vol.CIIIV, 241–54. Paris and New York: Presses universitaires de France, April 2000.

Mishory, Alexander, 'Le "reportage" réaliste d'un observateur objectif: le suite anglaise de Théodore Géricault', in *Géricault – dessins et estampes des collections de l'École des beaux-arts.* Paris: École nationale supérieure des beaux-arts, 1997.

Mollien, Gaspar, *Découverte des sources du Sénégal et de la Gambie en 1818.* Paris: C. Delagrave, 1889.

Mollien, Gaspar, *Travels in the Interior of Africa to the Sources of the Senegal and Gambia Performed by Command of the French Government in the year 1818.* London: H. Colburn & Co., 1820.

Moncrieff, William, *The Shipwreck of The Medusa, or, The Fatal Raft!* London, 1830.

Monestier, Alain and Cheyronnaud, Jacques, *Le Fait divers.* Paris: Éditions de la Réunion des musées nationaux, 1982.

Morenas, Joseph Elzéar, *Pétition contre la traite des Noirs présentée à la Chambre des Députés le 14 juin 1820.* Paris: Chez Corréard, 1820.

Morenas, Joseph Elzéar, *Précis historique de la traite des Noirs et de l'esclavage colonial.* Paris, 1828.

Morenas, Joseph Elzéar, *Seconde Pétition contre la traite des Noirs, présentée à la Chambre des Députés le 19 mars 1821.* Paris, 1821.

Mullens, W.H., 'William Bullock's London Museum', *Museums Journal,* No.17. London: October 1917.

Musée Renan-Scheffer, *La Nouvelle Athènes – le quartier Saint-Georges, de Louis XV à Napoléon III.* Paris: Musée Renan-Scheffer, 1984.

Nazarieux, Charles-Pierre de, *Mémoire pour la Société coloniale philanthropique, présenté à son excellence Mgr. le Ministre Secrétaire d'État de la Marine et des colonies par MM. les membres composant la Commission administrative de la Société coloniale.* Paris, November 25th, 1816.

Néret, Jean-Alexis, *Histoire Illustrée de la Librairie.* Paris: Lamarre, 1953.

Nettement, Alfred M., *Souvenirs de la Restauration.* Paris: Jacques Lecoffre et Cie, 1858.

Newman, Edgar Leon, *Historical Dictionary of France from the 1815 Restoration to the Second Empire*, 2 vols. Westport, Conn.: Greenwood Press, 1987.

Nicolson, Benedict, 'The "Raft" From the Point of View of Subject Matter', *The Burlington Magazine*, Vol.CXVI, No.617, 241–9. London, August 1954.

Nochlin, Linda, 'Géricault or the Absence of Women', in *Géricault, Conférences et colloques du Louvre*, Vol.1. Paris: La documentation française, 1996.

Noon, Patrick, 'Colour and Effect – Anglo-French Painting in London and Paris', in *Crossing the Channel, British and French Painting in the Age of Romanticism*, edited by Patrick Noon. London: Tate Publishing, 2003.

Parson, *Premier rapport de M. Parson, chef de la délégation envoyée au Cap-Verd par la Société-coloniale-philanthropique à l'effet de reconnoître les lieux les plus propres à la fondation des colonies agricoles* – 2ᵉ édition avec des Notes par M. Sévigny. Paris: Au bureau de la Société coloniale philanthropique, 1817.

Pescay, François Fournier de, 'Calenture', in *Dictionnaire des sciences médicales, par une société de médecins et de chirurgiens*, edited by Nicolas Philibert Adelon, Vol.2, 475–9. Paris, 1812.

Pescay, François Fournier de, 'Notice sur la Calenture, maladie particulière aux gens de mer', in *Annales des faits et des sciences militaires: faisant suite aux 'Victoires et conquêtes des Français de 1792 à 1815'*, edited by Jean Denis Barbié du Bocage, 4 vols. Paris, March 1818.

Planta, Edward, *A New Picture of Paris* or *The Stranger's Guide to the French Metropolis*. London: Samuel Leigh, July 1814.

Quotidienne, La. Paris, 1815–47.

Rabaroust, Marie Antoine, 'Récit inédit du naufrage de La Méduse', *L'Intermédiaire des Chercheurs*, No.45. Paris, January 10th, 1902.

Rabbe, Alphonse, 'Nécrologie, Géricault peintre d'histoire', *La Pandore, Journal des spectacles, des letters, des arts, des moeurs et des modes*, No.198. Paris, January 29th, 1824.

Bibliography

Rang, Sander (Alexandre Rang des Adrets, *dit* Sander Rang), *Voyage au Sénégal, Naufrage de la Méduse*. Paris: Éditions E.P.I., 1946.

Resnick, Daniel P., *The White Terror and the Political Reaction after Waterloo*. Cambridge, Mass.: Harvard University Press, 1966.

Riding, Christine, 'The Raft of the Medusa in Britain – Audience and Context', in *Crossing the Channel, British and French Painting in the Age of Romanticism*, edited by Patrick Noon. London: Tate Publishing, 2003.

Riley, James, *Loss of American Brig 'Commerce' wrecked on the Western Coast of Africa in the month of August 1815*. London: J. Murray, 1817.

Robert, Louis, 'Une odyssée atroce: le Radeau de la Méduse. La tragique origine d'une thèse de médecine', *La Presse Médicale*, No.51. Paris: Masson, August 8th, 1953.

Rosenblum, Robert, *Modern Painting and the Northern Romantic Tradition*. London: Thames and Hudson, 1975, pbk 1978.

Rosenthal, Donald A., 'Géricault's Expenses for the Raft of the Medusa, *Art Bulletin*, Vol.LXII. New York: College Art Association of America, December 1980.

Ryan, Maureen, 'Liberal Ironies, Colonial Narratives and the Rhetoric of Art: Reconsidering Géricault's *Radeau de la Méduse*, in *Théodore Géricault – The Alien Body: Tradition in Chaos*, edited by Serge Guilbaut, Maureen Ryan and Scott Watson. Vancouver: Morris and Helen Belkin Art Gallery, 1997.

Sagne, Jean, *Géricault*. Paris: Fayard, 1991.

Sagne, Jean, 'Géricault et l'opinion libérale', in *Géricault, Conférences et colloques du Louvre*, Vol.II. Paris: La documentation française, 1996.

Salgari, Emilio and Motta, Luigi, *Le Naufrage de la Méduse'*. Paris: J. Ferenczi et fils, 1926.

Savigny, Jean-Baptiste-Henri, *Journal des débats*. Vendredi, September 1816.

Savigny, Jean-Baptiste-Henri, *L'affreuse vérité de M. Savigny: second chirurgien de la frégate la Méduse, naufragé du radeau, miraculeusement sauvé par l'Argus le 17 juillet 1816*. Documents assembled and presented by Denis Escudier. Saint-Jean D'Angely: Bordessoules, 1991.

Savigny, Jean-Baptiste, *Observations sur les effets de la faim et de la soif éprouvées après le naufrage de la frégate du roi 'La Méduse' en 1816* (Paris May 26th, 1818), in Escudier, Denis, *L'affreuse vérité de M. Savigny: second chirurgien de la frégat la 'Méduse', naufragé du radeau, miraculeusement sauvé par l'Argus le 17 juillet 1816.* Saint-Jean D'Angely: Bordessoules, 1991.

Savigny, J.B. Henry and Corréard, Alexandre, *Narrative of a Voyage to Senegal in 1816.* London: Henry Colburn, 1818.

Savigny, Jean-Baptiste-Henri and Corréard, Alexandre, *Naufrage de la frégate la Méduse, faisant partie de l'expédition du Sénégal, en 1816.* Paris, 1817.

Savigny, Michel, 'Henri Savigny', *L'Intermédiaire des Chercheurs*, No.934, column 1010. Paris: May 30th, 1901.

Scheffer, Charles-Arnold, *De l'État de la liberté en France.* Brussels: Demat, 1818.

Scott, John, of Gala, *Paris Revisited in 1815, by way of Brussels.* London: Longman, Hurst, Rees, Orme & Brown, 1816.

Sells, Christopher, 'After *The Raft of the Medusa*: Gericault's Later Projects', *The Burlington Magazine*, Vol.CXXVIII, No.1001, 563–71. London, August 1986.

Sells, Christopher, 'New Light on Géricault, his Travels and his Friends, 1816–23', *Apollo*, Vol.CXXII, No.292. London, June 1986.

Sells, Christopher, 'Two Letters from Gericault to Madame Horace Vernet', *The Burlington Magazine*, Vol.CXXXI, No.1032, 216–18. London: March 1989.

Sévigny, P.H.J., *Mémoire au Conseil d'État pour la Société-coloniale-philanthropique de la Sénégambie, exposant les avantages politiques et commerciaux qui peuvent résulter pour la France de la fondation de cette nouvelle colonie, ainsi que les faits relatifs à l'établissement de la Société-coloniale.* Paris: Société-coloniale-philanthropique, 1817.

Shankland, Peter and Havers, The Rt. Hon. Sir Michael, Q.C., *Murder with a Double Tongue.* London: Souvenir Press, 1990.

Bibliography

Shelley, Mary, *Frankenstein* (1819). London: Wordsworth Editions, 1993.

Simon, Robert, 'Géricault and *l'affaire Fualdès*', in *Géricault, Conférences et colloques du Louvre*, Vol.1. Paris: La documentation française, 1996.

Simon, Robert, 'Géricault and the *fait divers*', in *Géricault, Conférences et colloques du Louvre*, Vol.1. Paris: La documentation française, 1996.

Simpson, Brian A.W., *Cannibalism and the Common Law: The Story of the Tragic Last Voyage of the Mignonette and the Strange Legal Proceedings to Which it Gave Rise*. Harmondsworth: Penguin, 1986.

Spitzer, Alan B., *Old Hatred and Young Hopes – The French Carbonari against the Bourbon Restoration*. Cambridge, Mass.: Harvard University Press, 1971.

Spitzer, Alan B., *The French Generation of 1820*. Princeton, New Jersey: Princeton University Press, 1987.

Stendhal (Henri Beyle), *Racine et Shakespeare*. Paris, 1823.

Sue, Eugène, *La Salamandre* (1845). Paris: Éditions des Autres, 1979.

Thomas, Hugh, *The Slave Trade*. London: Papermac, 1998.

Thompson, E.P., *The Making of the English Working Class*. New York: Vintage Books, 1963.

Times, The. London, 1816–22.

Titeux, Eugène, *Histoire de la Maison militaire du roi de 1814 à 1830*. Paris: Baudry, 1890.

Touches, Gicquel des, 'Souvenirs d'un marin de la République', *Revue des Deux-Mondes*, Parts I & II, Vol.28. Paris, 1905.

Tronchet, Louis, *Picture of Paris, being a complete guide to all the public buildings and curiosities in that metropolis*. London: Sherwood, Neely and Jones, 1815.

Tulard, Jean, 'Naufrage et cinéma', in *Le Naufrage – actes du colloque tenu à l'Institut catholique de Paris 28–30 Jan. 1998*, edited by Buchet & Thomasset. Paris: Honoré Champion, 1999.

Tulard, Jean, and Garros, Louis, *Itinéraire de Napoléon au jour le jour 1769–1821*. Paris: le Grand livre du mois, 2002.

Twyman, Michael, *Lithography 1800–1850*. London: Oxford University Press, 1970.

311

Vallery-Radot, Pierre, 'L'anatomie et la psychiatrie dans la vie et l'oeuvre de Géricault', *La Presse médicale*, 66, No.27. Paris: Masson, April 5th, 1958.

Vaughan, William, *Romantic Art*. London: Thames and Hudson, 1978.

Vayre, Pierre, *Les Larrey. Dominique, Hippolyte . . . et les autres*. Paris: Editions Glyphe, 2005.

Villeneuve, Roland, *Histoire du cannibalisme*. Paris, 1965.

Walvin, James, *England, Slaves and Freedom 1776–1838*. London: Macmillan, 1986.

Werdet, Edmond, *De la librairie française: son passé, son présent, son avenir*. Paris: Dentu, 1860.

Whitney, Wheelock, *Gericault in Italy*. New Haven and London: Yale University Press, 1997.

Wright, Beth S., *Painting and History During the French Restoration – Abandoned by the Past*. Cambridge: Cambridge University Press, 1997.

Wrigley, Richard, *The Origins of French Art Criticism from the Ancient Regime to the Restoration*. Oxford: Clarendon Press, 1993.

Zelle, Carsten, 'Théorie du naufrage: avant Géricault', in *Géricault, Conférences et colloques du Louvre*, Vol.1. Paris: La documentation française, 1996.

Index

Medusa

Index

Géricault, Georges-Nicolas, 15, 16, 238

Géricault, Théodore
appearance, 6, 17
childhood and youth, 7, 14–17
growing bond with Alexandrine Caruel, 15–17
studies art, 17, 18
dalliance with Mlle Montgolfier, 18
begins artistic career, 18–19
begins affair with Alexandrine, 19–20, 21, 50
in the Musketeers, 20
during *Cent-Jours*, 20–1
leaves Musketeers, 49
change in attitudes, 49
enters competition for *Prix de Rome*, 50
Italian trip, 50–1, 130–4, 135
returns to France, 134–5, 157–8
interest in Fauldès affair, 165, 167, 168
develops absorption with crime and catastrophe, 165
continues affair with Alexandrine, 166–7
and Alexandrine's pregnancy, 167, 169, 170
chooses to focus on *The Medusa*, 167–8
end of relationship with Alexandrine, 170
birth of son, 171
researches subject of *The Medusa*, 171–2
drawn to episodes on the raft, 172
studies human misery in streets of Paris 174–5
studies body parts, 1–5, 173, 175–7
paints *The Raft of the Medusa*, 178, 179–82, 185–7
and Corréard, 2, 3–4, 5, 181–2, 210, 235, 236, 259–60
exhibits *The Raft of the Medusa* at the Salon, 187–90
upset by unfavourable reaction, 190–1
retreats to the country, 191–2
returns to Paris, 192
exhibition in London, 195, 197, 202–4, 205–6
stays in London, 199, 200–1
exhibition in Dublin, 206–7
spends another period in London, 207–9
returns to France, 209–10
becomes involved in struggle for abolition of slave trade, 235–6
accident and illness, 236–7, 237–8
loses money, 238
sells paintings, 238
last weeks, 238–9
death, 239
funeral, 240
and Romantic movement, 253–4
sale of works and effects, 254

321

Index

Index

Medusa

332

Index

includes Corréard's letter of gratitude to British ambassador, 151
and Mlle Schmaltz, 159–60
quotations from, 38, 58, 108, 111, 148, 160, 246, 247–8
second edition published, 170, 171
used by Géricault, 172, 179
Corréard's intentions in later editions, 184
translation published in England, 76, 193–4, 195, 201
third edition published, 205
and panorama of the wreck of *The Medusa*, 207
pirated in *History of Shipwrecks*, 215
engraving of Corréard's cell included in, 221
and African culture, 223–4
black survivor mentioned in, 236
accuracy of account challenged, 36, 245, 246, 248–50
self-justification in, 246–8
and Coudein's report, 251
problems relating to, 252
Sicily, 204
Sistine Chapel, 132
Smyrna, 242, 256
Societé philanthropiqe du Cap-Vert, 10, 14, 30, 36, 39, 80, 98, 121, 127, 147, 250
Soubise, 243
Spain, 7, 204
and West Africa, 117
Staël, Madame de, 193
Stafford, Marquis of, 202

Stendhal, 135
Racine et Shakespeare, 135
Straits of Antioch, 35
Straits of Gaspar, 194
Stuart, Sir Charles, 145
Surabaya, 55
Switzerland, 50

Talleyrand, Charles-Maurice de, 225
Tenerife, 41–2, 43
Ternate, H.M.S., 194–5
Thames, River, 201, 209
Théâtre Italien, Paris, 186
Thirteenth Report of the Directors of the African Institution, 235
Thistlewood, Arthur, 199–200
Thomas, Honoré, 115, 250
Tiger, The, 107
Times, The, 145, 146, 193, 202, 204, 231
Tobago, 12
Touche-Lavillette Valéry *see* Lavillette (Touche-Lavillette), Valéry
Touches, Giquel des, 24, 26, 27, 33–4, 39, 149, 243
Toulon, 12
Trafalgar, 12, 23, 33, 34
Trazas tribe, 123
Trianon Gallery, 17–18
Tropic of Cancer, 43, 44
Tuileries, Paris, 8, 205
Turner, J.M.W., 186

Uffizi, Florence, 134
ultras (ultra-Royalists), 9, 21, 22–3, 48, 49, 136–7, 139, 157, 162, 164, 165, 189, 196, 205, 209–10, 217, 222